H E B R

MODERN

BOOK 1

A1-**C**1

MW00934675

JACOB ELI GOODSON

TABLE OF CONTENTS

INTRODUCTION

Americans know of Hebrew as the language of the Old Testament. Hebrew had been a living language, that is, it was spoken as a native language by a community of people, at least until the First Century, B.C., and possibly for several centuries after that. But even though it ceased to be a living language in this sense, a large and important body of literature has remained in constant daily use for prayer and study.

During the Middle Ages and into the Renaissance Hebrew served as a lingua franca for Jews throughout the world, and the literature was expanded by scholars and poets. Hebrew thus was kept in continuous familiarity, and in the last century successful efforts were begun to revive it as a modern language.

Today Hebrew is the official language of the State of Israel. It is being taught to immigrants speaking a wide variety of native languages, and the goal is to have all the inhabitants learn to speak it.

To be sure, modern Hebrew is different from the Biblical language. The phonology (sound system) has been simplified, and new syntactic patterns and vocabulary have been developed to express concepts not dreamed of two thousand years ago. But the modern language is unmistakably the descendant of the language of the Psalms and the prophets.

The sounds of modern Hebrew are fairly easy for Americans to learn. Since only a minority of the present population are native speakers of Hebrew, foreign accents can hardly be called rare, and one should not feel the slightest embarrassment in making even halting efforts to speak it.

PURPOSE

It should be stated very clearly at the outset that this book is not intended as an elementary text for the study of the Bible or other Hebrew literature. It is also not intended as a reference grammar of Hebrew. There are a number of good books on the market to fulfill those needs. This book is intended as a training manual, designed to teach a non-speaker of Hebrew to speak and comprehend with some degree of fluency an acceptable form of the modern language. Its relationship to a reference grammar is analogous to the relationship of a program of calisthenics to a textbook on physiology. The student is not supposed to read this book in order to find out about Hebrew; he is supposed to work at the material presented here until he can speak Hebrew, and he will have to work hard.

The goal of this course is performance. One "knows" Hebrew in the same sense that one "knows" how to drive a car. It is not necessary to be an automotive engineer or to know the technical terms for the parts of a car in order to be a good driver. Many excellent drivers even have wrong notions about the mechanical aspects of an automobile. Similarly, it is not necessary to be able to discuss accurately and comprehensively the grammar of a language in order to speak it fluently and correctly. Intensive drilling will produce the proper habits. When the student participates in conversation easily and fluently with a minimum of either "accent" or of conscious effort then he has achieved the goal of the course.

Emphasis on the spoken language does not mean that reading and writing are to be ignored or downgraded in overall importance for the educated speaker. These latter skills are a separate problem which in the initial stages of study are treated as secondary.

Many students who use this book will already be familiar with the Hebrew alphabet and writing system. For those who are not it is suggested that work on reading be postponed until Unit 10 is completed. Classes will of course, vary in their ability to absorb the material, and the instructor should feel free to adjust this schedule.

However, it is felt highly probable, on the basis of a large body of experience with many languages, including Hebrew, that the total competence of the student will be greater if he starts with the spoken language and then adds the written form rather than vice versa. Students who already know how to read will profit greatly if they concentrate exclusively on the spoken language for at least the first ten units.

STYLE OF HEBREW USED

The language presented here as a model for students to imitate is the ordinary informal speech of educated native Israelis. This is different from the Hebrew usually taught outside of Israel, and students who have already learned some Hebrew may have to make some adjustments.

Modern Hebrew is a living language and as such it is changing daily. Slang expression, coinages, variant pronunciations, and grammatical innovations are characteristic of any living language. Furthermore, Hebrew is spoken and written in a variety of styles. These vary from highly formal to highly informal.

Formal spoken style is very similar to the literary style and is more like the Hebrew that is taught traditionally. Formal style is used, as the name implies, for public speaking, official meetings, radio news broadcasts, or other occasions where the speaker would use deferential or deliberate speech.

Informal spoken style is that used by native speakers in ordinary, relaxed conversation. It is often more rapid than the formal style and is the speech which seems most "natural" to native Israelis.

There is a highly informal style which contains much slang, contractions and dropping of sounds, and is fairly rapid. The student should not attempt to learn it until he is fairly fluent in the ordinary informal style.

The informal speech used in this text is tempered with features of more formal speech. These are included because the non-native speaker will be expected to have learned them, and their use will not seem affected.

It is interesting to note that the speakers who provided the material for this book often insisted that one should not use forms or expressions which they, in fact, did. This occasionally led to long discussions about what to include in the book, and sometimes no final decision was reached. Thus, for a example, the forms /birer/ and /otxem/ "you" are included in the material as well as the 'correct' forms /berar/ and /etxem/. In such cases the student will find that either choice will be acceptable in conversation.

METHODS AND PROCEDURE

The Native Speaker

Since the emphasis is on speech throughout the course, an indispensable component is the voice of an instructor whose native language is Hebrew. The student should not attempt to use these materials without either a native instructor or recordings of a native instructor's voice. The method of instruction incorporates guided imitation, repetition, memorization, pattern practice, and conversation.

The instructor performs the following functions:

(a) He serves as a _model_ for imitation and a source for elicitation of material. In this his ability to repeat without change and his endless patience are most important.

(b) He _corrects_ mistakes of all kinds: pronunciation, grammar, and vocabulary. Tape recordings are an extremely useful tool, but they cannot correct the student.

(c) He _drills_ the student. He conducts, and may himself devise, drills and exercises designed to fix new language patterns in the habits of the learner.

(d) He _converses_ with the student. He acts out prepared conversations with the student. It is here that his intelligence, imagination, and skill are most important.

It is to be noted that _explanation_ is not listed as a normal function of the instructor. In general, explanation of the language is held to a minimum. Using the language and talking about it are different things.

The native speaker has under his control the vast array of possible sentences of the language, knows when to use them, and recognizes and responds to them when used by others. In this sense only the native speaker really _knows_ the language. For this reason he is the most satisfactory model, corrector, and conversation partner.

However, the native speaker is to a great extent unaware of the structural patterns of his language because he learned them at an early age and has not thought much about them. The educated man is overtly familiar only with those patterns of grammar, style, and pronunciation which are emphasized in his education. These are usually only a small fraction of the total structure of the language, and by no means the most important for the English-speaking student. The native speaker's explanations about his language may be satisfactory, or correct but inadequate, or even completely false or misleading. For these reasons the student should not rely on the native speaker as an explainer. Normally, the course is conducted under the supervision of a scientific linguist who provides whatever explanations are necessary. .

Intensiveness

Not only is a large total of instructional hours necessary, but concentrated study is essential. Experience has shown that greater concentration of contact hours, especially at the beginning of a language course, yields far better results than dispersal of the same number of hours of over a long period of time. The maximum load per day for efficient learning is highly variable, some students reaching the point of diminishing returns with four contact hours and others being able to work up to eight or more.

The size of the class is another important consideration. As in many learning situations, the learning of a second language proceeds more thoroughly and rapidly if it takes place in a small group. This provides greater variety in drill and conversation, more speaking time for each student per class hour, and allows the instructor to give more attention to each individual. The maximum figure for effective learning varies with the personality types of the students, the skill of the instructor, and other factors, but the number six serves as a standard, across-the-board maximum.

At the other extreme, a class consisting of a single student is feasible and may be very successful, but it usually proves better to have several students for drill and conversation. In the regular intensive courses at the norm is about four.

The drill techniques described below assume that the class will have no more than six students. For larger classes the instructor will have to devise various types of choral drills and responses and to rely more on tape recordings to give the individual student practice in speaking.

An important aspect of the method is OVERLEARNING, that is, learning sentences so thoroughly that they come out automatically. Any 'thinking in the language' then consists of thinking about <u>what</u> to say and not about <u>how</u> to go about saying it. This cannot be accomplished unless the student spends a lot of time practicing.

MATERIAL

The material for the spoken Hebrew section of the course is divided into units which consist of the following parts: Basic Conversations, additional vocabulary, vocabulary drills, verb drills, grammar notes and drills, rapid response drills, and review conversations.

Basic Conversations

The Basic Conversation is the core of each unit. It consists of a set of sentences in dialogue form, which is to be completely memorized by the student. After having <u>overlearned</u> these sentences the student proceeds to intensive drilling based on the sounds, constructions, and vocabulary contained in the sentences, then to prepared or guided conversations, and finally to free conversation on topics covered in the sentences and expanded by the grammatical points covered in the grammar sections.

The sentence is the natural <u>unit</u> of speech. All languages have sentences, and sounds and forms of a language normally appear within sentences. It is clear that the student must learn to use sentences readily, no matter how this learning is accomplished.

In learning whole sentences the student acquires words and grammatical patterns simultaneously. Experience has shown that having the student first learn words and rules and then produce sentences by combining the words according to the rules is an inefficient way to learn. For most people a grammatical pattern is learned (in the sense that it is "internalized" and can readily be used) more rapidly by thoroughly learning illustrative sentences which embody it than by having it presented as a rule.

Furthermore, the pronunciation and grammatical form of words or other units of the language may be quite different in isolated citation from what they are in connected speech, and since the connected speech form is far more frequent it normally deserves far more attention and drill than the citation form.

The sentences of the Basic Conversation are presented in three parallel columns. The column on the right gives the Hebrew sentence in the Hebrew alphabet. The column on the left gives an English equivalent (not necessarily a literal translation) of the Hebrew sentence. The middle column is a transcription of the Hebrew sentence. Since the Hebrew spelling is given without vowel points the student will have to rely on the transcription for rendition of the pronunciation. The Hebrew in the right hand column is given mainly for the benefit of the instructor who will find it more familiar to read than the transcription, although the student may use it for reading practice later.

After each sentence a "breakdown" of the new words is given. The English translations of these entries tend to be more literal than those given for the Basic Sentences themselves, and are more like the entries to be found in a dictionary.

The technique for teaching the Basic Sentences is a "build-up" scheme in which each longer sentence or group of sentences is broken up into short pieces, and then each piece is presented <u>last piece first</u> and cumulatively, until the student can speak the entire sentence or group of sentences. When the entire sentence is built up it is repeated by the instructor and student.

The pieces to be presented are printed on separate lines. For example, the group: /todá rabá. šlomí tóv. umá šlomxa?/ "Thank you very much. I'm fine. And how are you?" is written in the book like this:

Thank you very much.	todá rabá.	.תודה רבה.
I'm fine.	šlomí tóv.	.שׁלומי טוב
And how are you?	umá šlomxá?	?ומה שׁלומך

It is presented to the student as follows:

Instructor or Tape:	umá šlomxá?
Student:	umá šlomxá?
Instructor or Tape:	šlomí tóv. umá šlomxá?
Student:	šlomí tóv. umá šlomxá?
Instructor or Tape:	todá rabá. šlomí tóv. umá šlomxá?
Student:	todá rabá. šlomí tóv. umá šlomxá?
Instructor or Tape:	todá rabá. šlomí tóv. umá šlomxá? (repetition)
Student:	todá rabá. šlomí tóv. umá šlomxá?

As much as possible the sentences have been divided into natural sounding pieces. However, the instructor will still have to achieve skill in presenting the pieces with the intonation that they have within the entire sentence. The repetitions of these partial sentences should not be dull and mechanical, but should be an accurate model for the student to imitate in a natural conversation.

The instructor's pronunciation may vary somewhat from that indicated by the transcription. The student should imitate the instructor, but the instructor should not try to impose a "bookish" or supposedly "correct" pronunciation if it is not completely natural to him in ordinary, relaxed speech.

For the benefit of the instructor the Basic Sentences are printed in larger type than the vocabulary entries after each sentence. The instructor does not drill the vocabulary entries; they are given for the student's reference.

After acceptable imitation and accurate pronunciation of the Basic Sentences have been achieved they are assigned for <u>memorization</u> outside of class or repeated in class until memorized. Repetition outside of class, preferably using recorded materials as a guide, must be continued to the point of over learning, as mentioned above. As a final step, the students act out the entire Basic Conversation from memory, with the instructor or with other students. Only when the Basic Sentences have been mastered to this extent can they be considered to provide an adequate basis for grammatical drills and for control of the spoken language.

Some Basic Conversations are rather long, and are therefore broken up into sections which cover several units. After the section in each succeeding unit is mastered it may be combined with the sections from preceding units for review and practice of longer conversations.

Additional Vocabulary

Appropriate additional vocabulary is presented in this section which
follows the Basic Conversation. New words or expressions are always presented
within sentences, and the student is not required to memorize lists of new
words as such. Items are included in this section to give material for
expanded or varied conversation or to present paradigms to be learned before
a grammatical explanation is given.

Vocabulary Drills and Verb Drills

It is not assumed that a student will automatically be able to extend
the rules to all new forms encountered. Therefore, further opportunities are
presented to practice the manipulations. Whenever, for example, an adjective
is introduced in a Basic Sentence or Additional Vocabulary all other forms
(masculine, feminine, singular, plural) will be drilled in this section. Whenever a new verb is introduced the entire conjugation is drilled, as far as is
practicable. These drills not only reinforce the grammatical patterns, but
also give an opportunity to illustrate different meanings and the use of forms
in different contexts.

Grammar Notes and Drills

All explanation of the structure of Hebrew - sounds, forms, constructions,
or style, - is kept to a minimum in the course. When a grammatical point is
to be made clear by a supervising linguist or in a Grammar Note, this is done (a)
after examples of the point have appeared in Basic Sentences, (b) by calling
attention to these instances and adding other illustrations, and (c) by a
simple, clear statement. Then, most important of all , the point is reinforced
by drills.

Historical explanations or appeals to "logic" are generally avoided, but
contrast with similar or conflicting patterns of English is usually indicated.

It is generally wasteful to spend a great deal of time on grammatical
explanations. Even if they explain what IS said, rather than somebody's idea
of what SHOULD be said, it is still largely wasted motion in that the student
does not participate and does not master the point. The time spent in
explaining a point is usually better spent in drilling that point with carefully
selected, natural sentences exemplifying it.

On the other hand, the attempt to rule out all explanation and to teach
everything by a "direct method" completely in Hebrew also wastes time. Very
often a simple point which takes endless repetitions of various sentences before
the student gets the hang of it can be explained briefly and effectively in
English and then drilled systematically.

The Grammar Notes do not cover all possibilities. The instructor will be
sure to find exceptions to each explanation or contexts in which the explanation
is contradicted. The Grammar Notes are intended as guides, and the student
should not expect them to be comprehensive for all cases.

Some explanations are not given in traditional order. Thus, for example,
the first and second person forms of the past tense of verbs are drilled
separately from the third person forms, and the complete past tense of verbs is
then drilled without regard to binyan, or conjugation. The complete paradigm
of each binyan is not presented until Units 21-25, although references are made
to them and various verbs are drilled in preceding units. Also, the pi'el is
presented before the kal since the former is a simpler conjugation in modern
Hebrew and because most new verbs are coined in the pi'el.

Terminology

In line with the desire to keep explanations simple, no wild forays into novel terminology are made. All students will recognize such familiar terms as "past tense", "imperative", "gender", etc. Certain other terms which may not be so familiar are "construct state", "radical", and "dual", but these are traditionally used in grammars of Hebrew. Also, some Hebrew grammatical terms are used, such as "lamed hey verb", "pi'el", etc.

Nevertheless, the student may find some of the terms to be strange, especially if he has had no grammatical training embodying the practices of modern scientific linguistics. New terminology has arisen in order to be able to make more objective statements about language, and some of it is used here as a matter of course. Thus, for example, "forms" are said to "occur"; groups of consonants with no intervening vowel are called "consonant clusters"; etc. The most unfamiliar terminology may be the phonetic descriptions of consonants and vowels, such as "affricate", "low central vowel", etc.

The student should keep in mind that he does not have to learn terminology or to talk about Hebrew. It is far better and more pertinent for him to be a good mimic than to know what a voiced velar fricative is.

Rapid Response Drills

In Rapid Response Drills students answer in quick succession questions on the Basic Conversation of the unit. The instructor may vary these questions by having the students take the parts of various actors in the Basic Conversation and asking them direct questions about their parts.

Review Conversations

The Review Conversations give the student opportunity to improvise brief conversations, starting with models given in the text. The sample conversations given in this book may be used both for testing comprehension and for conversation practice. Complete directions for using the Review Conversations for conversation practice are given in Unit 1. Later the instructor and students are left to their own ingenuity in changing and expanding them.

DRILLS

Drills are not tests.

All drills are planned to be easily and rapidly answered. In class they are to be done orally with the students' books closed. Answers are available in the textbook. The drills are not puzzles; they are not to be "figured out" but merely to be spoken for speed and accuracy. They are opportunities to practice new forms or sequences in new contexts. If the student has difficulty this may reflect an inadequate mastery of the Basic Conversations or of previous drills. In any case, it is of no great importance whether or not he can figure them out by himself. The goal is to learn to speak Hebrew accurately and fluently, and this aim can be achieved only by correct repetition of the forms and patterns involved. The instructor should supply the correct response whenever the student hesitates too long or does not answer correctly.

In the earlier units of the course the drills are given in the Hebrew spelling and in transcription so that the student may follow the drills when using the tape recordings. It is assumed, however, that the student will have learned to read Hebrew by the time Unit 20 is completed. After Unit 21, therefore, the transcription is omitted in the drills. Translations are given for the first set of responses in each drill.

The instructor should check to see if the students understand what is going on by stopping at random points in a drill and asking a student to translate the last response.   It is best to ask a student other than the one who just responded.   The instructor should do this only once in a while so that a maximum amount of time is given to the students to speak Hebrew.

Substitution Drills

The purpose of this type of drill is to present variations in form, such as for gender, number, person, without the student having to do any manipulations at all other than to repeat what the instructor has said and to fit it into the model sentence.

A substitution drill is done as follows: The model sentence is given by the instructor and then repeated by the students.   The instructor then gives a form which is to be substituted into the model sentence.   The student responds with the entire sentence with the new form substituted.   The instructor reinforces the correct response by repeating the student's response.

In the tape recordings of drills a blank interval is left for the student to respond.   The correct response is then given.   If the student has not responded correctly he will hear something different from what he himself has said.   This will serve as a correction from the instructor.   If he has responded correctly then the repetition will reinforce the proper habits.

Further instructions for doing substitution drills and substitution-agreement drills are given with examples in Unit 1.

Substitution-Agreement Drills

The purpose of this type of drill is to elicit a variation determined by the cue from the instructor.   The instructor gives the student a substitution to make in the model sentence, and this substitution requires the student to make a change elsewhere in the sentence.   These subsequent changes are the points being drilled.

A substitution-agreement drill is done in the same way as a simple substitution drill.   It will usually require more repetitions for mastery since the student must make more than one change in the model sentence.

Expansion Drills

The purpose of expansion drills is to give the student practice in producing longer utterances while maintaining a certain grammatical context.

The instructor gives the student a model sentence.   The student repeats this model sentence and adds another sentence to make a longer utterance.   For example:

Instructor: hú gár bemalón dán.

Student: hú gár bemalón dán, vehamišpaxá šeló tagía beód šavúa.

Instructor: He's staying at the Dan Hotel.

Student: He's staying at the Dan Hotel, and his family will arrive in a week.

In this case the reference to the subject of the first sentence is maintained in the added sentence: /hú - šeló/ "he - his".

The instructor repeats the entire response of the student. After the drill has been done a number of times the instructor may omit this repetition in order to speed up the drill in class.

Transformation Drills

The purpose of transformation drills is to give the student practice in shifting from one tense to another, from one conjugation to another, from singular to plural, etc., or simply to paraphrase. The student must eventually be able to make all grammatical manipulations automatically, and this type of drill is most helpful.

The instructor gives a sentence and the student responds with another sentence, determined by the instructions given for the particular drill. The instructor should give the first reponse so that the student will understand what sort of transformation he is supposed to make.

Response Drills

The purpose of response drills is to simulate a situation which may occur in a real conversation. The question and response is extracted from such a possible conversation in order to concentrate on the grammatical points which must be drilled.

Response drills differ from real conversation in that the student is instructed to give only one possible answer. The instructor should give the first response so that the student will know what his responses to subsequent questions should be.

Translation Drills

The purpose of translation drills is to familiarize the student with the idiom of Hebrew or with characteristic constructions of Hebrew whose literal English translation might be misleading. Translations drills are comparatively few in number in the course, but all drills may be used as translation exercises by asking for spot translations into English as explained above.

TRANSLATIONS

Two kinds of translations are used in this text, literal and free. The latter is often more in the nature of an English equivalent, that is, what would be said in English in an equivalent situation rather than a linguistic translation.

A beginning student often has the impression that the literal meaning is the "true" meaning and that any other meaning is necessarily secondary or wrong. This misunderstanding should be avoided. By comparing literal and free translations, the student will learn how much the translation depends on context. A word, expression, or construction may have several translations, depending on other words in the sentence, the grammatical structure of the two languages involved, and the social situation in which the conversation takes place. For example, the literal translation of /ma šlomxa/ is "What is your peace?" We have translated this as "How are you?", which is what an English speaker says in the same situation. Conversely, though, the literal equivalent of the English, /eyx ata?/, is used in Hebrew but only as a rejoinder to a previous greeting.

In the drills various possible translations are deliberately used to free the student from the idea that there is only one correct translation.

TESTS

The ultimate test is the ability to engage in a conversation in Hebrew and to speak and comprehend accurately, fluently, and easily. Most students, though, will appreciate some measurement of their performance during the course. Certain tests are built into the course material itself, and depend on the instructor's judgment in proceeding to new material. That is, the instructor should not proceed to new material until the students have mastered the old. A decision to proceed is thus a satisfactory mark of performance.

Intensive language training is usually very tedious, and the instructor should resist pressure from the students to go on to a new unit if he feels that they need more practice on the old.

The Basic Conversations and Additional Vocabulary must be memorized and overlearned. Any hesitation on the part of a student means that he does not know the material.

The Review Conversations also serve as a test for comprehension and of the ability of the students to use the limited amount of material learned up to that point.

For further testing two other types are suggested below and some examples of each are given in the section on tests.

Interpreter Situations

These require three persons - the instructor, who pretends to know no English, the student, who acts as the interpreter, and a third person who, ideally, knows no Hebrew, but who may be another student pretending to know no Hebrew. The interpreter is the one being tested and his ability to serve in that function with accuracy will be readily apparent. In later stages of the course an error on his part may lead the conversation far off the track or reduce it to an absurdity. Students usually enjoy these interpreter situations once they become familiar with the technique.

Taped Tests

None of the above tests will give the student a number grade. Suggestions for tests which can be marked and a number or percentage grade given are included in the section on tests. These tests require a tape recorder for the student to record his answers. If the school is equipped with a language laboratory, then the entire class may be tested at one time. The tapes are then listened to and marked by the instructor.

The supervising linguist and instructor will, of course, want to devise additional tests which the student will not be able to see beforehand.

The student should not be required on any test to discuss Hebrew grammar per se or to list conjugations or the like. Questions such as "What is the feminine singular imperative of /ba/ 'he came'?" are to be avoided. Instead, the student should be told "Tell that girl to come over here." If he responds with /bói héna/, then he knows the form. Otherwise, he does not.

READINGS

Material for instruction and practice in reading Hebrew is given in a special section at the end of the material for spoken Hebrew. This does not mean that such instruction should wait until the spoken material is completed. Indeed, it is expected that reading will begin about the time Unit 11 is started.

After the explanation of the Hebrew alphabet some simple recognition drills are given. These may be supplemented or replaced by flashcard drills in class. Once the students have learned to recognize all the letters and the most frequent sequences, then they may go back to the earlier units and read the Basic Conversations, drills, and Review Conversations.

Resumés of the Basic Conversations from Unit 11 on are then given in the reading section. These becomes progressively longer and more difficult. Occasionally new vocabulary is supplied in these resumés. The material in the spoken Hebrew does not assume this additional vocabulary, but it may, of course, be used in Review Conversations and the like.

Following the series of resumés is a series of short paragraphs, some of which are based on actual news articles. These are intended to bridge the gap between a fixed written text and free conversation, Progressive stages of different types of questions follow these paragraphs. All of this is in Hebrew, and the student practices reading and free conversation this way.

At the very end are some reading selections taken from newspapers and other periodicals. They are presented as examples of material which the student will see in normal encounters in Israel. The supervising linguist and instructor may prepare additional materials to supplement them and to cover a range of subject matter more pertinent to particular classes or individual students.

SUMMARY

The text provides for the assimilation of all basic forms and patterns of the language by the guided imitation, memorization, and manipulation of a large number of sentences and by practice in confronting several widely occurring everyday situations. Actual living use of the language is a necessary adjunct of the course. The instructor should therefore encourage his students from the start to use Hebrew in every way possible, above and beyond what is provided for in the text. After the first few days of work both students and instructor should avoid the use of English in the classroom. Only by constant use of the skill he is learning can the student hope to master it and retain it as a useful tool.

Transcription

In addition to the Hebrew spelling the material in this course is written in a transcription meant to help the student listen. It is an attempt to put down on paper the sounds that the instructor will say, or that will be heard on the recordings. It should be emphasized that the transcription is just a reminder of what is said and not a substitute for it.

The transcription is based for the most part directly on spoken Hebrew and is not a transliteration of ordinary Hebrew spelling. Thus, for example, /k/ is used for both כ and ק , and /t/ is used for both ט and ת. Transcriptions are set off in slash lines / / except in the Basic Conversations and Additional Vocabulary. Slash lines are also omitted where they would clutter the text.

Some departures are made from a slavish transcription of the spoken language. The definite article is spelled /ha-/ even though the /h/ is often dropped in connected speech. Root consonants which assimilate to other consonants in clusters are spelled consistently. For example, /tisgor/ "you will close" is spelled with /s/ although /tizgor/ would represent the actual pronunciation more accurately. The departures were made ad hoc to eliminate possible confusion and then only when the normal pronunciation may be easily read from the varied transcription.

Students may be familiar with other transcription and transliteration systems which are in use. sh is used where we use š and ch or kh where we use x . The system used here avoids ambiguities in the use of letters, and students will have no trouble adopting it. However, commonly used transliterations will be found in the English translations: For example, chala, Moshe, etc.

TABLE OF SYMBOLS

Consonants:

Voiceless:	p	t	k	c	č	f	s	š	x	h

Voiced:	b	d	g	j	v	z	ž	r

Nasal: m   n

Lateral: l

Glide: y

Open juncture: '

Vowels: i   e   a   o   u

Stress: Strong   ´   Weak   (unmarked)

The correspondences of these symbols with the letters of the Hebrew alphabet is given in the section on Readings.

In the following drills attention will be paid mainly to those Hebrew sounds or groups of sounds which are very different from their English counterparts. The examples in the drills are not to be memorized. The English translations are given only for reference.

CONSONANTS

/l/ The articulation represented by this letter differs from the articulations represented by the letter in English, especially at the end of a syllable. The Hebrew articulation is a lateral, with the tongue touching the gum ridge behind the upper teeth. The tongue is somewhat tenser than in English. The Hebrew articulation is essentially the same at the end as at the beginning of a syllable, whereas in English the tongue is retroflexed with the tip approaching the gum ridge but not making definite contact.

The Hebrew /l/ should be thoroughly learned since substitution of the English or American articulation gives one a "thick" accent to the Israeli ear.

li	"to me"	šalom	"hello"	el	"to"		
lo	"to him"	šeli	"mine"	al	"on"		
la	"to her"	šelo	"his"	kol	"all"		
lánu	"to us"	šelánu	"ours"	gadol	"big"		
lev	"heart"	milon	"dictionary"	meíl	"coat"		
				kilkul	"malfunction"		
				klal	"generalization"		
				menahel	"director"		
				gidel	"he raised"		
				gódel	"size"		

/x/ Voiceless velar fricative.

The articulation represented by this letter does not exist in English, and, therefore, may give some difficulty to students. However, it is extremely important that students master it and do not substitute /h/ or /k/ for it.

The tongue is brought back toward the soft palate, but instead of stopping the passage of air, as with /k/, a friction sound is made between the back of the tongue and the soft palate, similar to the noise made in clearing the throat.

Some speakers use an Arabicized pronunciation of /x/ when spelled ח . This pronunciation is affected on the radio, also. However, it is not used in general speech and will not be heard on the accompanying tapes.

xam	"warm"	léxem	"bread"	oréax	"guest"
xalav	"milk"	óxel	"food"	eyx	"how"
xom	"heat"	exad	"one"	šlomex	"(greeting)"
xódeš	"month"	axal	"he ate"	šelax	"yours"
xéci	"half"	šaxav	"he lay"	namux	"short"
xika	"waited"	axim	"brothers"	maclíax	"succeeds"
xuc	"outside"	axot	"sister"	tox	"inside"
xiduš	"renewal"				
xadaš	"new"				
xex	"palate"				
xaxam	"smart"				
šlomxa	"(greeting)"				
xémed	"delight"				
xaval	"pity"				
xut	"thread"				

/r/   Voiced velar fricative.

The articulation of the tongue is similar to that of /x/, but it is accompanied by voicing of the vocal cords. Some speakers use a tongue-tip trill instead of the velar fricative. The trill is also generally used on radio, in the theater, etc. Students may use the trill, but for most native Israelis the velar fricative will sound more "natural".

ram	"high"	laruc	"to run"	šoter	"policeman"
rax	"soft"	teruc	"excuse"	xaver	"friend"
rišon	"first"	dérex	"way"	séfer	"book"
rikud	"dance"	érev	"evening"	ir	"city"
réga	"minute"	arox	"long"	sar	"minister"
régel	"foot"	garim	"live"	kar	"cold"
rúax	"wind"	xaverim	"friends"	or	"light"
roš	"head"	šagrirut	"embassy"	barur	"clear"
rak	"only"	šagrir	"ambassador"	lira	"pound"

/p/   Voiceless Bilabial stop.

This consonant is quite similar to the English articulation. It occurs at the end of words only rarely, and these are all loan words or abbreviations used as words.   At the end of words the lips are released. Before a stressed vowel it is not as strongly aspirated as the English counterpart.

po	"here"	bapina	"on the corner"	jip	"jeep"

/t/   Voiceless alveolar stop.

This sound is also similar to the English, except that at the end of a word it must be released.   Before a stressed vowel it is not as strongly aspirated as the English counterpart.

tov	"good"		omédet	"stands"
matay	"when"		menahélet	"directress"
et	"time"		šévet	"tribe"
at	"you"(f.s.)		záit	"olive"
ot	"letter"		báit	"house"
šélet	"sign"		štut	"foolishness"
safot	"languages"		xut	"thread"
kapot	"spoons"		rut	"Ruth"

/k/   Voiceless velar stop.

This consonant, too, is similar to the English articulation except that at the end of a word it must be released.   Before a stressed vowel it is not as strongly aspirated as the English counterpart.

kol	"all"	amok	"deep"	dévek	"glue"
sakana	"danger"	xok	"law"	ravak	"bachelor"
rak	"only"	bakbuk	"bottle"	xarak	"insect"
sakik	"small bag"	šotek	"keeps quiet"		
sélek	"beet"	šok	"thigh"	matok	"sweet"
tadlik	"kindle"	šuk	"market"	pihuk	"yawn"
émek	"valley"	porek	"unloads"	xélek	"part"

/c/ Voiceless alveolar affricate.

This consonant is a combination of the articulation /t/ and /s/ functioning as a unit ts.   Practice is usually required when /c/ occurs at the beginning of a word or after a consonant.

The single symbol /c/ is used because between vowels the sequence /-ts-/ is broken up into /-t + s-/ when syllabified. /c/, on the other hand, goes with the second syllable as a unit.

/huca/	"he was taken out"	הוצא
/hutsa/	"she was flown"	הוטסה

koc	"thorn"	cav	"turtle"	cafon	"north"
yoec	"advisor"	cava	"army"	cara	"trouble"
ec	"tree"	cédek	"justice"	came	"thirsty"
lauc	"to advise"	cécef	"shell"	carud	"hoarse"
káic	"summer"	cémed	"pair"	coek	"hollers"
acic	"flowerpot"	céva	"color"	cofe	"scout"
tocéret	"product"	cimuk	"raisin"	coléa	"lame"
kacav	"butcher"	cincénet	"jar"	colélet	"submarine"
tocaa	"result"	cipor	"bird"	cur	"rock"
mecit	"lighter"	cir	"represen- tative"	cuk	"cliff"

/y/ This sound is similar to the English glide and forms diphthongs with preceding vowels.

   /iy/   /ey/   /ay/   /oy/   /uy/

The diphthong /iy/ is rare and tends to be reduced to /i/ when it occurs.

   /tiyšan/   ⟶   /tišan/ "you will sleep."

At the beginning of a word the sequence /yi/ tends to be reduced to /i/

   /yisrael/   ⟶   /israel/

/'/ Open Juncture

The open juncture /'/ has an English counterpart which is not usually written.   It is the "catch" that occurs between vowels in the exclamation "oh - oh" or the separation of syllables the second of which begins with a vowel, as in the sequence "an aim" as opposed to "a name", or in "grade A" as opposed to "gray day".

/'/ occurs mainly in slow or deliberate speech.   In ordinary conversation it is elided or barely audible.

/'/ is spelled א or ע . The latter has an Arabicized pronunciation which is used by some speakers but which is not heard generally.   It does not occur on the accompanying tapes.

The following pairs are given as illustrations.   They should not require much practice on the part of the English-speaking student.

/lirot/	"to shoot"	לירות	/lir'ot/	"to see"	לראות
/maca/	"he found"	מצא	/mac'a/	"she found"	מצאה
/nasa/	"he travelled"	נסע	/nas'a/	"she travelled"	נסעה
/mila/	"word"	מלה	/mil'a/	"she filled"	מלאה

For the pronunciation of vowels when the intervening /'/ is elided see the note on vowel clusters.

/h/ This sound is similar to the English counterpart, except that it tends to be dropped in rapid speech.   Before stressed vowels it is usually retained.

When /h/ is dropped it is replaced by zero, not /'/.

/lehakir/ ⟶   /leakir/ "to recognize" להכיר (not /le'akir/)

The /h/ is generally kept in the transcription since the student might just as well retain it until he acquires a natural-sounding rapid speech. It will not seem affected or bookish.

The student should be aware in listening to other speakers that the dropping of /'/ and /h/ will produce homonyms.

/gahar/	⟶	/gaar/	"he crouched"	גהר
/ga'ar/	⟶	/gaar/	"he scolded"	גער

The following consonants are infrequent and occur only in loan-words and proper names.

/č/ as the ch in English cheese.

/čizbat/   "tall tale"   צ'יזבט

/j/ as in English jeep.

/jip/   "jeep"   ג'יפ

/ž/ as the s in English measure or the j in French.

/žaket/   "jacket"   ז'קט
/bež/   "beige"   בז'

Consonant Clusters

In ordinary speech two adjacent consonants within a word will tend to be either both voiced or both voiceless.   If there is a sequence voiced - voiceless, such as / - zk -/, or voiceless-voiced, such as /- sg -/ then the first will assimilate to the second.   In slow or very careful speech the distinction may be maintained.

Slow speech voiced-voiceless		Normal speech	
/tizkor/	תזכור	/tiskor/	"you will remember"

voiceless-voiced

/tisgor/	תסגור	/tizgor/	"you will close"

This will often produce homonyms, or forms which in slow speech are distinguishable but in normal speech are not.   For example, the singular forms of these verbs are always distinguishable:

/yexapes/   "he will seek"   יחפש

/yexabes/   "he will launder"   יכבס

The plural forms, though, will usually sound the same:

| | /yexapsu/ | "they will seek." | יחפשו |
| (/yexabsu/ →) | /yexapsu/ | "they will launder " | יכבסו |

English speakers should have no difficulty learning such pronunciations, though in English the second consonant often assimilates to the first rather than the reverse: "observe" is pronounced <u>obzerve,</u> rather than <u>opserve.</u> The student should be aware of the possibilities since the occurrences are quite common, but context usually relieves any ambiguity.

The four consonants which do not have voiceless counterparts /m, n, l, y/ (See chart) as well as /r/ and /v/ do not cause the assimilation of a preceding voiceless consonant.

| | /masve/ | "veil" | not | */mazve/ |
| | /nifrad/ | "separated" | not | */nivrad/ |

/c/ assimilates to a following voiced consonant, also: /hicbía/ "voted" הצביע often sounds like /hidzbía/.

The above examples show medial consonant clusters, that is, clusters between vowels.   Clusters also occur initially (at the beginning of a word) and finally (at the end of a word).   Medial and final clusters should give the English speaker no particular difficulty.

Initial Consonant Clusters

Some initial clusters are similar to their English counterparts and should not present any pronunciation problems,

/pl/	-	/plitim/	"refugees"	פליטים
/tr/	-	/truma/	"contribution"	תרומה
/kl/	-	/klita/	"absorption"	קליטה

Many frequently occurring initial clusters will be unfamiliar and will require practice.   Some examples are given below, but many more will occur in the course material.

The most common error that English speakers make is to insert a vowel between the consonants.

/pt/	-	/ptax/	"open"	פתח
		/ptixa/	"opening"	פתיחה
/pn/	-	/pne/	"turn"	פנה
		/pnim/	"interior"	פנים
/tm/	-	/tmarim/	"dates"	תמרים
		/tmuna/	"picture"	תמונה
/tl/	-	/tluya/	"dependent"	תלויה
		/tlišut/	"detachment"	תלישות
/kt/	-	/któvet/	"address"	כתובת
		/ktana/	"small"	קטנה
/cr/	-	/crixa/	"necessary"	צריכה
		/cror/	"bundle"	צרור
/cf/	-	/cfat/	"Safed"	צפת
		/cfoni/	"northern"	צפוני

/cv/	–	/cvat/	"pliers"	צבת
		/cvai/	"military"	צבאי
/bd/	–	/bdika/	"examination"	בדיקה
		/bdixa/	"joke"	בדיחה
/bg/	–	/bgadim/	"clothes"	בגדים
		/bgida/	"treason"	בגידה
/dl/	–	/dli/	"bucket"	דלי
		/dlatot/	"doors"	דלתות
/dv/	–	/dvaš/	"honey"	דבש
		/dvora/	"bee"	דבורה
/gv/	–	/gvéret/	"Mrs."	גברת
		/gvina/	"cheese"	גבינה
/gd/	–	/gdola/	"big"	גדולה
		/gdud/	"troop"	גדוד

Clusters of Three Consonants

Medial clusters of three consonants are rare. When they occur as a result of grammatical patterning then a vowel (usually /e/) is inserted between the second and third consonants. When clusters of three consonants occur initially the vowel /i/ is usually inserted between the first and second consonants. These insertions are discussed in a number of places in the text.

The clusters of three consonants which do occur are mainly in recent loan-words or proper names:

/split/   "(banana) split"

Non-Permissible Clusters

Some sequences of consonants do not occur in Hebrew. These are called non-permissible clusters. For the most part, restrictions are limited to initial clusters.

When a grammatical pattern would ordinarily produce a cluster, but the cluster is non-permissible, then a vowel is inserted, usually /e/. If the first of the two consonants is /h/, /x/, or /'/ then the inserted vowel is usually /a/.

Examples of non-permissible clusters occurring in a grammatical pattern are:

m.s.		f.s.	
/gadol/	"big"	/gdola/	
/yaxol/	"able"	/yexola/	for */yxola/
/xazak/	"strong"	/xazaka/	for */xzaka/
/'acuv/	"sad"	/'acuva/	for */'cuva/
/na'im/	"pleasant"	/ne'ima/	for */n'ima/

The insertion of such vowels is discussed and drilled for each particular grammatical pattern.

Some non-permissible initial clusters are permissible medially. The addition of a prefix may, therefore, give two possible forms with the same meaning.

/rexov álenbi/   "Allenby Road"
/berexov álenbi/   "On Allenby Road"
        or
/birxov álenbi/

(The shorter form is often the more formal or literary style.)

VOWELS

The vowels of modern Hebrew are harder to master than the consonants. Students who have already learned some Hebrew traditionally may find that they have to un-learn some of the pronunciations.

In stressed syllables the vowels are very similar to the five vowels of Spanish. In unstressed syllables the vowels are generally reduced or centralized. In rapid speech vowels may be dropped entirely.

The student will find that the instructor's pronunciation of vowels will shift when going from deliberate speech to normal speed speech. Often the instructor is unaware of these changes and when asked to repeat or slow down he will produce a somewhat unnatural utterance. The student should be aware of this tendency and imitate the normal speed utterance. Speaking whole sentences at normal speed rather than choppy groupings of individual words will help the student in this regard.

/i/ High front vowel, tenser than the i of English bit

im	"with"	lištot	"to drink"	ani	"I"
iš	"man"	naim	"pleasant"	mi	"who"
iša	"woman"	máim	"water"	bli	"without"
ir	"city"	tikansi	"enter"	kli	"dish"
bišvili	"for me"	adoni	"sir"		

/e/ This symbol represents a vowel which has a range covering several English vowel phonemes. In stressed position followed by a consonant or at the end of a word it is similar to e of English bet.

Students should be very careful not to replace it with /ey/ at the end of a word - /kafe/ does not sound like the English café. The final /e/ is like the e of bet with the t cut off.

bet	"second letter"	bétax	"sure"	nae	"nice"
omed	"stands"	yafe	"pretty"	kafe	"coffee"
oxel	"eats"	et	"time"	roe	"sees"

In primary stress position before a vowel it is slightly higher and followed by a y glide.

| yodéa | "knows" | šoméa | "hears" | koréa | "tears" |

In other positions it is more centralized, like the e of democracy.

meod	"very"	lamádeti	"I studied"
meot	"hundreds"	dérex	"way"
mevin	"understands"	beséder	"O.K."
késef	"money"	bevakaša	"please"
yéled	"boy"		

/a/ Low central vowel

This vowel is pronounced like the o in American English hot. Before voiced consonants this vowel is shorter than the similar English vowel. At the end of a word it is glottalized, that is, has a "clipped" ending.

In unstressed syllables, especially before a strongly stressed syllable it tends to be centralized, like the e of English below.

at	"you" f.s.	amad	"stood"
rak	"only"	gag	"roof"
šamaš	"custodian"	az	"strong"
mamaš	"really"	kala	"bride"
ahav	"loved"	xala	"twist bread"
ad	"until"	téva	"nature"

/o/ Low-mid back vowel.

This vowel is similar to the ou of cough as pronounced by many Americans. Listen to the tapes or the native instructor to get the exact pronunciation. Be careful not to substitute a diphthong such as the o of note . Before voiced consonants it is shorter that the similar English vowel. At the end of a word it is glottalized.

In unstressed syllables, especially before a strongly stressed syllable it tends to be centralized, like the e of English below.

kof	"monkey"	bóker	"morning"	oto	"him"
tov	"good"	boker	"herdsman"	lo	"no"
sof	"end"	óxel	"food"	o	"or"
xódeš	"month"	oxel	"eats"	šlómo	"Solomon"
yom	"day"	ohev	"loves"		

/u/ High back vowel

This vowel is slightly higher than the oo of shook. Be careful not to substitute a diphthong with a w-off-glide such as the oo of food.

šuk	"market"	yifnu	"they will turn"
šuv	"again"	yištu	"they will drink"
šiput	"jurisdiction"	šávu	"they returned"
sulam	"ladder"	bánu	"in us"
sidur	"arrangement"	banu	"they built"
ud	"firebrand"	kanu	"they bought"
uf	"fly away"	avdu	"they worked"
uc	"advise"	kúmu	"get up"
hu	"he"	úru	"wake up"

Vowel Clusters

All combinations of two vowels occur. The Hebrew spelling may indicate that /'/, /h/, or /y/ should occur between them, and in deliberate speech these consonants will usually be heard. In ordinary speech, however, vowel clusters occur with a smooth transition between them. English speakers will have to practice these vowel clusters in order to achieve a proper Israeli pronunciation.

In the transcriptions these clusters are generally written without the consonants which are indicated by the Hebrew spelling. Appropriate reminders are given at various points in the text.

In pronouncing the following examples for the students to imitate, the instructor should be relaxed and informal in his pronunciation.   Otherwise he will tend to insert a consonant and the practice will have lost its point.

Elision of /'/, /h/, and /y/ does not mean that the speech is "sloppy" or "corrupt".   In slow or emphatic speech they must occur.   But in normal, everyday, "natural" speech they are dropped by native speakers of Hebrew. Maintaining these consonants in this informal style will sound awkward.

paam	"time"
taavor	"you will cross"
laalot	"to go up"
báit	"house"
israel	"Israel"
naim	"pleasant"
menaalin	"directors"
leexol	"to eat"
neima	"pleasant"
meod	"very"
beemet	"really"
yoec	"counsellor"
yoacim	"counsellors"
bóu,	"come"
šavúa	"week"
batúax	"sure"
šeuit	"beans"
maašaa	"What time is it?"

STRESS AND INTONATION

A complete description of stress and intonation patterns would be very complicated and of little help in the actual learning of them. The instructor should present the sentences as naturally as possible, and the student should do his best to mimic closely.

The following comments will explain the general occurrence of stress on individual words and in connected speech.   The learning of the Basic Sentences and the acting out of the conversations constitute the drills on stress and intonation.

In the transcription an accent mark ´ indicates a syllable which may receive strong stress.   In words of more than one syllable the placement of stress is meaningful.

In individual words, particularly when pronounced in isolation, the stress is usually on the last syllable or on the next to the last syllable.   In most cases the placement of stress is a part of the grammatical pattern, but in others it must be memorized as part of the individual word.   For example, the /-ti/ and /-ta/ suffixes of the past tense are never stressed: /amárti/ "I said", /amárta/ "you said".   On the other hand the following pairs of words are distinguished from each other by the stress placement.

/oxél/	"(he is) eating"	/óxel/	"food"
/šlomó/	" his peace"	/šlómo/	"Solomon"
/emcá/	" I will find"	/émca/	"middle"
/banú/	" they built"	/bánu/	"in us"

In some words of three or more syllables the stress is on the last syllable but two: /mášehu/ "something",   /míšehu/ "someone"
       /ótobus/ "bus"   ,   /amérika/ "America"

(In general, loan-words tend to retain the stress where it was in the language from which it was borrowed.)

Only the main stress of a word is indicated. Of the unstressed (unmarked) syllables some will seem louder than others. English has similar patterns of "secondary" and "tertiary" stresses, and there is no need to drill the pronunciation - provided the main stress is properly placed:

/ledabér/   "to speak"   and not */lédaber/.

From Unit 18 on the stress mark ´ is placed on a word only when the stress is <u>not</u> on the last syllable.

Reduction of Stress

In ordinary connected speech many words, particularly the prepositions with pronominal suffixes, lose the stress which they have when spoken in isolation: /tagíd li/ "tell me". In effect, these words are pronounced as one word with the stress on the next to last syllable.

Style Differences in Placement of Stress

The placement of stress differs in formal style in some words and grammatical patterns. In general, a stress on the next to last syllable is shifted to the last syllable in these forms. For example:

<u>Informal</u>	<u>Formal</u>	
/šmóne/	/šmoné/	"eight"
/hi báa/	/hi baá/	"she is coming"
/amártem/	/amartém/	"you said"

Intonation Marks

Intonation is indicated only in a very broad way by the use of punctuation marks at the end of a phrase or sentence.

A period indicates a falling intonation. Questions which begin with a question-word (who, what, etc.) generally have a falling intonation at the end and are therefore marked with a period, <u>not</u> with a question mark.

A question mark indicates a rising intonation. Yes-or-no questions and rejoinder questions (And how are you?) generally have a rising intonation at the end.

A comma indicates a possible pause with a relatively sustained intonation. A hyphen indicates a hesitation pause, usually with a sustained or rising intonation.

An exclamation mark indicates an exclamation with increased loudness.

<u>Note</u>: These marks are used in this manner <u>only</u> in the transcription. In the English and Hebrew spellings the standard punctuation is used.

TAPE RECORDINGS

The tape recordings which accompany <u>Hebrew Modern   have the</u> following format:

(1) Basic Conversation

   (a)   <u>Dialogue for Learning.</u> The first presentation of the Basic Sentences are built up from the partial utterances, as described in the Introduction. Each full sentence is said twice.   The student repeats everything he hears at this step. He may follow in his book.

   (b)   <u>Dialogue for Fluency.</u> Each complete Basic Sentence is given with space for repetition.   The student should not need his book here.

   (c)   <u>Dialogue for Comprehension.</u> The Basic Conversation is spoken at normal speed by a group of Hebrew speakers as you might overhear it.   The student just listens with his book closed.

   (d)   <u>Alternating Drill.</u> The Basic Conversation is presented at normal speed with one speaker's part missing.   The Student speaks the missing part. He thus conducts a conversation with the tape recording.

   The Basic Conversation is then presented with the other speaker's part missing. The student supplies the part.   He thus practices participating in the entire conversation.

   In some Basic Conversations a third speaker has a small part.   In such cases the entire conversation is not repeated with this small part missing.

(2) Additional Vocabulary

   The sentences in the Additional Vocabulary section are presented with build-ups if necessary.

(3) Drills

   (a)   <u>Substitution Drills, Substitution-Agreement Drills.</u> The first, or "model" sentence is given with spaces for repetition. Then a substitution cue is given with space for the student to respond with the new sentence.   The correct response is then given on the tape. The student may follow in the book.

   (b)   <u>Expansion Drills, Transformation Drills, Response Drills.</u> The cue sentence is given with space for the response sentence.   The tape then gives the correct response sentence.   The student should look in the book to see what his response should be.   Only the translation of the first cue-response in given.

Note: In using the tapes the student should not go through an entire tape at one sitting especially when doing the drill sections.   Instead he should do a few drills, rewind the tape, and do them again until he can do them perfectly without using the book.

   Translation Drills, Rapid Response Drills, and Review Conversations are not recorded.

   Occasionally circumstances required the use of a woman's voice to record a man's part and vice versa. This should not disturb the student.

1.1 <u>Greetings</u> (Two men meet)

MR. WILLIAMS

Hello, Moshe.	šalóm mošé.		שָׁלוֹם, משה.
How are you?	má šlomxá.		מה שלומך?
peace, welfare		šalóm (m)	שלום
what		má	מה
the welfare of		šlóm-	שלום-
you, your (m.s.)		-xá (m.s.)	ך-

MOSHE

Thank you very much.	todá rabá.		תודה רבה.
I'm fine.	šlomí tóv.		שְׁלוֹמִי טוֹב.
And how are you?	umá šlomxá?		ומה שלומך?
thanks		todá (f)	תודה
much		rabá (f)	רבה
me, my		-í	י-
and		u-	ו

MR. WILLIAMS

Fine.	tóv.		טוב.
How is	má šlóm		מה שלום
the family?	hamišpaxá.		המשפחה?
the		ha-	ה-
family		mišpaxá (f)	משפחה

MOSHE

All right.	beséder.		בסדר.
How is	má šlóm		מה שלום
your wife?	ištexá.		אשתך?
in		be-	ב-
order		séder (m)	סדר
wife, woman		išá (f)	אשה

MR. WILLIAMS

She's fine, too.	gám šlomá tóv.		גם שלומה טוב.
Excuse me.	slixá.		סליחה.
I have to	aní muxráx		אני מוכרח
run.	larúc.		לרוץ.
too, also		gám	גם
her		-á	ה-
pardon (noun)		slixá (f)	סליחה
I		aní	אני
have to, must		muxráx (m.s.)	מוכרח
to		la-	ל-
run		rúc	רוץ

MOSHE

Oh, yes!	ó -- kén!		או -- כן!
It's late already.	kvár meuxár.		כבר מאוחר.
Goodbye.	šalóm.		שלום.
yes		kén	כן
already		kvár	כבר
late		meuxár	מאוחר

MR. WILLIAMS

So long.	šalóm.	שלום.
Be seeing you.	lehitraót.	להתראות.
to see again	lehitraót	להתראות

1.2 Greetings (Two women meet)

MRS. WILLIAMS

Hello, Miriam.	šalóm, miryám.	שלום, מרים.
How are you?	má šloméx.	מה שלומך?
you, your (f.s.)	-éx	־ך

MIRIAM

Thank you very much.	todá rabá.	תודה רבה.
I'm fine.	šlomí tóv.	שלומי טוב.
And how are you?	umá šloméx?	ומה שלומך?

MRS. WILLIAMS

| Fine. | tóv. | טוב. |
| How is the family? | má šlóm hamišpaxá. | מה שלום המשפחה? |

MIRIAM

All right.	beséder.	בסדר.
How is	má šlóm	מה שלום
your husband?	baaléx.	בעלך?
husband	báal (m)	בעל

MRS. WILLIAMS

He's fine, too.	gám šlomó tóv.	גם שלומו טוב.
Excuse me.	slixá.	סליחה.
I have to	aní muxraxá	אני מוכרחה
run.	larúc.	לרוץ.
him, his	-ó	־ו
have to, must	muxraxá (f.s.)	מוכרחה

MIRIAM

| Oh, yes! It's late already. | ó -- kén! kvár meuxár. | או ־ כן! כבר מאוחר. |
| So long. | šalóm. | שלום. |

MRS. WILLIAMS

| So long. Be seeing you. | šalóm. lehitraót. | שלום. להתראות. |

1.3 ADDITIONAL VOCABULARY

We are fine.	šloménu tóv.	שלומנו טוב.
How are you? (m.pl.)	má šlomxém.	מה שלומכם?
How are you? (f.pl.)	má šlomxén.	מה שלומכן?
How are they? (m.pl.)	má šlomám.	מה שלומם?
How are they? (f.pl.)	má šlomán.	מה שלומן?

Mr. Carmi	már kármi	מר כרמי
Mr. Carmi (alternate form)	adón kármi	אדון כרמי
Miss or Mrs. Carmi	gvéret kármi	גברת כרמי
It is early.	mukdám.	מוקדם.

1.4 Classroom Expressions

In this section we introduce a few additional Hebrew phrases which will be used in class. They should be practiced until the pronunciation is learned, but since they will be used constantly in class they can be memorized without special effort.

Some of the expressions are given in more than one form, differing in gender or number. Their use will depend on the make-up of the class, and the instructor may find it necessary to introduce additional variations not included here.

1. Close the door.
   (said to a man)   sgór et hadélet.   סגור את הדלת.
   (said to a woman)   sigrí et hadélet.   סגרי את הדלת.

2. Sit down, please.
   (said to a man)   šév, bevakašá.   שב, בבקשה.
   (said to a woman)   šví, bevakašá.   שבי, בבקשה.
   (said to men or both) švú, bevakašá.   שבו, בבקשה

3. Quiet, please.   šéket, bevakašá.   שקט, בבקשה.

4. Open your books.
   (said to men or both) pitxú et hasfarím.   פתחו את הספרים.
   (said to women)   ptáxna et hasfarím.   פתחנה את הספרים.

5. Speak louder.
   (said to a man)   dabér yotér bekól.   דבר יותר בקול.
   (said to a woman)   dabrí yotér bekól.   דברי יותר בקול.

6. All together.   kulám beyáxad.   כולם ביחד.

7. Again.   ód hapáam.   עוד הפעם.

8. Do you understand?
   (said to a man)   atá mevín?   אתה מבין?
   (said to a woman)   át meviná?   את מבינה?

9. I don't understand.
   (said by a man)   aní ló mevín.   אני לא מבין.
   (said by a woman)   aní ló meviná.   אני לא מבינה.

10. I don't know.
    (said by a man)   aní ló yodéa.   אני לא יודע.
    (said by a woman)   aní ló yodáat.   אני לא יודעת.

11. Please translate.
    (said to a man)   targém, bevakašá.   תרגם, בבקשה.
    (said to a woman)   targemí, bevakašá.   תרגמי, בבקשה.

12. How do you say   éyx omrím   איך אומרים
    table in Hebrew?   table beivrít.   table בעברית?

GRAMMAR DRILLS

1.5 Masculine and Feminine

Compare the following sets of corresponding sentences from conversations 1.1 and 1.2:

a. šalóm, mošé. má šlomxá. — Hello, Moshe. How are you?
šalóm, miryám. má šloméx. — Hello, Miriam. How are you?

b. má šlóm ištexá. — How is your wife?
má šlóm baaléx. — How is your husband?

Note that forms differ when a man or woman is being spoken to. It is important that the student learn the corresponding forms at the outset. There are a number of patterns of these corresponding forms, which will be referred to by their traditional names, masculine and feminine. All nouns in Hebrew, whether or not referring to beings with sex, are members of one or the other class. These will be designated (m) or (f) in the vocabulary listings.

Throughout the course the various corresponding forms required by each gender will be drilled.

The following drills should be thoroughly learned. The student should not have to be corrected afterwards on the use of the proper forms. Such errors will produce a reaction similar to that felt by English speakers on hearing the following: "How is your brother?"
"She is fine, thank you."

The cue words in the following drills are names of men and women. Include the name in the response so as to fix firmly the connection of form and sex of person spoken to. The instructor may vary the drill by using the names of members of the class or by introducing other Hebrew names such as /avígdor/(man) and /xána/ (woman).

The drills are to be done as follows:

Instructor: šalóm mošé má šlomxá.
Student: (repeats) šalóm mošé. má šlomxá.
Instructor: miryám
Student: šalóm miryám. má šloméx.
Instructor: (repeats) šalóm miryám. má šloméx.
már kóhen

A. šalóm mošé. má šlomxá. — שלום, משה. מה שלומך?

miryám	šalóm miryám. má šloméx.	מרים
már kóhen	šalóm már kóhen. má šlomxá.	מר כהן
gvéret Williams	šalóm gvéret Williams. má šloméx.	גב׳ וויליאמס
gvéret káspi	šalóm gvéret káspi. má šloméx.	גב׳ כספי
már Williams	šalóm már Williams. má šlomxá.	מר וויליאמס
avígdor	šalóm avígdor. má šlomxá.	אביגדור
xána	šalóm xána. má šloméx.	חנה
már káspi	šalóm már káspi. má šlomxá.	מר כספי
mošé	šalóm mošé. má šlomxá.	משה

B. <u>má šlóm ištexá, már Williams.</u>   מה שלום אשתך, מר וויליאמס?

   <u>gvéret Williams</u>   má šlóm baaléx, gvéret Williams.   גב' וויליאמס

   <u>már kóhen</u>   má šlóm ištexá, már kóhen.   מר כהן

   <u>gvéret kármi</u>   má šlóm baaléx, gvéret kármi.   גב' כרמי

   <u>xána</u>   má šlóm baaléx, xána.   וחנה

   <u>mošé</u>   má šlóm ištexá, mošé.   משה

   <u>már Williams</u>   má šlóm ištexá, már Williams.   מר וויליאמס

1.6 Pronominal Suffixes - Singular Set

There are several sets of pronouns indicating person, gender, and number. The following occur as suffixes to singular nouns and to certain prepositions. They will be referred to as the singular set.

When suffixed to nouns they are often translated as possessives.

     má šlom<u>xá</u>.   (literally) What is <u>your</u> peace?
     má šlóm ište<u>xá</u>.   How is <u>your</u> wife?
     šlom<u>í</u> tóv.   (literally) <u>My</u> peace is good.

Except for certain stereotyped expressions as these, though, the suffixing of nouns to indicate possession is more formal in style.

When suffixed to prepositions they are usually translated as the objects of the prepositions. This will be discussed later on.

A. Substitution Drill

   má šlomxá.   How are you?   מה שלומך?
     šloméx   שלומך.
     šlomxém   שלומכם
     šlomám   שלומם
     šlomán   שלומן
     šlomó   שלומו
     šlomxén   שלומכן
     šlomá   שלומה

B. Substitution Drill

   šlomí tóv.   I'm fine.   שלומי טוב.
     šloménu   שלומנו
     šlomó   שלומו
     šlomán   שלומן
     šlomá   שלומה
     šlomám   שלומם

C. Response Drill

   Instructor: má šlomxá.   Student: šlomí tóv.   מה שלומך?
         má šlomxém.   šloménu tóv.   מה שלומכם?
         má šlomám.   šlomám tóv.   מה שלומם?
         má šlomó.   šlomó tóv.   מה שלומו?
         má šlomxén.   šloménu tóv.   מה שלומכן?
         má šlomá.   šlomá tóv.   מה שלומה?
         má šloméx.   šlomí tóv.   מה שלומך?

D. Response Drill

Instructor: má šlóm baaléx.	Student: šlomó tóv.	?מה שלום בעלך
má šlóm ištexá.	šlomá tóv.	?מה שלום אשתך
má šlóm hamišpaxá.	šlomá tóv.	?מה שלום המשפחה
má šlóm baalá.	šlomó tóv.	?מה שלום בעלה
má šlóm ištó.	šlomá tóv.	?מה שלום אשתו

[Note: In the form /ištexá/ the /-e-/ is inserted for phonological reasons, to break up the three-consonant cluster /-štx-/, which would otherwise result.]

1.7 Alternate forms of nouns before suffixes

Many nouns have an alternate form when occurring with a pronominal suffix.

| šalóm | 'welfare' | ' šlomí | 'my welfare' |
| išá | 'wife' | iští | 'my wife' |

Compare, on the other hand: báal   'husband'   baalí   'my husband'

It is very difficult to predict which nouns will have such alternate forms or what the alternate form will be. The student should simply drill these as they occur in the text until he has mastered them.

When a suffixed noun occurs in a Basic Sentence the independent form of the noun will be given in the vocabulary breakdown, and, as much as possible, drills will be provided.

REVIEW CONVERSATIONS

The purpose of the Review Conversations is to lead the student into free conversation within the range of the vocabulary and grammatical patterns which he has learned. Students should keep their books closed while the instructor follows the procedure suggested here.

1. With the class just listening, the instructor reads the conversation in as natural a manner as possible. The instructor repeats the conversation until the class understands it completely.

2. The instructor rereads the conversation several times with half the class repeating one role and half the other role.

3. The two halves of the class exchange roles and Step 2 is repeated.

4. The instructor takes the first part and acts out the conversation with the class.

5. The class and instructor exchange roles and repeat Step 4.

6. Individual students are assigned the various roles in turn until all have taken both parts in the conversation.

7. Individual students make substitutions freely, including whatever changes may be necessary elsewhere in the conversation. These free conversations should not be prolonged more than four minutes or so. This will give all the students an opportunity to try their hand at the same situation. The instructor should refrain from adding a lot of vocabulary at this point.

A: šalóm, gvéret kóhen. má šloméx.   ?א: שלום, גברת כהן. מה שלומך

B: todá. šlomí tóv, umá šlomxá?   ?ב: תודה. שלומי טוב. ומה שלומך

A: gám šlomí tóv, todá.   .א: גם שלומי טוב, תודה

B: má šlóm mošé.   ?ב: מה שלום משה

A: aní ló yodéa.   .א: אני לא יודע

_____

C: má šlóm ištexá, már kármi.   ?ג: מה שלום אשתך, מר כרמי

D: beséder, todá. má šlóm baaléx?   ?ד: בסדר, תודה. מה שלום בעלך

C: šlomó tóv. má šlóm hamišpaxá?   ?ג: שלומו טוב. מה שלום המשפחה

D: tóv, todá. slixá. meuxár.   .ד: טוב, תודה. סליחה. מאוחר

C: ó, gám aní muxraxá larúc. šalóm.   .ג: או, גם אני מוכרחה לרוץ. שלום

D: šalóm, lehitraót.   .ד: שלום, להתראות

7

E: šalóm, már Williams.   ה: שלום, מר ווילי אמס.

    šalóm, gvéret Williams.   má šlomxém.   שלום, גברת ווילי אמס. מה שלומכם?

F: todá rabá. šloménu tóv.   ו : תודה רבה. שלומנו טוב.

    má šloméx, gvéret zahávi.   מה שלומך, גברת זהבי?

E: beséder.   má šlóm hamišpaxá?   ה: בסדר. מה שלום המשפחה?

F: slixá. aní ló mevín.   ód hapáam,   ו : סליחה. אני לא מבין. עוד הפעם

    bevakašá.   בבקשה.

E: má šlóm hamišpaxá.   ה: מה שלום המשפחה?

F: šlomá tóv, todá.   ו : שלומה טוב, תודה.

———————

G: šalóm, már kármi.   ז : שלום, מר כרמי.

H: o! šalóm, mošé! má šlomxá.   ח: או ו שלום, משה! מה שלומך?

G: šlomí tóv. má šlóm hamišpaxá.   ז : שלומי טוב. מה שלום המשפחה?

H: beséder. sgór et hadélet, bevakašá.   ח: בסדר. סגור את הדלת, בבקשה.

G: ken.   slixá.   ז : כן. סליחה.

———————

I: már Williams, šév, bevakašá.   ט: מר ווילי אמס, שב, בבקשה.

J: ód hapáam, bevakašá. aní ló mevín.   י: עוד הפעם, בבקשה. אני לא מבין.

I: šév, bevakašá.   ט: שב, בבקשה.

J: ó kén. aní mevín. todá.   י : או כן. אני מבין. תורה.

———————

K: slixá, miryám. aní muxráx larúc.   כ: סליחה, מרים. אני מוכרח לרוץ.

L: ló. šév, bevakašá. mukdám.   ל: לא. שב, בבקשה. מוקדם.

K: ló, todá. meuxár.   כ: לא, תודה. מאוחד.

L: tóv. lehitraót.   ל: טוב. להתראות.

———————

M: šéket, bevakašá.   מ: שקט, בבקשה.

N: slixá. dabér yotér bekól.   נ: סליחה. דבר יותד בקול.

M: šéket! atá mevín?   מ: שקט! אתה מבין?

N: tóv. aní mevín. slixá.   נ: טוב. אני מבין. כליחה.

2.1   Introductions   (Two men are introduced)

MR. CASPI

Mr. Cohen,	már kóhen,	מר כהן,
please meet	takír bevakašá	תכיר בבקשה
Mr. Williams.	et már Williams.	את מר ווילליאמס.
you will know	takír (m.s.)	תכיר
(preposition indicating	et	את
object of verb)		

MR. COHEN

I'm very happy	naím li meód	נעים לי מאד
to meet you,	lehakír otxá,	להכיר אותך,
Mr. Williams.	már Williams.	מר ווילליאמס.
pleasant	naím (m.s.)	נעים
to me	li	לי
very	meód	מאד
to know (a person)	lehakír	להכיר
you (m.s., obj.)	otxá (m.s.)	אותך

MR. WILLIAMS

How do you do,	naím meód,	נעים מאד,
Mr. Cohen.	már kóhen.	מר כהן.

MR. CASPI

Mr. Williams	már Williams	מר ווילליאמס
is Counsellor of	hú yoéc	הוא יועץ
the American Embassy.	hašagrirút	הישגרירות
	haamerikáit.	האמריקאית.
he, it	hú	הוא
counsellor, adviser	yoéc (m)	יועץ
embassy	šagrirút (f)	שגרירות
American	amerikái (m.s.)	אמריקאי

MR. COHEN

When	matáy	מתי
did you arrive	higáta	הגעת
in the country,	laárec,	לארץ,
Mr. Williams?	már Williams.	מר ווילליאמס.
when (interrogative)	matáy	מתי
you arrived (m.s.)	higáta (m.s.)	הגעת
country	érec (f)	ארץ

MR. WILLIAMS

I arrived	higáti	הגעתי
two days ago,	lifnéy yomáim,	לפני יומיים,
Mr. Cohen.	már kóhen.	מר כהן.
I arrived	higáti	הגעתי
before, ago	lifnéy	לפני
day	yóm (m)	יום
two days	yomáim	יומיים

2.2 Introductions (Two women are introduced)

MRS. CASPI

Mrs. Cohen,	gvéret kóhen,	גברת כהן,
please meet	takíri bevakašá	תכירי בבקשה
Mrs. Williams.	et gvéret Williams.	את גברת וויל'אמס.
you will know (f.s.)	takíri (f.s.	תכירי

MRS. COHEN

I'm very happy	naím lí meód	נעים לי מאד
to meet you,	lehakír otáx,	להכיר אותך,
Mrs. Williams.	gvéret Williams.	גברת וויל'אמס.
you (f.s.,obj.)	otáx (f.s.)	אותך

MRS. WILLIAMS

How do you do,	naím meód,	נעים מאד,
Mrs. Cohen.	gvéret kóhen.	גברת כהן.

MRS. CASPI

Mrs. Williams	gvéret Williams	גברת וויל'אמס
is the wife	hí ištó	היא אשתו
of the Counsellor	šel yoéc	של יועץ
of the American Embassy.	hašagrirút	השגרירות
	haamerikáit.	האמריקאית.
she, it	hí	היא
of	šél	של

MRS. COHEN

When	matáy	מתי
did you arrive	higát	הגעת
in the country,	laárec,	לארץ,
Mrs. Williams?	gvéret Williams.	גברת וויל'אמס?
you arrived (f.s.)	higát (f.s.)	הגעת

MRS. WILLIAMS

I arrived	higáti	הגעתי
two days ago,	lifnéy yomáim,	לפני יומיים,
Mrs. Cohen.	gvéret kóhen.	גברת כהן.

2.3 ADDITIONAL VOCABULARY

I arrived yesterday.	higáti etmól.	הגעתי אתמול.
I arrived the day before yesterday.	higáti šilšóm.	הגעתי שלשום.
I arrived a week ago.	higáti lifnéy šavúa.	הגעתי לפני שבוע.
week	šavúa (m)	שבוע
I arrived two weeks ago.	higáti lifnéy švuáim.	הגעתי לפני שבועיים.
I arrived a month ago.	higáti lifnéy xódeš.	הגעתי לפני חודש.
month	xódeš (m)	חודש
I arrived two months ago.	higáti lifnéy xodšáim.	הגעתי לפני חודשיים.

GRAMMAR DRILLS

2.4 Equational Sentences

Compare the following sentences and their English translations:

    a. má šlomxá   (literally)   What is your peace?

    b. šlomí tóv   (literally)   My peace is good.

    c már Williams hú yoéc   Mr. Williams is the Counsellor
       hašagrirút haamerikáit.   of the American Embassy.

Note that the Hebrew equivalent of the English sentence pattern "A is B" is "A B". The Hebrew equivalent for the English present tense forms am, is and are is the juxtaposition of the two parts of the sentence. Such sentences are called equational sentences.

In Sentence c the form /hú/ 'he' is a pleonastic subject.

Now compare the following sentences and their translations:

    d. meuxár.   It is late.

    e. naím meód.   It is very pleasant.

In these sentences the English has not only a verb form, but this verb requires a subject, in this case the impersonal pronoun it. The Hebrew sentences are complete as they stand.

A. Substitution Drill

<u>hú</u> amerikái.	He is an American.	הוא אמריקאי.
aní		אני
mošé hú		משה הוא
már Williams		מר וויל־יאמס
baalá		בעלה

B. Substitution Drill

<u>hí</u> amerikáit.	She is an American.	היא אמריקאית.
aní		אני
iští		אשתי
gvéret Williams		גברת וויל־יאמס
miryám hí		מרים היא

C. Substitution Drill

<u>hú</u> yoéc hašagrirút.	He is the Counsellor of the Embassy.	הוא יועץ השגרירות.
aní		אני
már Williams hú		מר וויל־יאמס הוא
baalá		בעלה

D. Substitution Drill

<u>meuxár</u> meód.	It is very late.	מאוחר מאד.
mukdám		מוקדם
naím		נעים

2.5 The Direct Object Preposition /et ~ ot-/

The preposition /et/ preceded a direct object of a verb when the object is definite. An object is definite in any of the following cases:
a. It is preceded by the definite article prefix /ha-/ 'the';
b. It has a pronoun suffix, e.g., /iští/ 'my wife';
c. It is a proper name, e.g., /mošé/ 'Moshe';
d. It is the first noun of a noun-noun construction in which the second noun is definite, e.g., /yoéc hašagrirút/ 'the Counsellor of the Embassy';
  [The grammar of this last case will be discussed in detail later.]
e. It is an interrogative or demonstrative, e.g. /má/ 'what', /zé/ 'this'.

When the object of the verb is not definite, then the preposition does not occur. Compare: sgór et hadélet.   Close the door.
                        sgór délet.   Close a door.

The sequence /et ha-/ is often contracted in ordinary speech to /ta-/.
        /sgór tadélet./   /pitxú tasfarím./

The singular set of pronominal suffixes is used with this preposition, but the preposition has the alternate form /ot-/ when occuring with a suffix.
    naím li meód lehakír <u>otxá.</u>   naím li meód lehakír <u>otáx.</u>
Some speakers use a regularized form of the latter - /otéx/. The first person plural form is /otánu/ rather than */oténu/. These variants of the pronominal suffixes, /-áx/ and /-ánu/, occur with certain other prepositions.
    The second person plural forms are either /otxém, otxén/ or /etxém, etxén/. The latter, however, are considered rather literary and somewhat stilted, though these are the only ones occurring in the classical language.

A. Substitution Drill
                Please meet Mr. Williams.
    takír bevakašá et már Williams.   תכיר בבקשה את מר וויל'אמס.
                gvéret Williams   גברת וויל`אמס
                mošé   משה
                hayoéc   היועץ
                hamišpaxá   המשפחה
                iští   אשתי
                yoéc hašagrirút   יועץ השגרירות
                baalá   בעלה
                ištó   אשתו
                xána   חנה

B. Substitution Drill

    sgór et hadélet.   Close the door.   סגור את הדלת.
        hasfarím   הספרים

C. Substitution Drill

    pitxú et hadélet.   Open the door.   פתחו את הדלת.
        hasfarím   הספרים
        hašagrirút   השגרירות

D. Substitution Drill
                I'm very happy to meet you.
    naím li meód lehakír otxá.   נעים לי מאד להכיר אותך.
                otáx   אותך
                otó   אותו
                et már Williams   את מר ווילאמס
                et ištó   את אשתו

12

E. Substitution-Agreement Drill

I'm very happy to meet you, Mr. Williams.

naím li meód lehakír otxá, már Williams.   נעים לי מאד להכיר אותך, מר ווילאמס.

gvéret kóhen	naím li meód lehakír otáx, gvéret kóhen.	גב' כהן
gvéret Williams	naím li meód lehakír otáx, gvéret Williams.	גב' ווילאמס
már káspi	naím li meód lehakír otxá, már káspi.	מר כספי
mošé	naím li meód lehakír otxá, mošé.	משה
miryám	naím li meód lehakír otáx, miryám.	מרים
gvéret zahávi	naím li meód lehakír otáx, gvéret zahávi.	גברת זהבי
már óren	naím li meód lehakír otxá, már óren.	מר אורן
xána	naím li meód lehakír otáx, xána.	חנה
avígdor	naím li meód lehakír otxá, avígdor.	אביגדור

נעים לי מאד להכיר אותך...

13

REVIEW CONVERSATIONS

A: šalóm, gvéret Williams.
    takíri bevakašá et iští.

א: שלום, גברת וויל**י**אמס.
תכירי בבקשה את אשתי.

B: naím li meód lehakír otáx
    gvéret zahávi. má šloméx.

ב: נעים לי מאד להכיר אותך,
גברת זהבי. מה שלומך?

C: gám lí naím lehakír otáx.

ג: גם לי נעים להכיר אותך.

D: miryám. takíri et baalá šel sára.

ד: מרים. תכירי את בעלה של שרה.

E: naím li meód lehakír otxá, már zahávi.

ה: נעים לי מאד להכיר אותך, מר זהבי.

F: naím meód.

ו: נעים מאד.

G: má šloméx, miryám.
    matáy higát lašagrirút.

ז: מה שלומך, מרים?
מתי הגעת לשגרירות?

H: higáti lifnéy yomáim, már Williams.
    takír bevakašá et baalí.

ח: הגעתי לפני יומיים, מר ווילי**א**מס.
תכיר בבקשה את בעלי.

G: naím li meód lehakír otxá, már kóhen.

ז: נעים לי מאד להכיר אותך, מר כהן.

I: naím meód, már Williams.

ט: נעים מאד, מר ווילי**א**מס.

J: matáy higáta laárec, már Jones.

י: מתי הגעת לארץ, מר ג'ונס?

K: higáti etmól.

כ: הגעתי אתמול.

J: gám aní higáti etmól.

י: גם אני הגעתי אתמול.

L: atára. matáy higát letèl avív.

ל: עטרה. מתי הגעת לתל אביב?

M: higáti lifnéy xódeš.
    matáy higáta lašagrirút, davíd.

מ: הגעתי לפני חודש.
מתי הגעת לשגרירות, דוד?

L: higáti šilšóm.

ל: הגעתי שלשום.

N: davíd. sgór et hadélet, bevakašá.

נ: דוד. סגור את הדלת, בבקשה.

O: et má?

ע: את מה?

N: et hadélet.

נ: את הדלת.

O: ó kén. slixá.

ע: או, כן. סליחה.

3.1 <u>Introductions, contd.</u> (Two men)

MR. COHEN

How did you come?	éx higáta.	איך הגעת?
By plane or	beavirón ó	באוירון או
by ship?	beoniá.	באוניה?

	how	éx, éyx	איך
	airplane	avirón (m)	אוירון
	or	ó	או
	ship	oniá (f)	אוניה

MR. WILLIAMS

I came	higáti	הגעתי
by plane	beavirón	באוירדרן
to Lydda.	lelúd.	ללוד.
Lydda (place name)	lúd, lód	לוד

MR. COHEN

How	éx	איך
were you impressed	hitrašámta	התרשמת
by Lydda?	milúd.	מלוד?

| | you were impressed | hitrašámta (m.s.) | התרשמת |
| | from, by | mi-, me- | מ- |

MR. WILLIAMS

Lydda is	lúd hú	לוד הוא
a beautiful and	nemál teufá	נמל תעופה
modern airport.	yafé	יפה
	vexadíš.	וחדיש.

	port	namál, namél (m)	נמל
	flight	teufá (f)	תעופה
	beautiful, pretty	yafé (m.s.)	יפה
	and	ve-	ו-
	modern	xadíš (m.s.)	חדיש

MR. COHEN

I hope that	aní mekavé še-	אני מקווה ש-
you like our country.	arcénu	ארצנו
	mócet xén	מוצאת חן
	beeynéxa.	בעיניך.

	hope	mekavé (m.s.,pres.)	מקווה
	that (conjunction)	še-	ש-
	find	mocét (f.s.,pres.)	מוצאת
	favor, charm	xén (m)	חן
	eye	áin (f)	עין
	[two] eyes	eynáim	עיניים
	your (m.s.) eyes	eynéxa	עיניך

MR. WILLIAMS

Oh, yes.	ó kén.	או, כן.
The country is	haárec	הארץ
very pretty.	yafá meód.	יפה מאד.
beautiful, pretty	yafá (f.s.)	יפה

15

3.2 Introductions, contd. (Two women)

MRS. COHEN

How did you come?	éx higát.	?איך הגעת
By plane or	beavirón ó	באוירון או
by ship?	beoniá.	?באוניה

MRS. WILLIAMS

I came	higáti	הגעתי
by plane	beavirón	באוירון
to Lydda.	lelúd.	.ללוד

MRS. COHEN

How	éx	איך
were you impressed	hitrašámt	התרשמת
by Lydda?	milúd.	?מלוד
you were impressed	hitrašámt (f.s.)	התרשמת

MRS. WILLIAMS

Lydda is	lúd hú	לוד הוא
a beautiful and	nemál teufá	נמל תעופה
modern airport.	yafé	יפה
	vexadíš.	.וחדיש

MRS. COHEN

I hope that	aní mekavá še-	—אני מקורה ש
you like our country.	arcénu	ארצנו
	mócet xén	מוצאת חן
	beeynáix.	.בעיניך
hope (present)	mekavá (f.s.,pres.)	מקורה
your (f.s.) eyes	eynáix	עיניך

MRS. WILLIAMS

Oh, yes.	ó kén.	.או, כן
The country is	haárec	הארץ
very pretty.	yafá meód.	.יפה מאד

3.3 ADDITIONAL VOCABULARY

How did you come?		
(said to men or both)	éx higátem.	?איך הגעתם
(said to women)	éx higáten.	?איך הגעתן
We came by plane.	higánu beavirón.	.הגענו באוירון
I like the country.	haárec mócet xén beeynáy.	.הארץ מוצאת חן בעיני
He likes the country.	haárec mócet xén beeynáv.	.הארץ מוצאת חן בעיניו
She likes the country.	haárec mócet xén beeynéha.	.הארץ מוצאת חן בעיניה
We like the country.	haárec mócet xén beeynéynu.	.הארץ מוצאת חן בעינינו
You (m.pl.) like the country.	haárec mócet xén beeyneyxém.	.הארץ מוצאת חן בעיניכם
You (f.pl.) like the country.	haárec mócet xén beeyneyxén.	.הארץ מוצאת חן בעיניכן
They (m) like the country.	haárec mócet xén beeyneyhém.	.הארץ מוצאת חן בעיניהם
They (f) like the country.	haárec mócet xén beeyneyhén.	.הארץ מוצאת חן בעיניהן

GRAMMAR DRILLS

3.4 Alternate Forms of Nouns

In Grammar Section 1.6 it was noted that some nouns have an alternate form when occurring with suffixes. Some nouns also have an alternate form when occurring as the first noun in a noun-noun sequence. Some examples of this are:

| šalóm | 'welfare' | šlóm hamišpaxá | 'the welfare of the family' |
| namál | 'port' | nemál teufá | 'airport' |

Compare, on the other hand:

    yoéc   'counsellor'   yoéc hašagrirút   'the Counsellor of the Embassy'

As with suffixed nouns, it is difficult to predict which nouns will have an alternate form or what the alternate form will be. It may or may not be the same form of the noun which occurs with suffixes (except for stress placement), e.g., /šlomí/ and /šlóm hamišpaxá/.

When a noun occurs in a Basic Sentence as the first noun in such a sequence the independent form will be given in the vocabulary breakdown.

3.5 Dual Number in Nouns

In addition to singular and plural as grammatical numbers Hebrew has a noun suffix, /-áim/, which indicates dual number. Some examples are:

yóm	'day'	yomáim	'two days'
šavúa	'week'	švuáim	'two weeks'
xódeš	'month'	xodšáim	'two months'
áin	'eye'	eynáim	'[two] eyes'

This suffix occurs with a limited number of nouns and in a few other forms. These nouns include parts of the body which come in pairs, doubled numbers and units of time, paired articles of clothing, and a few other items. It is not otherwise used to indicate two of something. Except for this suffix, dual nouns are treated as plurals. Verbs and adjectives used with them have plural forms, and the plural set of pronominal suffixes is also used. (See Section 3.6)

3.6 Pronominal Suffixes - Plural Set

In Section 1.6 the singular set of pronominal suffixes was discussed. Another set of pronominal suffixes occurs with plural (and dual) nouns and with certain prepositions. The form of the noun preceding these suffixes is often a special plural alternate, and this alternation will be drilled later. Often however, the only indication of the number of the noun is the pronominal suffix.

    eyní   'my eye'   eynáy   'my eyes'

[Note: As in many other instances, /ev/ is sometimes shortened to /e/. This may cause some confusion in the first and second person plural suffixes of the two sets.]

A. Substitution Drill

haárec mócet xén beeynáy.	I like the country.	הארץ מוצאת חן בעיני.
beeynéxa		בעיניך
beeynáix		בעיניך
beeynáv		בעיניו
beeynéha		בעיניה
beeynéynu		בעינינו
beeyneyxém		בעיניכם
beeyneyxén		בעיניכן
beeyneyhém		בעיניהם
beeyneyhén		בעיניהן

B. Expansion Drill

 The student repeats the question of the instructor and asks the second question.
    Instructor: How are you?
    Student: How are you? How do you like the country?

                                                    מה שלומך?

    má šlomxá, éx mócet xén beeynéxa haárec.
    má šlóm ištexá, éx mócet beeynéha haárec.
    má šlóm hamišpaxá, éx mócet xén beeynéha haárec.
    má sloméx, éx mócet xén beeynáix haárec.
    má šlomxém, ex mócet xén beeyneyxém haárec.
    má šlóm baaléx, éx mócet xén beeynáv haárec.
    má šlomá, éx mócet xén beeynéha haárec.
    má šlomxén, éx mócet xén beeyneyxén haárec.
    má šlóm davíd, éx mócet xén beeynáv haárec.
    má šlomó, éx mócet xén beeynáv haárec.
    má šlomám, éx mócet xén beeyneyhém haárec.

C. Response Drill

Instructor:	Student:
How are you?	Fine. I like the country.
má šlomxá.	tóv. haárec mócet xén beeynáy.
má šlóm davíd.	tóv. haárec mócet xén beeynáv.
má šlomxém.	tóv. haárec mócet xén beeynéynu.
má šlóm ištexá.	tóv. haárec mócet xén beeynéha.
má šlóm mošé veištó.	tóv. haárec mócet xén beeyneyhém.
má sloméx.	tóv. haárec mócet xén beeynáy.
má šlóm xána umiryám.	tóv. haárec mócet xén beeyneyhén.

D. Transformation Drill - Pronominal Suffixes, singular and Plural Sets

Instructor:	Student:
His country is very beautiful.	He likes the country.
arcó yafá meód.	haárec mócet xén beeynáv.
arcí yafá meód.	haárec mócet xén beeynáy.
arcénu yafá meód.	haárec mócet xén beeynéynu.
arcám yafá meód.	haárec mócet xén beeyneyhém.
arcexá yafá meód.	haárec mócet xén beeynéxa.
arcéx yafá meód.	haárec mócet xén beeynáix.
arcá yafá meód.	haárec mócet xén beeynéha.
arcexém yafá meód.	haárec mócet xén beeyneyxém.

E. Transformation Drill - Repeat Drill D in reverse.

                              18

F. Substitution-Agreement Drill

In the following drill responses by men should begin with /aní mekavé/ and those of women should begin with /aní mekavá/. The instructor should repeat the correct answer of the particular student.

aní mekavé šearcénu mócet xén beeynéxa, már Williams.

gvéret Williams	aní mekavé šearcénu mócet xén beeynáix, gvéret Williams.	גב' וויל־יאמס
már kóhen	aní mekavé šearcénu mócet xén beeynéxa, már kóhen.	מר כהן
gvéret Smith	aní mekavé šearcénu mócet xén beeynáix, gvéret Smith.	גב' סמיט
már Jones	aní mekavé šearcénu mócet xén beeynéxa, már Jones.	מר ג׳ונס
gvéret Fuller	aní mekavé šearcénu mócet xén beeynaíx, gvéret Fuller.	גב' פולר
gvéret Jones	aní mekavé šearcénu mócet xén beeynáix, gvéret Jones.	גב' ג׳ונס
már Williams	aní mekavé šearcénu mócet xén beeynéxa, már Williams.	מר וויל− יאמס

אה כן. הארץ יפה מאד...

19

REVIEW CONVERSATIONS

A: šalóm, david. matáy higáta laárec.   א: שלום, דוד. מתי הגעת לארץ?

B: higáti etmól beoniá lexáyfa.   ב: הגעתי אתמול באניה לחיפה.

A: éx hitrašámta mehanamál?   א: איך התרשמת מהנמל?

B: hanamál xadíš veyafé.   ב: הנמל חדיש ויפה.

C: matáy higáta lašagrirút, már Jones.   ג: מתי הגעת לשגרירות, מר ג'ונס?

D: higáti lifnéy šavúa, miryám.   ד: הגעתי לפני שבוע, מרים.

C: aní mekavá šehašagrirút mócet xén   ג: אני מקוה שהשגרירות מוצאת חן
     beenéxa.   בעיניך.

D: kén. hašagrirút meód mócet xén beenáy.   ד: כן. השגרירות מאד מוצאת חן בעיני.

E: gvéret kóhen. éyx higát laárec.   ה: גברת כהן, איך הגעת לארץ?

F: higáti beoniá lexáyfa.   ו: הגעתי באניה לחיפה.

E: aní mekavé šehitrašámt mehaoniá.   ה: אני מקוה שהתרשמת מהאניה.

F: ken. haoniá yafá meód.   ו: כן. האניה יפה מאד.

G: már Williams. matáy higáta.   ז: מר ויליאמס, מתי הגעת?

H: higáti etmól, már kóhen.   ח: הגעתי אתמול, מר כהן.

G: éyx higáta.   ז: איך הגעת?

H: higáti beavirón lelúd.   ח: הגעתי באוירון ללוד.

4.1 Housing Arrangements (Two men speaking)

MR. COHEN

Where	heyxán	היכן
are you staying,	atá gár,	אתה גר,
Mr. Williams?	már Williams.	מר וויל:אמס?
where	heyxán	היכן
you	atá (m.s.)	אתה
reside	gár (m.s. pres.)	גר

MR. WILLIAMS

I'm staying	aní gár	אני גר
in the meantime	beynatáim	בינתיים
at the Dan Hotel.	bemalón dán.	במלון דן.
meanwhile	beynatáim	בינתיים
hotel	malón (m)	מלון

MR. COHEN

Very good.	tóv meód.	טוב מאד.
It's close	zé karóv	זה קרוב
to the Embassy.	lašagrirút.	לשגרירות.
it, this, that	zé (m)	זה
near, close	karóv (m.s.)	קרוב

MR. WILLIAMS

Yes, that's right.	kén. naxón.	כן. נכון.
correct	naxón (m.s.)	נכון

MR. COHEN

And where	veeyfó	ואיפה
do you plan	atá mitkonén	אתה מתכונן
to live?	lagúr?	לגור?
where	eyfó, éyfo	איפה
plan	mitkonén (m.s. pres.)	מתכונן
to reside	lagúr	לגור

MR. WILLIAMS

There will be arranged	yesudár	יסודר
for us	avurénu	עבורנו
a house in Ramat Gan.	báit beramát gán.	בית ברמת גן.
will be arranged	yesudar (3.m.s.)	יסודר
for, on behalf of	avúr	עבור
house	báit (m)	בית

MR. COHEN

	haím	האם
Have you seen	raíta	ראית
the house?	et habáit?	את הבית?
(yes-or-no question introducer)	haím	האם
you saw	raíta (m.s.)	ראית

MR. WILLIAMS

No. But	16. áx	לא. אך
I've heard that	šamáti še-	שמעתי שֶ-
the house is	habáit	הבית
big and beautiful.	gadól veyafé.	גדול ויפה.
but	áx	אך
I heard	šamáti	שמעתי
big, large, great	gadól (m.s.)	גדול

MR. COHEN

When will	matáy tagía	מתי תגיע
your family arrive?	hamišpaxá šelxá.	המשפחה שלך?
will arrive	tagía (3.f.s.)	תגיע
of you, yours	šelxá (m.s.)	שלך

MR. WILLIAMS

My family	hamišpaxá šelí	המשפחה שלי
will arrive in	tagía beód	תגיע בעוד
about a month.	kexódeš yamím.	כחודש ימים.
of me, mine	šelí	שלי
still, yet	ód	עוד
approximately, as	ke-	כ-
days	yamím	ימים
	(pl. of /yóm/)	יום

4.2 Housing Arrangements (Two women speaking)

MRS. COHEN

Where	heyxán	היכן
are you staying,	át gára,	אֻו גרה,
Mrs. Williams?	gvéret Williams.	גברת ווילי־אמס?
you (f.s)	át (f.s.)	את
reside (f.s.pres.)	gára (f.s.pres.)	גרה
		.

MRS. WILLIAMS

I'm staying	aní gára	אני גרה
in the meantime	beynatáim	בינתיים
at the Dan Hotel.	bemalón dán.	במלון דן.

MRS. COHEN

Very good.	tóv meód.	טוב מאד.
It's close	zé karóv	זה קרוב
to the Embassy.	lašagrirút.	לשגרירות.

MRS. WILLIAMS

Yes, that's right.	kén. naxón.	כן. נכון.

MRS. COHEN

And where	veeyfó	ואיפה
do you plan	át mitkonénet	את מתכוננת
to live?	lagúr?	לגור?
plan	mitkonénet (f.s. pres.)	מתכוננת

MRS. WILLIAMS

There will be arranged	yesudár	יסודר
for us	avurénu	עבורנו
a house in Ramat Gan.	báit beramát gán.	בית ברמת גן.

MRS. COHEN

Have you seen	haím raít	האם ראית
the house?	et habáit?	את הבית?
you saw	raít (f.s.)	ראית

MRS. WILLIAMS

No. But	ló. áx	לא. אך
I've heard that	šamáti še-	שמעתי ש-
the house is	habáit	הבית
big and beautiful.	gadól veyafé.	גדול ויפה.

MRS. COHEN

When will	matáy tagía	מתי תגיע
the rest of your	yéter hamišpaxá	יתר המשפחה
family arrive?	šeláx.	שלך?
rest, remainder	yéter	יתר
of you, yours	šeláx (f.s.)	שלך

MRS. WILLIAMS

My family	hamišpaxá šelí	המשפחה שלי
will arrive in	tagía beód	תגיע בעוד
about a month.	kexódeš yamím.	כחודש ימים.

4.3 ADDITIONAL VOCABULARY

His house is very nice.	habáit šeló yafé meód.	הבית שלו יפה מאד.
Her house is very nice.	habáit šelá yafé meód.	הבית שלה יפה מאד.
Our house is very nice.	habáit šelánu yafé meód.	הבית שלנו יפה מאד.
Your (m.pl.) house is very nice.	habáit šelaxém yafé meód.	הבית שלכם יפה מאד.
Your (f.pl.) house is very nice.	habáit šelaxén yafé meód.	הבית שלכן יפה מאד.
Their (m) house is very nice.	habáit šelahém yafé meód.	הבית שלהם יפה מאד.
Their (f) house is very nice.	habáit šelahén yafé meód.	הבית שלהן יפה מאד.

We (m) live in Haifa.	ánu garím bexáyfa.	אנו גרים בחיפה.
You (m.pl.) live in Haifa.	atém garím bexáyfa.	אתם גרים בחיפה.
They (m) live in Haifa.	hém garím bexáyfa.	הם גרים בחיפה.

We (f) live in Haifa.	ánu garót bexáyfa.	אנו גרות בחיפה.
You (f.pl.) live in Haifa.	atén garót bexáyfa.	אתן גרות בחיפה.
They (f) live in Haifa.	hén garót bexáyfa.	הן גרות בחיפה.

GRAMMAR NOTES

4.4   The Preposition /šel/ 'of'

Examine these sentences which have occurred in the text:

hí ištó šel yoéc haságrirút.   She is the wife of the Counsellor of the
                                      Embassy.

matáy tagía hamišpaxá šelxá.   When will your family arrive?

habáit šeló yafé meód.   His house is very nice.

Note that the preposition /šel/ indicates a genitive or possessive
relationship of the noun following it or pronoun affixed to it with the noun
preceding it.
This is the most frequent construction in spoken Hebrew indicating such a
possessive relationship. The preposition may often be equated to the English
preposition of as in the first example above.
The noun preceding /šel/ is made definite with /ha-/ or with a pronominal
suffix /ištó/. The latter is not used when a pronoun is suffixed to /šel/ itself.
The difference is primarily one of style.

haišá šel már Williams   The wife of Mr. Williams
ištó šel már Williams   The wife of Mr. Williams

The construction with the suffixed preposition is synonymous with the
suffixed noun construction.

habáal šelá naím meód.   Her husband is very pleasant.
baalá naím meód.   Her husband is very pleasant.

When the noun preceding /šel/ is indefinite the usual English equivalent is
a prepositional phrase construction.

avirón šelánu.   An airplane of ours.

The singular set of pronominal suffixes is used with /šel/, with variations
in the feminine second person singular, /šeláx/, and in the plural suffixes.
(compare /otáx/ and /otánu/.)

A.   Substitution Drill.

My house is very modern.

habáit šelí xadíš meód.   .הבית שלי חדיש מאד
      šelxá   שלך
      šeláx   שלך
      šeló   שלו
      šelá   שלה
      šelánu   שלנו
      šelaxém   שלכם
      šelaxén   שלכן
      šelahém   שלהם
      šelahén   שלהן

24

B. Transformation Drill

Instructor: Student:
Mr. Carmi's plane is in Lydda.   His plane is in Lydda.

haavirón šel már kármi belúd.   haavirón šeló belúd.   ‏האוירון של מר כרמי בלוד.‏
haavirón šel xána belúd.   haavirón šelá belúd.   ‏האוירון של חנה בלוד.‏
haavirón šel mošé veléa belúd.   haavirón šelahém belúd.   ‏האוירון של משה ולאה בלוד.‏
haavirón šel hayoéc belúd.   haavirón šeló belúd.   ‏האוירון של היועץ בלוד.‏
haavirón šel hašagrirút belúd.   haavirón šelá belúd.   ‏האוירון של השגרירות בלוד.‏
haavirón šel baaléx belúd.   haavirón šeló belúd.   ‏האוירון של בעלך בלוד.‏
haavirón šel iští belúd.   haavirón šelá belúd.   ‏האוירון של אשתי בלוד.‏

C. Transformation Drill

My wife is very pretty.

Instructor: Student:
iští yafá meód.   haišá šelí yafá meód.   ‏אשתי יפה מאד.‏
ištó yafá meód.   haišá šeló yafá meód.   ‏אשתו יפה מאד.‏
ištexá yafá meód.   haišá šelxá yafá meód.   ‏אשתך יפה מאד.‏

D. Transformation Drill - Repeat Drill C in reverse.

E. Transformation Drill

Her husband is staying at the Dan Hotel.

Instructor: Student:
baalá gár bemalón dán.   habáal šelá gár bemalón dán.   ‏בעלה גר במלון דן.‏
baaléx gár bemalón dán.   habáal šeláx gár bemalón dán.   ‏בעלך גר במלון דן.‏
baalí gár bemalón dán.   habáal šelí gár bemalón dán.   ‏בעלי גר במלון דן.‏

F. Transformation Drill - Repeat Drill E in reverse.

G. Transformation Drill

Our country is very beautiful.

Instructor: Student:
arcénu yafá meód.   haárec šelánu yafá meód.   ‏ארצנו יפה מאד.‏
arcí yafá meód.   haárec šelí yafá meód.   ‏ארצי יפה מאד.‏
arcó yafá meód.   haárec šeló yafá meód.   ‏ארצו יפה מאד.‏
arcám yafá meód.   haárec šelahém yafá meód.   ‏ארצם יפה מאד.‏
arcán yafá meód.   haárec šelahén yafá meód.   ‏ארצן יפה מאד.‏
arcexém yafá meód.   haárec šelaxém yafá meód.   ‏ארצכם יפה מאד.‏
arcexén yafá meód.   haárec šelaxén yafá meód.   ‏ארצכן יפה מאד.‏
arcá yafá meód.   haárec šelá yafá meód.   ‏ארצה יפה מאד.‏

H. Transformation Drill - Repeat Drill G in reverse.

I. Transformation Drill

Instructor: Student:
He lives in Haifa.   His family lives in Haifa.

hú gár bexáyfa.	hamišpaxá šeló gára bexáyfa.	הוא גר בחיפה.
hí gára bexáyfa.	hamišpaxá šelá gára bexáyfa.	היא גרה בחיפה.
ánu garím bexáyfa.	hamišpaxá šelánu gára bexáyfa.	אנו גרים בחיפה.
hém garím bexáyfa.	hamišpaxá šelahém gára bexáyfa.	הם גרים בחיפה.
aní gár bexáyfa.	hamišpaxá šelí gára bexáyfa.	אני גר בחיפה.
hén garót bexáyfa.	hamišpaxá šelahén gára bexáyfa.	הן גרות בחיפה.

J. Transformation Drill - Repeat Drill I. in reverse.

K. Expansion Drill

Instructor: He is staying at the Dan Hotel.
Student: He is staying at the Dan Hotel, and his family will arrive in a week.

hú gár bemalón dán.vehamišpaxá šeló tagía beód šavúa.	הוא גר במלון דן.
hém garím bemalón dán.vehamišpaxá šelahém tagía beód šavúa.	הם גרים במלון דן.
aní gár bemalón dán.vehamišpaxá šelí tagía beód šavúa.	אני גר במלון דן.
hí gára bemalón dán.vehamišpaxá šelá tagía beód šavúa.	היא גרה במלון דן.
ánu garím bemalón dán.vehamišpaxá šelánu tagía beód šavúa.	אנו גרים במלון דן.
hayoéc gár bemalón dán.vehamišpaxá šeló tagía beód šavúa.	היועץ גר במלון דן.
hú veištó garím bemalón dán.vehamišpaxá šelahém	הוא ואשתו גרים במלון דן.
tagía beód šavúa.	

L. Transformation Drill

Instructor: Student:
I like the country.   My country is very pretty.

haárec mócet xén beeynáy.	haárec šelí yafá meód.	הארץ מוצאת חן בעיני.
haárec mócet xén beeynéxa.	haárec šelxá yafá meód.	הארץ מוצאת חן בעיניך.
haárec mócet xén beenáix.	haárec šeláx yafá meód.	הארץ מוצאת חן בעיניך.
haárec mócet xén beeynéynu.	haárec šelánu yafá meód.	הארץ מוצאת חן בעינינו.
haárec mócet xén beeyneyxém.	haárec šelaxém yafá meód.	הארץ מוצאת חן בעיניכם.
haárec mócet xén beeynéha.	haárec šelá yafá meód.	הארץ מוצאת חן בעיניה.
haárec mócet xén beeyneyxén.	haárec šelaxén yafá meód.	הארץ מוצאת חן בעיניכן.

M. Response Drill

Instructor: Student:
Where is your family staying? My family is staying at the Dan Hotel.

heyxán gára hamišpaxá šelxá.	hamišpaxá šelí gára bemalón dán.	היכן גרה המשפחה שלך?
heyxán gára hamišpaxá šeló.	hamišpaxá šeló gára bemalón dán.	היכן גרה המשפחה שלו?
heyxán gára hamišpaxá šelaxém.	hamišpaxá šelánu gára bemalón dán.	היכן גרה המשפחה שלכם?
heyxán gára hamišpaxá šeláx.	hamišpaxá šelí gára bemalón dán.	היכן גרה המשפחה שלך?
heyxán gára hamišpaxá šelahén.	hamišpaxá šelahen gára bemalón dán.	היכן גרה המשפחה שלהן?

4.5 The Preposition /avúr/ 'for', on behalf of'

The preposition /avúr/ is used with the singular set of pronominal suffixes.
yesudár avurénu báit berámat gán.

A. Substitution Drill

A house will be arranged for me.

yesudár avurí báit.   יסודר עבורי בית.
        avurxá   עבורך
        avuréx   עבורך
        avuró   עבורו
        avurá   עבורה
        avurénu   עבורנו
        avurxém   עבורכם
        avurxén   עבורכן
        avurám   עבורם
        avurán   עבורן

B. Transformation Drill
        Instructor: A house will be arranged for Mr. Williams.
        Student: A house will be arranged for him.

yesudár avúr már Williams báit.   yesudár avuró báit. יסודר עבור מר ווילאמס בית.
yesudár avúr miryám báit.   yesudár avurá báit.   יסודר עבור מרים בית.
yesudár avúr yaakóv veléa báit.   yesudár avurám báit. יסודר עבור יעקב ולאה בית.
yesudár avúr hamišpaxá šeló báit. yesudár avurá báit.   יסודר עבור המשפחה שלו בית.
yesudár avúr hayoéc báit.   yesudár avuró báit.   יסודר עבור היועץ בית.

C. Transformation Drill
        Instructor: His house will be arranged.
        Student: A house will be arranged for him.

habáit šeló yesudár.   yesudár avuró báit.   הבית שלו יסודר.
habáit šelxá yesudár.   yesudár avurxá báit.   הבית שלך יסודר.
habáit šelánu yesudár.   yesudár avurénu báit. הבית שלנו יסודר.
habáit šelí yesudár.   yesudár avurí báit.   הבית שלי יסודר.
habáit šeláx yesudár.   yesudár avuréx báit.   הבית שלך יסודר.
habáit šelá yesudár.   yesudár avurá báit.   הבית שלה יסודר.
habáit šelahém yesudár.   yesudár avurám báit.   הבית שלהם יסודר.
habáit šelaxém yesudár.   yesudár avurxém báit. הבית שלכם יסודר.
habáit šel davíd yesudár.   yesudár avúr davíd báit. הבית של דוד יסודר.

D. Transformation Drill - Repeat Drill C in reverse.

4.6 Contraction of /le- + ha-/ 'to the'

        Examine the underlined forms in the following:
            lelúd   'to Lydda'
            hašagrirút   'the embassy'
            lašagrirút   'to the embassy'
        Note that the preposition /le-/ and the definite article /ha-/ contract to
/la-/. This is an obligatory contraction.
        When /ha-/ is a verb prefix or is simply the first syllable of a word (but
not the definite article) then the contraction is not made: /lehakír/ 'to know'.
        The preposition has the alternate form /la-/ with certain verb infinitives:
/larúc, lagúr/. However, it is not a contraction of /leha-/ in these cases.

27

REVIEW CONVERSATIONS

A: heyxán atá gár, már Williams?   א: היכן אתה גר, מר ווילאמס?

B: aní veiští garím bemalón beynatáim.   ב: אני ואשתי גרים כמלון בינתיים.

A: bemalón dán?   א: כמלון דן?

B: kén. zé karóv lašagrirút.   ב: כן. זה קרוב לשגרירות.

A: haím atá mitkonén lagúr betél avív?   א: האם אתה מחכונן לגור בתל אביב?

B: ló. aní mitkonén lagúr berámat gán.   ב: לא. אני מחכונן לגור כרמת גן.

A: haím yesudár avurxém báit?   א: האם יסודר עבורכם כית?

B: kén. áx ló raíti otó.   ב: כן. אך לא ראיתי אותו.

C: haím hamišpaxá šelxá betél avív?   ג: האם המשפחה שלך בתל אביב?

D: ló. hamišpaxá šelí beamérika.   ד: לא. המשפחה שלי באמריקה.

C: matáy tagía hamišpaxá laárec?   ג: מתי תגיע המשפחה לארץ?

D: beód xódeš.   ד: כעוד חורש.

E: haím raíta et habáit šel már kármi?   ה: האם ראית את הכית של מר כרמי?

F: kén. vehitrašamtí meód mehabáit.   ו: כן. והתרשמתי מאד מהבית.

E: šamáti šehabáit gadól.   ה: שמעתי שהבית גדול.

F: kén. naxón. habáit gadól vexadíš.   ו: כן. נכון. הכית גדול וחדיש.

G: heyxán át mitkonénet lagúr, atára.   ז: היכן את מחכוננת לגור, עטרה.

H: aní ló yodáat. beynatáim   ח: אני לא יודעת. בינתיים
    aní gára bemalón.   אני גרה כמלון.

G: ló yesudár avuréx báit?   ז: לא יסודר עבורך כית?

H: kén. šamáti šeyesudár báit.   ח: כן. שמעתי שיסודר כית.
    áx aní ló yodáat eyfó umatáy.   אך אני לא יודעת איפה ומתי.

I: dálya, raít et hayoéc haamerikái?   ט: דליה, ראית את היועץ האמריקאי?

J: kén. hú naím meód.   י: כן. הוא נעים מאד.

I: éyfo hú gár?   ט: איפה הוא גר?

J: hú veištó garím bemalón dán.   י: הוא ואשתו גרים כמלון דן.

I: raít et ištó?   ט: ראית את אשתו?

J: ló. áx šamáti šehí yafá meód.   י: לא. אך שמעתי שהיא יפה מאד.

5.1 Speaking Hebrew (Men)

MR. COHEN

Tell me,	emór li	אמור לי,
please.	bevakašá.	בבקשה.
Where did you learn	heyxán lamádeta	היכן למדת
to speak such a	ledabér ivrít	לדבר עברית
beautiful Hebrew?	kol káx yafá.	כל כך יפה?

	tell, say	emór (m.s. imv.)	אמור
	you learned	lamádeta (m.s.)	למדת
	to speak	ledabér	לדבר
	all	kól	כל
	so, as much	kol káx	כל כך

MR. WILLIAMS

I learned	lamádeti	למדתי
to speak Hebrew	ledabér ivrít	לדבר עברית
in America.	beamérika.	באמריקה.

	I learned	lamádeti	למדתי

MR. COHEN

In which	beéyze	באיזה
school	bet séfer	בית ספר
did you study?	lamádeta.	למדת?

	which	éyze (m)	איזה
	book	séfer (m)	ספר
	school	bet séfer	בית ספר

MR. WILLIAMS

In the school	bevét haséfer	בבית הספר
of languages of	lesafót šel	לשפות של
our State Department	misrád haxúc šelánu.	משרד החוץ שלנו.

	language	safá (f)	שפה
	languages	safót (f.pl.)	שפות
	office	misrád (m)	משרד
	outside	xúc	חוץ

MR. COHEN

You did well	tóv meód asíta	טוב מאד עשית
to learn Hebrew	šelamádeta ivrít	שלמדת עברית
before	lifnéy še-	לפני ש-
you came here.	báta héna.	באת הנה.

	you did	asíta (m.s.)	עשית
	you came	báta (m.s.)	באת
	[to] here, hither	héna	הנה

You speak	atá medabér	אתה מדבר
Hebrew	ivrít	עברית
just like	mamáš kmó	ממש כמו
an Israeli.	israelí.	ישראלי.

	speak	medabér (m.s.pres.)	מדבר
	really, just	mamáš	ממש
	like	kmó	כמו

MR. WILLIAMS

Don't exaggerate.	ál tagzím.	אל תגזים.
Like an Israeli	kmó israelí	כמו ישראלי
as yet	adáin	עדיין
I don't speak.	eynéni medabér.	אינני מדבר.

don't	ál (neg.part.)	אל
you will exaggerate	tagzím	תגזים
as yet	adáin	עריין
not	éyn (neg.part.)	אין
I don't	eynéni	אינני

MR. COHEN

You speak	atá medabér	אתה מדבר
very well.	yafé meód.	יפה מאד.

MR. WILLIAMS

I'm happy	aní saméax	אני שמח
with the results.	mehatocaót.	מהתוצאות.

happy	saméax	שמח
result	tocaá (f)	תוצאה
results	tocaót (f.pl.)	תוצאות

5.2 Speaking Hebrew (Women)

MRS. COHEN

Tell me,	imrí li	אמרי לי
Please, please	bevakašá.	בבקשה.
Where did you learn	heyxán lamádet	היכן למדת
to speak such a	ledabér ivrít	לדבר עברית
beautiful Hebrew?	kol káx yafá.	כל כך יפה?

tell, say (imv.)	imrí	אמרי
you learned	lamádet (f.s.)	למדת

MRS. WILLIAMS

I learned	lamádeti	למדתי
to speak Hebrew	ledabér ivrít	לדבר עברית
in America.	beamérika.	באמריקה.

MRS. COHEN

In which	beéyze	באיזה
school	bet séfer	בית ספר
did you study?	lamádet?	למדת?

MRS. WILLIAMS

In the school	bevét haséfer	בבית הספר
of languages of	lesafót šel	לשפות של
our State Department.	misrád haxúc šelánu.	משרד החוץ שלנו.

<u>MRS. COHEN</u>

You did well	tóv meód asít	טוב מאד עשית
to learn Hebrew	šelamádet ivrít	שלמדת עברית
before	lifney še-	לפני שָ-
you came here.	bát héna.	באת הנה.
you did	asít (f.s.)	עשית
you came	bát (f.s.)	באת

You speak	át medabéret	את מדברת
Hebrew	ivrít	עברית
just like	mamáš kmó	ממש כמו
an Israeli	israelít.	ישראלית.
speak	medabéret (f.s.pres.)	מדברת
Israeli	israelít (f)	ישראלית

<u>MRS. WILLIAMS</u>

Don't exaggerate.	ál tagzími.	אל תגזימי.
Like an Israeli	kmó israelít	כמו ישראלית
as yet	adáin	עדיין
I don't speak.	eynéni medabéret.	אינני מדברת.
you will exaggerate	tagzími (f.s.)	תגזימי

<u>MRS. COHEN</u>

| You speak | at medabéret | את מדברת |
| very well. | yafé meód. | יפה מאד. |

<u>MRS. WILLIAMS</u>

I'm happy	aní smexá	אני שמחה
with the results.	mehatocaót.	מהתוצאות.
happy	smexá (f.s.)	שמחה

31

GRAMMAR NOTES

5.3 Past Tense of Verbs - First and Second Persons

Compare the underlined forms in the following sentences:

1. matáy <u>higáta</u> laárec, már Williams.
    matáy <u>higát</u> laárec, gvéret Williams.

2. heyxán <u>lamádeta</u> ledabér ivrít kol káx yafá.
    heyxán <u>lamádet</u> ledabér ivrít kol káx yafá.

3. tóv meód <u>asíta</u> šelamádeta ivrít lifnéy šebáta héna.
    tóv meód <u>asít</u> šelamádet ivrít lifnéy šebát héna.

Note that in speaking to a man the forms end in /-ta/, and in speaking
to a woman they end in /-t/. Now compare the following forms as spoken by
either a man or a woman.

4. <u>higáti</u> lifnéy yomáim.

5. <u>lamádeti</u> ledabér ivrít beamérika.

Note that these forms end in /-ti/. Comparison with some plural verb
forms yields three more suffixes.

/-nu/ 'we' <u>higánu</u> lifnéy yomáim.

/-tem/ 'you' (m.pl.) matáy <u>higátem</u> laárec.

/-ten/ 'you' (f.pl.) matáy higáten laárec.

These pronominal suffixes are affixed to the past tense stems of all verbs.
Given a past tense form with any of these suffixes, the other five may be
derived by substitution.
    The third person forms of the past tense will not be drilled until later.
    The third person forms involve changes in the stem, whereas the first and
second person forms differ only in the suffixes.
    The independent pronouns may be used with the first and second person past
tense forms for contrast, insistence, etc.

<u>aní</u> higáti héna etmól.   <u>I</u> got here yesterday.
matáy <u>atá</u> higáta.   When did <u>you</u> get here?

A. Substitution Drill

When did you get here?

matáy higáta héna.   ?מתי הגעת הנה
      higát   הגעת
      higátem   הגעתם
      higáten   הגעתן

B. Substitution Drill

In which school did you study?

beéyze bet séfer lamádeta.   באיזה בית ספר למדת?
                lamádet   למדת
                lamádetem   למדתם
                lamádeten   למדתן

C. Expansion Drill

Instructor: You came yesterday.
Student: You did well that you came yesterday.

báta etmól.   tóv asíta šebáta etmól.   טוב עשית שבאת אתמול.   באת אתמול.
bánu etmól.   tóv asínu šebánu etmól.   טוב עשינו שבאנו אתמול. באנו אתמול.
bát etmól.   tóv asít šebát etmól.   טוב עשית שבאת אתמול.   באת אתמול.
báti etmól.   tóv asíti šebáti etmól.   טוב עשיתי שבאתי אתמול. באתי אתמול.
bátem etmól.   tóv asítem šebátem etmól.   טוב עשיתם שבאתם אתמול. באתם אתמול.
báten etmól.   tóv asíten šebáten etmól.   טוב עשיתן שבאתן אתמול. באתן אתמול.

D. Expansion Drill

Instructor: I arrived yesterday.
Student: I arrived yesterday, and I'm
             staying at the Savoy Hotel.

higáti etmól,   veaní gár bemalón savóy.   ואני גר כמלון סבוי.   הגעתי אתמול.
higátem etmól, veatém garím bemalón savóy. ואתם גרים כמלון סבוי. הגעתם אתמול.
higánu etmól,   veánu garím bemalón savóy.   ואנו גרים כמלון סבוי. הגענו אתמול.
higát etmól,   veát gára bemalón savóy.   ואת גרה כמלון סבוי.   הגעת אתמול.
higáten etmól, veatén garót bemalón savóy. ואתן גרות כמלון סבוי. הגעתן אתמול.
higáta etmól.   veatá gár bemalón savóy.   ואתה גר כמלון סבוי.   הגעת אתמול.

Note: Women students may respond with
       /aní gára/ and /ánu garót/.

E. Expansion Drill

Instructor: Hello, David.
Student: Hello, David. When did you get here?

šalóm davíd.   matáy higáta héna.   שלום, רוד. מתי הגעת הנה?
šalóm sára.   matáy higát héna.   שלום, שרה. מתי הגעת הנה?
šalóm, már kármi.   matáy higáta héna.   שלום, מר כרמי. מתי הגעת הנה?
šalóm, xána. šalóm, léa. matáy higáten héna.   שלום,חנה. שלום,לאה. מתי הגעתן הנה?
šalóm, avígdor.   matáy higáta héna.   שלום, אביגדור. מתי הגעת הנה?
šalóm, mošé, šalóm, dóv.   matáy higátem héna.   שלום,משה. שלום,דב. מתי הגעתם הנה?
šalóm, gvéret kóhen.   matáy higát héna.   שלום, גברת כהן. מתי הגעת הנה?

33

F. Transformation Drill

Instructor: I was very impressed by the school.
Student: I saw that the school is modern and beautiful.

hitrašámti meód mibét haséfer.	.התרשמתי מאד מבית הספר
raíti šebét haséfer xadíš veyafé.	.ראיתי שבית הספר חריש ויפה
hitrašámnu meód mibét haséfer.	.התרשמנו מאד מבית הספר
raínu šebét haséfer xadíš veyafé.	.ראינו שבית הספר חריש ויפה
hitrašámtém meód mibét haséfer.	.התרשמתם מאד מבית הספר
raítem šebét haséfer xadíš veyafé.	.ראיתם שבית הספר חריש ויפה
hitrašámt meód mibét haséfer.	.התרשמת מאד מבית הספר
raít šebét haséfer xadíš veyafé.	.ראית שבית הספר חריש ויפה
hitrašámta meód mibét haséfer.	.התרשמת מאד מבית הספר
raíta šebét haséfer xadíš veyafé.	.ראית שבית הספר חריש ויפה
hitrašámten meód mibét haséfer.	.התרשמתן מאד מבית הספר
raíten šebét haséfer xadíš veyafé.	.ראיתן שבית הספר חריש ויפה

This drill may be varied by making it an expansion drill.

    Instructor: hitrašámti meód mibét haséfer.
    Student: hitrašámti meód mibét haséfer. raíti šebét haséfer xadíš
        veyafé.

G. Transformation Drill

Instructor: You live in Tel Aviv.
Student: You have seen the Dan Hotel.

atém garím betél avív.	raítem et malón dán.	.אתם גרים בתל אביב
át gára betél avív.	raít et malón dán.	.את גרה בתל אביב
aní gár betél avív.	raíti et malón dán.	.אני גר בתל אביב
ánu garím betél avív.	raínu et malón dán.	.אנו גרים בתל אביב
atá gár betél avív.	raíta et malón dán.	.אתה גר בתל אביב
atén garót betél avív.	raíten et malón dán.	.אתן גרות בתל אביב

This drill may be varied by making it an expansion drill.

    Instructor: atém garím betél avív.
    Student: atém garím betél avív. raítem et malón dán.

H. Transformation Drill

Instructor: I learned to speak Hebrew in America.
Student: I studied Hebrew before I came here.

lamádeti ledabér ivrít beamérika.	.למדתי לדבר עברית באמריקה
lamádeti ivrít lifnéy šebáti héna.	.למדתי עברית לפני שבאתי הנה
lamádnu ledabér ivrít beamérika.	.למדנו לדבר עברית באמריקה
lamádnu ivrít lifnéy šebánu héna.	.למדנו עברית לפני שבאנו הנה
lamádeta ledabér ivrít beamérika.	.למדת לדבר עברית באמריקה
lamádeta ivrít lifnéy šebáta héna.	.למדת עברית לפני שבאת הנה
lamádet ledabér ivrít beamérika.	.למדת לדבר עברית באמריקה
lamádet ivrít lifnéy šebát héna.	.למדת עברית לפני שבאת הנה
lamádeten ledabér ivrít beamérika.	.למדתן לדבר עברית באמריקה
lamádeten ivrít lifnéy šebáten héna.	.למדתן עברית לפני שבאתן הנה
lamádetem ledabér ivrít beamérika.	.למדתם לדבר עברית באמריקה
lamádetem ivrít lifnéy šebátem héna.	.למדתם עברית לפני שבאתם הנה

I.   Transformation Drill

Instructor: I heard that Haifa is very beautiful.
Student: I haven't seen Haifa.

     šamáti šexáyfa yafá meód.   שמעתי שחיפה יפה מאד.
         ló raíti et xáyfa.   לא ראיתי את חיפה.
     šamátem šexáyfa yafá meód.   שמעתם שחיפה יפה מאד.
         ló raítem et xáyfa.   לא ראיתם את חיפה.
     šamát šexáyfa yafá meód.   שמעת שחיפה יפה מאד.
         ló raít et xáyfa.   לא ראית את חיפה.
     šamánu šexáyfa yafá meód.   שמענו שחיפה יפה מאד.
         ló raínu et xáyfa.   לא ראינו את חיפה.
     šamáta šexáyfa yafá meód.   שמעת שחיפה יפה מאד.
         ló raíta et xáyfa.   לא ראית את חיפה.
     šamáten šexáyfa yafá meód.   שמעתן שחיפה יפה מאד.
         ló raíten et xáyfa.   לא ראיתן את חיפה.

J.   Transformation Drill - Repeat Drill I in reverse.

    Drills I and J may be varied by making them expansion drills.

      Instructor: šamáti šexáyfa yafá meód.
      Student: šamáti šexáyfa yafá meód, áx ló raíti otá.

      Instructor: ló raíti et xáyfa.
      Student: ló raíti et xáyfa, áx šamáti šehí yafá meód.

    In the following drills the instructor supplies the independent pronoun
as a cue, and the student responds with an entire sentence. The instructor
may vary the drills by requiring the students to include the independent
pronoun in the response.

      Instructor: báti héna lifnéy yomáim.
      Student: báti héna lifnéy yomáim.
      Instructor: atá
      Student: báta héna lifnéy yomáim. (or) atá báta héna lifnéy
                                         yomáim.

K.   Substitution Drill

    I came here two days ago.

    <u>báti héna lifnéy yomáim.</u>   <u>באתי הנה לפני יומיים.</u>

    atá - ánu - át - atém   אתה - אנו - את - אתם

    atén - ánu - atá - aní   אתן - אנו - אתה - אני

L.   Substitution Drill

    You did well to get to Israel a month ago.

    <u>tóv asíta šehigáta laárec lifnéy xódeš.</u> <u>טוב עשית שהגעת לארץ לפני חודש.</u>

    aní - át - atém - ánu   אני - את - אתם - אנו
    át - atén - aní - atá   את - אתן - אני - אתה

M. Substitution Drill

We've heard him and we've seen him.

<u>šamánu otó veraínu otó.</u>   .שמענו אותו וראינו אותו

   aní - át - atá - aní   אני - את - אתה - אני
   atém - atá - atén - ánu   אתם - אתה - אתן - אנו

N. Substitution - Agreement Drill

When did you arrive in the country, Mr. Williams?

<u>matáy higáta laárec, már Williams.</u>   ?מתי הגעת לארץ, מר ויליאמס

<u>gvéret fúler</u>	matáy higát laárec, gvéret fúler.	<u>גב' פולר</u>
<u>miryám</u>	matáy higát laárec, miryám.	<u>מרים</u>
<u>avígdor</u>	matáy higáta laárec, avígdor.	<u>אביגדור</u>
<u>gvéret kóhen</u>	matáy higát laárec, gvéret kóhen.	<u>גב' כהן</u>
<u>már óren</u>	matáy higáta laárec, már óren.	<u>מר אורן</u>
<u>gvéret káspi</u>	matáy higát laárec, gvéret káspi.	<u>גב' כספי</u>
<u>már Williams</u>	matáy higáta laárec, már Williams.	<u>מר ויליאמס</u>

5.4 Alternation /mi- ~ me-/ 'from'

The prefixed preposition /mi-/ 'from' has the alternate form /me-/ when immediately followed by a vowel or by /h/.

         éx hitrašámta <u>mi</u>lúd.
         aní saméax <u>me</u>hatocaót.

Many speakers, especially in more formal speech, use /me-/ before /x/ and /r/.

         <u>me</u>xáyfa.
         <u>me</u>rámat gán.

5.5 Consonant Alternation /b ~ v/

The consonant /b/ often alternates with /v/ when not initial in the word.

         <u>b</u>ét haséfer   'the school'
         be<u>v</u>ét haséfer   'in the school'

In this particular case the alternation in the second example is optional in informal speech - both /bebét haséfer/ and /bevét haséfer/ are heard. In other cases, particularly in verbs, the alternation is required. The patterns of alternation are rather complicated and are not consistent for all levels of speech nor for all speakers. For the time being the student should simply memorize each particular example as it occurs in the text. [Note: The instructor may insist that students make the optional alternations since it is supposedly 'correct' to do so. Students should interpret 'correct' to mean 'more formal' and not spend much time on this point.]

REVIEW CONVERSATIONS

A. heyxán lamádeta ledabér ivrít,
   már Williams.

א: היכן למדת לדבר עברית,
   מר וויליאמס?

B. lamádeti ivrít beamérika.

ב: למדתי עברית באמריקה.

A. tóv asíta šelamádeta ivrít.

א: טוב עשית שלמדת עברית.

B. kén, aní saméax mehatocaót.

ב: כן, אני שמח מהתוצאות.

C. hitrašámti meód mibét haséfer lesafót.

ג: והתרשמתי מאד מבית הספר לשפות.

D. kén. zé bét séfer tóv.

ד: כן. זה ביח ספר טוב.

C. gám aní lamádeti ivrít bevét séfer
   lesafót.

ג: גם אני למדתי עברית בבית ספר
   לשפות.

D. ó? atá ló israelí?

ד: או! אתה לא ישראלי?

C. ló. bátı héna mehungárya.

ג: לא. באתי הנה מהונגריה.

E. át medabéret ivrít kmó israelít.

ה: את מדברת עברית כמו ישראלית.

F. ál tagzím. kmó israelít
   eynéni medabéret.

ו: אל תגזים. כמו ישראלית
   אינני מדברת.

E. át medabéret yafé meód.

ה: את מדברת יפה מאד.

F. todá rabá.

ו: תודה רבה.

G. šamáti šehabáit šel mošé
   gadól veyafé.

ז: שמעתי שהבית של משה
   גדול ויפה.

H. ál tagzím. raíti et habáit,
   vehú ló kól káx gadól.

ח: אל תגזים. ראיתי את הבית,
   והוא לא כל כך גדול.

I. haím raítem et habáit šelánu?

ט: האם ראיתם את הבית שלנו?

J. ló, áx šamánu mimošé
   šehabáit šelaxém yafé meód.

י: לא. אך שמענו ממשה
   שהבית שלכם יפה מאד.

I. matáy raítem et mošé?

ט: מתי ראיתם את משה?

J. raínu otó lifnéy yomáim.

י: ראינו אותי לפני יומיים.

I. eyfó hú gár?

ט: איפה הוא גר?

J. aní ló yodéa. raínu otó
   bemisrád haxúc.

י: אני לא יודע. ראינו אותו
   במשרד החוץ.

37

K.   yaakóv. Šamáta? hayoéc
     haamerikái medabér ivrít.

כ: יעקב! שמעת? היועץ
האמריקאי מדבר עברית.

L.   kén. Šamáti. hú medabér yafé meód.

ל: כן, שמעתי. הוא מדבר יפה מאד.

K.   kmó israelí?

כ: כמו ישראלי?

L.   ló. ló kmó israelí.
     áx hú medabér tóv.

ל: לא. לא כמו ישראלי.
אך הוא מדבר טוב.

M.   raínu et habáit šelxá.

מ: ראינו את הבית שלך.

N.   éyx hitrašámtem.

נ: איך התרשמתם?

M.   hitrašámnu meód. habáit šelxá
     xadíš meód.

מ: התרשמנו מאד. הבית שלך
חדיש מאד.

N.   aní mekavé šegám avurxém
     yesudár báit yafé.

נ: אני מקווה שגם עבורכם
יסודר בית יפה.

M.   gám aní mekavé.

מ: גם אני מקווה.

6.1 Asking Directions (A man asks a man)

MR. WILLIAMS

Tell me, please,	emór lí bevakašá.	אמור לי, בבקשה,
how can I	éx aní yaxól	איך אני יכול
get from here	lehagía mikán	להגיע מכאן
to the main post office?	ladóar hamerkazí.	לדואר המרכזי??
can	yaxól (m.s.)	יכול
to arrive	lehagía	להגיע
here	kán	כאן
mail, post office	dóar (m)	דואר
central	merkazí (m.s.)	מרכזי

PASSERBY

Turn here	pné kán	פנה כאן
at the first corner	bapiná harišoná	בפינה הראשונה
to the right.	yemína.	ימינה.
turn	pné (m.s.imv.)	פנה
corner	piná (f)	פינה
first	rišoná (f.s.)	ראשונה
to the right	yemína	ימינה

MR. WILLIAMS

English	Transliteration	Hebrew
Yes-	kén-	-- כן

PASSERBY

English	Transliteration	Hebrew
Go	léx	לך
about four blocks,	kearbaá rexovót,	כארבעה רחובות,
and there	vešám	ושם
turn left.	tifné smóla.	תפנה שמאלה.
go	léx (m.s.imv.)	לך
four	arbaá (m)	ארבעה
street	rexóv (m)	רחוב
there	šám	שם
you will turn	tifné (m.s.)	תפנה
to the left	smóla	שמאלה

MR. WILLIAMS

English	Transliteration	Hebrew
Yes-	kén-	-- כן

PASSERBY

English	Transliteration	Hebrew
Continue straight	tamšíx yašár	תמשיך ישר
to the intersection.	ád lahictalvút.	עד להצטלבות.
you will continue	tamšíx (m.s.)	תמשיך
straight	yašár (m.s.)	ישר
until, up to	ád	עד
intersection	hictalvút (f)	הצטלבות

MR. WILLIAMS

English	Transliteration	Hebrew
The first	hahictalvút	ההצטלבות
intersection?	harišoná?	הראשונה?

PASSERBY

Yes. Go past	kén. avór	כן. עבור
the lights,	et haramzorím,	את הרמזורים,
and continue straight	vehamšéx yašár	והמשך ישר
to the post office building.	ád lebinyán hadóar.	עד לבנין הדואר.
cross, pass	avór (m.s.imv.)	עבור
traffic light	ramzór (m)	רמזור
continue	hamšéx (m.s.imv.)	המשך
building	binyán (m)	בנין

MR. WILLIAMS

Is it	haím zé	האם זה
far from here?	raxók mikán?	רחוק מכאן?
far	raxók (m.s.)	רחוק

PASSERBY

No, it's	ló. zé	לא. זה
not far.	ló raxók.	לא רחוק.

MR. WILLIAMS

Thank you very much,	todá rabá lexá,	תודה רבה לך,
sir.	adoní.	אדוני.
sir	adoní	אדוני

PASSERBY

Don't mention it.	ál ló davár.	על לא דבר.
on	ál	על
thing	davár (m.)	דבר

6.2 **Asking Directions** (A woman asks a woman)

MRS. WILLIAMS

Tell me, please,	imrí lí bevakašá.	אמרי לי, בבקשה,
how can I	éx aní yexolá	איך אני יכולה
get from here	lehagía mikán	להגיע מכאן
to the main post office?	ladóar hamerkazí.	לדואר המרכזי?
can	yexolá (f.s.)	יכולה

PASSERBY

Turn here	pní kán	פני כאן
at the first corner	bapiná harišoná	בפינה הראשונה
to the right.	yemína.	ימינה.
turn	pní (f.s.imv.)	פני

MRS. WILLIAMS

Yes-	kén-	כן --

PASSERBY

Go	lexí	לכי '
about four blocks,	kearbaá rexovót	כארבעה רחובות
and there	vešám	ושם
turn left.	tifní smóla.	תפני שמאלה.
go	lexí (f.s.imv.)	לכי
you will turn	tifní (f.s.)	תפני

MRS. WILLIAMS

Yes-	kén-	כן -- '

PASSERBY

Continue straight	tamšíxi yašár	תמשיכי ישר
to the intersection.	ád lahictalvút.	ער להצטלבות.
you will continue	tamšíxi (f.s.)	חמשיכי

MRS. WILLIAMS

The first	hahictalvút	ההצטלבות
intersection?	harišoná?	הראשונה?

PASSERBY

Yes. Go past	kén. ivrí	כן. עברי
the lights	et haramzorím	א.ת הרמזורים
and continue straight	vehamšíxi yašár	והמשיכי ישר
to the post office building.	ád lebinyán hadóar.	ער לבנין הדואר.
cross, pass	ivrí (f.s.imv.)	עברי
continue	hamšíxi (f.s.imv.)	המשיכי

MRS. WILLIAMS

Is it	haím zé	האם זה
far from here?	raxók mikán?	רחוק מכאן?

PASSERBY

No, it's	ló. zé	לא. זה
not far.	ló raxók.	לא רחוק.

MRS. WILLIAMS

Thank you very much,	todá rabí láx,	וורה רבה לך,
ma'am.	gvirtí.	גבירתי.
ma'am	gvirtí	גבירתי

PASSERBY

Don't mention it.	ál ló davár.	על לא דבר.

6.3 ADDITIONAL VOCABULARY

Continue straight.		
(said to men or both)	hamšíxu yašár.	המשיכו ישד.
(said to women)	hamšéxna yašár.	המשכנה יישד.

GRAMMAR NOTES

6.4 Stark Imperatives

Compare the underlined forms in the following sentences:

    a. sgór et hadélet.
        sigrí et hadélet.

    b. šév, bevakašá.
        šví, bevakašá.

    c. dabér, yotér bekól.
        dabrí, yotér bekól.

    d. targém, bevakašá.
        targemí, bevakašá.

    e. emór lí bevakašá. heyxán lamádeta ledabér ivrít.
        imrí lí bevakašá. heyxán lamádet ledabér ivrít.

    f. pné kán bapiná harišoná yemína.
        pní kán bapiná harišoná yeminá.

    g. léx kearbá rexovót.
        lexí kearbá rexovót.

    h. avór et haramzorím vehamšéx yašár.
        ivrí   et haramzorím vehamšíxi yašár.

The underlined words are imperative forms of verbs. They are termed 'stark imperatives' since their only function is as imperatives and to differentiate them from the 'gentle imperative' forms which function also as future tense forms.

There are a number of form classes of verbs in Hebrew, but the imperatives of all of them have certain similar characteristics. The masculine singular does not end in /-i/ and the feminine singular does. In some the /-i/ does not bear the stress /hamšíxi/, and in some it does /imrí, sigrí, pní/.
Examine now the plural forms which have occurred in the text.

    i. hamšíxu yašár.
        hamšéxna yašár.

Note that the masculine plural is identical to the feminine singular except for the final vowel, /-u/ instead of /-i/; and that the feminine plural is identical to the masculine singular except for the additional syllable /-na/. This criss-cross patterning occurs with all verbs in the stark imperative. Thus, given both singular forms, both plurals, both masculine forms, or both feminine forms, the other two may be easily derived.
The stress will always be on the corresponding syllable in the feminine singular and masculine plural: /hamšíxi - hamšíxu/ and /sigrí - sigrú/. The feminine plural suffix /-na/ is never stressed.
At this point the student will have to memorize the corresponding pairs. It will be a while before the patterns become sorted out. However, since the pattern of the stark imperative is one of the keys to the identification of a particular verb pattern the student will have lost nothing by memorizing and drilling them thoroughly now.

A.   Substitution Drill

Tell me, please, where is the post office?

emór lí bevakašá. éyfo hadóar.	אמור לי, בבקשה, איפה הדואר?
emórna	אמורנה
imrí	אמרי
imrú	אמרו
emór	אמור

B.   Substitution - Agreement Drill

In the following drill the instructor may vary the substitutions supplied as cues, alternating between the imperatives and the pronouns.

Tell me, please, where do you live?

emór lí bevakašá	eyfó atá gár.	אמור לי, בבקשה, איפה אתה גר?
emórna lí bevakašá.	eyfó atén garót.	אמורנה לי, בבקשה, איפה אתן גרות?
imrí lí bevakašá.	eyfó át gára.	אמרי לי, בבקשה, איפה את גרה?
imrú lí bevakašá.	eyfó atém garím.	אמרו לי, בבקשה, איפה אתם גרים?
imrí lí bevakašá.	eyfó át gára.	אמרי לי, בבקשה, איפה את גרה?
emór lí bevakašá.	eyfó atá gár.	אמור לי, בבקשה, איפה אתה גר?
imrú lí bevakašá.	eyfó atém garím.	אמרו לי, בבקשה, איפה אתם גרים?
emórna lí bevakašá.	eyfó atén garót.	אמורנה לי, בבקשה, איפה אתן גרות?
imrí lí bevakašá.	eyfó át gára.	אמרי לי, בבקשה, איפה את גרה?

C.   Substitution Drill

Go past the first intersection.

avór et hahictalvút harišoná.	עבור את ההצטלבות הראשונה.
avórna	עבורנה
ivrí	עברי
ivrú	עברו
avór	עבור
ivrí	עברי
ivrú	עברו

D.   Substitution Drill

Close the door, please.

sigrí et hadélet, bevakašá.	סגרי את הדלת, בבקשה.
sigrú	סגרו
sgór	סגור
sgórna	סגורנה
sigrú	סגרו
sigrí	סגרי
sgór	סגור

E.   Substitution Drill

Open the door, please.

pitxú et hadélet bevakašá.	פתחו את הדלת, בבקשה.
pitxí	פתחי
ptáxna	פתחנה
ptáx	פתח
pitxí	פתחי
pitxú	פתחו
ptáx	פתח

F.   Substitution Drill

The following drill may be varied by first going through the drill a few times using one verb as substitution cues and then a few times using the other verb as cues. When the forms are mastered the drill may be done by alternating the cues.

Turn left here and go straight.

pné kán yemína	veléx yašár.	ולך ישר.	פנה כאן ימינה
pní kán yemína	velexí yašár.	ולכי ישר.	פני כאן ימינה
pnú kán yemína	velexú yašár.	ולכו ישר.	פנו כאן ימינה
pnéna kán yemína	veléxna yašár.	ולכנה ישר.	פנינה כאן ימינה
pné kán yemína	veléx yašár.	ולך ישר.	פנה כאן ימינה
pnú kán yemína	velexú yašár.	ולכו ישר.	פנו כאן ימינה
pní kán yemína	velexí yašár.	ולכי ישר.	פני כאן ימינה

G.   Substitution Drill

Continue straight to the school.

hamšéx yašár ád lebét haséfer.	המשך ישר עד לבית הספר.
hamšíxu	המשיכו
hamšíxi	המשיכי
hamšéxna	המשכנה
hamšéx	המשך
hamšíxi	המשיכי

H.   Substitution - Agreement Drill

This drill may be varied by alternating the substitution cues as in Drill F.

Close the door and sit down, please.

sgór et hadélet	vešév bevakašá.	ושב, בבקשה.	סגור את הדלת
sigrú et hadélet	vešvú bevakašá.	ושבו, בבקשה.	סגרו את הדלת
sigrí et hadélet	vešví bevakašá.	ושבי, בבקשה.	סגרי את הדלת
sgórna et hadélet	vešévna bevakašá.	ושבנה, בבקשה.	סגורנה את הדלת
sgór et hadélet	vešév bevakašá.	ושב, בבקשה.	סגור את הדלת
sigrí et hadélet	vešví bevakašá.	ושבי, בבקשה.	סגרי את הדלת
sigrú et hadélet	vešvú bevakašá.	ושבו, בבקשה.	סגרו את הדלת

I. Substitution Drill

Please speak Hebrew.

dabér ivrít, bevakašá.   דבר עברית, בבקשה.
dabrí   דברי
dabrú   דברו
dabérna   דברנה
dabér   דבר

6.5 Gentle Imperatives

Compare the underlined forms in the following sentences:

a. takír bevakašá et már Williams.
    takíri bevakašá et gvéret Williams.

b. šám tifné smóla.
    šám tifní smóla.

c. tamšíx yašár ád lahictalvút.
    tamšíxi yašár ád lahictalvút.

Note that the masculine-feminine alternation is very much the same as in
the stark imperatives. In addition the forms have a prefix beginning with
/t-/. These are identical with the second person future tense forms but are
used as imperatives. They are termed 'gentle imperatives' since they are not
ordinarily used for direct positive commands, and have a gentler connotation.
The stark imperative is used for the whole range of simple request to direct
command.
        As with the stark imperatives, the corresponding pairs should be drilled
and memorized With the exception noted below the same criss-cross derivations
may be made to get the remaining forms.

                tifné (m.s.)   tifní (f.s.)
                tifnéna (f.pl.)   tifnú (m.pl.)

The exception is with verbs in which the final vowel of the masculine
singular is /-í-/. In most of these verbs the feminine plural has /-é-/, in
the others /-á-/.

                tamšíx   –   tamšéxna
                takír   –   takérna
(When the feminine plural has /-á-/, this will be especially noted.)

[In the vocabulary breakdown of the basic sentences the gentle
imperatives are translated as future forms. This is a convention adopted for
this text.]

The vowel of the prefix depends on the form class to which the verb
belongs. It may be /i, e, a, o/, but it is the same in all four forms. At
this point the substitution drills should be repeated until the vowel of the
prefix is memorized.

A. Substitution Drill

    Turn left at the first corner.

tifné smóla bapiná harišoná.	תפנה שמאלה בפינה הראשונה.
tifní	תפני
tifnú	תפנו
tifnéna	תפנינה
tifní	תפני
tifnú	תפנו
tifné	תפנה

B. Substitution Drill

    Cross the intersection.

taavór et hahictalvút.	תעבור את ההצטלבות.
taavrí	תעברי
taavrú	תעברו
taavórna	תעבורנה
taavrí	תעברי
taavór	תעבור
taavrú	תעברו

C. Substitution Drill

    Keep on speaking.   I understand.

tamšíx ledabér.	aní mevín.	תמשיך לדבר. אני מבין.
tamšíxi		תמשיכי
tamšíxu		תמשיכו
tamšéxna		תמשכנה
tamšíx		תמשיך
tamšíxi		תמשיכי

    Women students should respond with /aní meviná/.

D. Substitution Drill

    Please meet my wife (husband).

takír bevakašá et iští (baalí).	תכיר בבקשה את אשתי (בעלי).
takíri	תכירי
takíru	תכירו
takérna	תכרנה

46

E. Substitution - Agreement Drill

Moshe, please meet Mr. Oren.

mošé. takír bevakašá et már óren.   משה, תכיר בבקשה את מר אורן.

miryám   miryám. takíri bevakašá et már óren.   מרים
már káspi   már káspi. takír bevakašá et már óren.   מר כספי
már Williams már Williams. takír bevakaá et már óren.   מר ויליאמס
gvéret kóhen gvéret kóhen. takíri bevakašá et már óren. גברת כהן
xána   xána. takíri bevakašá et már óren.   חנה
avígdor   avígdor. takír bevakašá et már óren.   אביגדור

F. Substitution - Agreement Drill

This drill may be done first as two separate substitution drills, and then
varied by alternating the substitution cues as in Drill F, Section 6.4 above.

Drill 1. tisgór et hadélet.
Drill 2. tešév bešéket.
Drill 3. tisgór et hadélet vetešév bešéket.

Close the door and sit quietly.

tisgór et hadélet   vetešév bešéket.   תסגור את הדלת ותשב בשקט.
tisgerú et hadélet   vetešvú bešéket.   תסגרו את הדלת ותשבו בשקט.
tisgerí et hadélet   vetešví bešéket.   תסגרי את הדלת ותשבי בשקט.
tisgórna et hadélet   vetešévna bešéket.   תסגורנה את הדלת ותשכנה בשקט.
tisgór et hadélet   vetešév bešéket.   תסגור את הדלת ותשב בשקט.
tisgerí et hadélet   vetešví bešéket.   תסגרי את הדלת ותשכי בשקט.
tisgerú et hadélet   vetešvú bešéket.   תסגרו את הדלת ותשבו בשקט.

G. Substitution Drill

Open the office for me.

tiftáx et hamisrád avurí.   תפתח את המשרד עבורי.
tiftexí   תפתחי
tiftexú   תפתחו
tiftáxna   תפתחנה
tiftexí   תפתחי
tiftexú   תפתחו
tiftáx   תפתח

6.6 Negative Imperatives

The negative of both imperatives consists of the construction /ál/ +
gentle imperative.

ál tagzím.   'Don't exaggerate.'

47

A. Substitution Drill

   Don't exaggerate. The house isn't that big.

   ál tagzím. habáit ló kol káx gadól.   .אל תגזים; הבית לא כל כך גדול
      tagzími   תגזימי
      tagzímu   תגזימו
      tagzím   תגזים
      tagzémna   תגזמנה
      tagzími   תגזימי

B. Transformation Drill - Affirmative to Negative

   Instructor: Turn left here.
   Student: Don't turn left here.   :תלמיד   :מורה

      pné smóla.   ál tifné smóla.   .אל תפנה שמאלה   פנה שמאלה
      pní smóla.   ál tifní smóla.   .אל תפני שמאלה   פני שמאלה
      pnú smóla.   ál tifnú smóla.   .אל תפנו שמאלה   פנו שמאלה
      pnéna smóla.   ál tifnéna smóla.   .אל תפנינה שמאלה   פנינה שמאלה
      pné smóla.   ál tifné smóla.   .אל תפנה שמאלה   פנה שמאלה

C. Transformation - Expansion Drill

   Repeat Drill B with student adding /pné yemína./ 'Turn right'.

   Instructor: pné smóla.
   Student: ál tifné smóla. pné yemína.

D. Transformation Drill - Affirmative to Negative.

   Instructor: Go to the main post office.
   Student: Don't go to the main post office.

      léx ladóar hamerkazí.   ál teléx ladóar hamerkazí.   .לך לדואר המרכזי
      lexí ladóar hamerkazí.   ál telxí ladóar hamerkazí.   .לכי לדואר המרכזי
      léxna ladóar hamerkazí.   ál teléxna ladóar hamerkazí.   .לכנה לדואר המרכזי
      lexú ladóar hamerkazí.   ál telxú ladóar hamerkazí.   .לכו לדואר המרכזי
      lexí ladóar hamerkazí.   ál telxí ladóar hamerkazí.   .לכי לדואר המרכזי
      léx ladóar hamerkazí.   ál teléx ladóar hamerkazí.   .לך לדואר המרכזי

E. Transformation - Expansion Drill

   Repeat Drill D with student adding /léx lašagrirút./ 'Go to the embassy.'

   Instructor: léx ladóar hamerkazí.
   Student: ál teléx ladóar hamerkazí. léx lašagrirút.

F.   Transformation Drill - Affirmative to Negative

Instructor: Continue straight to the intersection.
Student: Don't continue straight.

hamšéx yašár ád lahictalvút.	ál tamšíx yašár.	המשך ישר עד להצטלבות.
hamšíxu yašár ád lahictalvút.	ál tamšíxu yašár.	המשיכו ישר עד להצטלבות.
hamšíxi yašár ád lahictalvút.	ál tamšíxi yašár.	המשיכי ישר עד להצטלבות.
hamšéxna yašár ád lahictalvút.	ál tamšéxna yašár.	המשכנה ישר עד להצטלבות.
hamšéx yašár ád lahictalvút.	ál tamšíx yašár.	המשך ישר עד להצטלבות.
hamšíxi yašár ád lahictalvút.	ál tamšíxi yašár.	המשיכי ישר עד להצטלבות.

G.   Transformation - Expansion Drill

Repeat Drill F with student adding /pné smóla./ 'Turn left.'

Instructor: hamšéx yašár ád lahictalvút.
Student: ál tamšíx yašár. pné smóla.

H.   Transformation Drill - Affirmative to Negative.

Instructor: Cross the lights.
Student: Don't cross the lights.

avór et haramzorím.	ál taavór et haramzorím.	עבור את הרמזורים.
ivrí et haramzorím.	ál taavrí et haramzorím.	עברי את הרמזורים.
avórna et haramzorím.	ál taavórna et haramzorím.	עבורנה את הרמזורים.
avór et haramzorím.	ál taavór et haramzorím.	עבור את הרמזורים.
ivrú et haramzorím.	ál taavrú et haramzorím.	עברו את הרמזורים.
ivrí et haramzorím.	ál taavrí et haramzorím.	עברי את הרמזורים.

I.   Transformation Drill - Negative to Affirmative

Instructor: Don't speak loudly.
Student: Speak loudly.

		תלמיד:	מורה:
ál tedabér bekól.	dabér bekól.	דבר בקול.	אל תדבר בקול.
ál tedabrú bekól.	dabrú bekól.	דברו בקול.	אל תדברו בקול.
ál tedabrí bekól.	dabrí bekól.	דברי בקול.	אל ודברי בקול.
ál tedabérna bekól.	dabérna bekól.	דברנה בקול.	אל תדברנה בקול.
ál tedaber bekól.	dabér bekól.	דבר בקול.	אל תדבר בקול.
ál tedabrí bekól.	dabrí bekól.	דברי בקול.	אל תדברי בקול.

J.   Transformation Drill - Affirmative to Negative

Repeat Drill I in reverse.

K.   Transformation - Expansion Drill

Drill I is repeated as follows.

Instructor: dabér bekól.
Student: ál tedabér bekól. dabér bešéket.

L. Substitution Drill

Don't say goodbye.

ál tomár šalóm.	אל תאמר שלום.
tomrí	תאמרי
tomárna	תאמרנה
tomrú	תאמרו
tomár	תאמר
tomrí	תאמרי

M. Expansion Drill

Instructor: <u>Don't say goodbye to me.</u>
Student: Don't say goodbye to me; say 'Be seeing you'.

<u>ál tomár lí šalóm.</u>	emór lí lehitraót.	אמור לי להתראות.	<u>אל תאמר לי שלום.</u>
<u>ál tomrí lí šalóm.</u>	imrí lí lehitraót.	אמרי לי להתראות.	<u>אל תאמרי לי שלום.</u>
<u>ál tomárna lí šalóm.</u>	emórna lí lehitraót.	אמורנה לי להתראות.	<u>אל תאמרנה לי שלום.</u>
<u>ál tomrú lí šalóm.</u>	imrú lí lehitraót.	אמרו לי להתראות.	<u>אל תאמרו לי שלום.</u>
<u>ál tomrí lí šalóm.</u>	imrí lí lehitraót.	אמרי לי להתראות.	<u>אל תאמרי לי שלום.</u>
<u>ál tomár lí šalóm.</u>	emór lí lehitraót.	אמור לי להתראות.	<u>אל תאמר לי שלום.</u>

N. Individual Transformation - Expansion Drill

In this drill the student contradicts the instructor and adds a further
instruction.

Instructor: Turn left here.
Student: Don't turn here. Continue straight.

Instructor: pné kán smóla.   מורה: פנה כאן שמאלה.
Student: ál tifné kán. hamšéx yašár.   תלמיד: אל תפנה כאן. המשך ישר.

léx ladóar hamerkazí.	לך לדואר המרכזי.
pní bapiná harišoná yemína.	פני כפינה הראשונה ימינה.
dabér anglít, bevakašá.	דבר אנגלית, בבקשה.
lexú lemalón dán.	לכו למלון דן.
avór et hahictalvút.	עבור את ההצטלבות.
ivrí et haramzorím.	עברי את הרמזורים.
hamšíxu yašár ád lašagrirút.	המשיכו ישר עד לשגרירות.
hamšíxi ledabér.	המשיכי לדבר.
pnú bahictalvút harišoná yemína.	פנו כהצטלבות הראשונה ימינה.

6.7 Contraction of /be- + ha-/ 'at the, in the'

When the preposition /be-/ is prefixed to a form with the definite article
prefix /ha-/, the two syllables are contracted to /ba-/.

hapiná harišoná	'the first corner'
bapiná harišoná	'at the first corner'

This contraction is similar to that of /le- + ha-/ to /la-/, described in
Section 4.6, and it is equally obligatory.

6.8 <u>Alternate forms /ve- ~ u-/ 'and'</u>

In formal speech the conjunction /ve-/ has the alternate form /u-/ before
the consonants /m, v, f/ and before consonant clusters.

> mošé <u>um</u>iryám.
> léx <u>usg</u>ór et hadélet.

In informal speech the form /u-/ is heard occasionally in these cases and
in stereotyped expressions, such as /umá šlomxá/ but the form /ve-/ is far
more frequently used. With some speakers there is free alternation of these
forms, and the student should be prepared for both.

> sigrú et hadélet <u>vešvú</u> bešéket.
> sigrú et hadélet <u>ušvú</u> bešeket.

Since the use of /u-/ in these cases is more formal, 'correct',
classical, or what have you, the instructor may insist on the student using it,
but the student may safely ignore these strictures in informal conversation.

6.9 <u>Loss of Final Stem Vowel in Verbs</u>

Compare the following pairs of forms:

> dabér   dabrí
> dabérna   dabrú
>
> šév   šví
> šévna   švú
>
> taavór   taavrí
> taavórna   taavrú

Note that the forms in the right-hand column have a suffix beginning with
a stressed vowel /-í, -ú/ and that the final vowel of the verb stem is
dropped. Now compare the following pairs:

> hamšéx   hamšíxi
> hamšéxna   hamšíxu
>
> takír   takíri
> takérna   takíru

In the forms of the right-hand column the suffix is not stressed, and the
final vowel of the stem remains.

When a suffix beginning with a stressed vowel is affixed to a verb, the
final vowel of the verb stem is dropped.

This is a general rule in verbs and allows but a few exceptions, which will
be stated when they occur.

When the dropping of this stem vowel results in a medial three-consonant
cluster, or in a non-permissible initial two-consonant cluster, then /-e-/
is inserted for phonological reasons.

> tiftáx   <u>tiftexí</u>   [for * /tiftxí/]
> targém   <u>targemí</u>   [for * /targmí/]
> léx   <u>lexí</u>   [for * /lxí/]

51

The latter pair is comparable to /šév ~ šví/ except that /šv-/ is a permissible initial cluster and /lx-/ is not. However, in the gentle imperative both verbs are more similar since there are no initial clusters.

tešév	tešví
teléx	telxí

When an initial three-consonant cluster results /-i-/ is usually inserted between the <u>first two</u>.

sgór	sigrí [for * /sgrí/]
ptáx	pitxí [for * /ptxí/]

6.10 Consonant Alternation /p ~ f/ in Related Forms

Examine the following pairs of forms:

ptáx	pné
tiftáx	tifné

In these pairs there is an alternation of the consonants /p/ and /f/. These two consonants often alternate in related forms (such as stark and gentle imperatives.) The patterns of the alternation are regular but somewhat complicated, and at this point the student should simply memorize them by drilling the forms.

REVIEW CONVERSATIONS

A. imrí lí bevakašá. éyx aní yaxól
   lehagía lemalón dán.

א: אמרי לי בבקשה, איך אני יכול
להגיע למלון דן?

B. léx kearbá rexovót, pné smóla,
   vetamšíx yašár ád lamalón.

ב: לך כארבעה רחובות, פנה שמאלה,
ותמשיך ישר עד למלון.

A. haím zé raxók?

א: האם זה רחוק?

B. ló, zé karóv.

ב: לא. זה קרוב.

C. dabér ivrít, bevakašá.

ג: דבר עברית, בבקשה.

D. atá medabér ivrít?

ד: אתה מדבר עברית?

C. kén. lamádeti bevét haséfer.

ג: כן. למדתי בבית הספר.

D. aní eynéni medabér kol káx tóv.

ד: אני אינני מדבר כל כך טוב.

C. léx lebét haséfer.

ג: לך לבית הספר.

D. leéyze bet séfer?

ד: לאיזה בית ספר?

C. lebét haséfer lesafót. kán bapiná.

ג: לבית הספר לשפות. כאן בפינה.

7.1 <u>Wandering Through Tel Aviv</u> (speaking to man passerby)

MR. WILLIAMS

Pardon me, sir.	tisláx li, adoní.	תסלח לי, אדוני,
I want	aní rocé	אני רוצה
to get	lehagía	להגיע
to the tourist office.	lemisrád hatayarút.	למשרד התיירות.
you will pardon	tisláx (m.s.)	תסלח
want	rocé (m.s.pres.)	רוצה
tourism	tayarút (f)	תיירות

PASSERBY

To the Government	lemisrád hatayarút	למשרד הת יירות
tourist office?	hamemšaltí?	הממשלתי?
governmental	memšaltí (m.s.)	ממשלתי

MR. WILLIAMS

Yes. Is it	kén. haím zé	כן. האם זה
far from here?	raxók mikán?	רחוק מכאן?

PASSERBY

No, it's not far.	ló. zé ló raxók.	לא, זה לא רחוק.
you are	atá nimcá	אתה נמצא
now next to	axšáv al yád	עכשיו על יד
the Mugrabi Theater,	kolnóa múgrabi.	קולנוע מוגרבי.
right?	naxón?	נכון?
situated, found	nimcá (m.s.)	נמצא
now	axšáv	עכשיו
next to, alongside	al yád	על יד
movie theater	kolnóa (m)	קולנוע

MR. WILLIAMS

Yes,	kén,	כן,
I think	aní xošév	אני חושב
so.	káx.	כך.
think	xošév (m.s.pres.)	חושב

PASSERBY

What do you mean,	má zot oméret,	מה זאת אומרת,
you think so?	atá xošév káx.	אתה חושב כך?
You don't see	atá ló roé	אתה לא רואה
that this is	šezé	שזה
the Mugrabi Theater?	kolnóa múgrabi?	קולנוע מוגרבי?
it, this	zót (f)	זאת
say	oméret (f.s.pres.)	אומרת
see	roé (m.s.pres.)	רואה

MR. WILLIAMS

Sir,	adoní.	אדוני.
speak a little	dabér kcát	דבר קצת
slower.	yotér leát.	יותר לאט.
a little, some	kcát	קצת

53

I'm new	aní xadáš	אני חדש
in the country.	baárec.	בארץ.
new	xadáš (m.s.)	חדש
I come	aní bá	אני בא
from America.	meamérika.	מאמריקה.
come	bá (m.s.pres.)	בא

PASSERBY

Oh, you're new in the country.	á- atá xadáš baárec?	אה, אתה חדש בארץ?
That's something else.	zé davár axér.	זה דבר אחר.
other	axér (m.s.)	אחר
So why didn't	áz láma ló	אז למה לא
you tell me	amárta lí	אמרת לי
before?	kódem?	קודם?
then, so	áz	אז
why	láma	למה
you said	amárta (2 m.s.)	אמרת
before, earlier	kódem	קודם

MR. WILLIAMS

When before?	matáy kódem.	מתי קודם?
You didn't give me	ló natáta lí	לא נתת לי
a chance to speak.	hizdamnút ledaber.	הזדמנות לדבר.
you gave	natáta (2 m.s.)	נתת
chance, opportunity	hizdamnút (f)	הזדמנות

7.2 _Wandering through Tel Aviv_ (speaking to woman passerby)

MRS. WILLIAMS

Excuse me, ma'am.	tislexí li, gvirtí.	תסלחי לי, גברתי,
I want	aní rocá	אני רוצה
to get	lehagía	להגיע
to the tourist office.	lemisrád hatayarút.	למשרד התיירות.
want	rocá (f.s. pres.)	רוצה

PASSERBY

To the Government	lemisrád hatayarút	למשרד התיירות
tourist office?	hamemšaltí?	הממשלתי?

MRS. WILLIAMS

Yes. Is it	ken. haím zé	כן. האם זה
far from here?	raxók mikán?	רחוק מכאן?

PASSERBY

No, it's not far.	ló. zé ló raxók.	לא. זה לא רחוק.
You are	át nimcét	את נמצאת
now next to	axšáv al yád	עכשיו על יד
the Mugrabi Theater,	kolnóa múgrabi.	קולנוע מוגרבי,
right?	naxón?	נכון?
situated, found	nimcét (f.s.)	נמצאת

54

MRS. WILLIAMS

Yes.	kén.	כן.
I think	aní xošévet	אני חושבת
so,	káx.	כך.
think	xošévet (f.s.pres.)	חושבת

PASSERBY

What do you mean,	má zot oméret,	מה זאת אומרת,
you think so?	át xošévet káx.	את חושבת כך?
You don't see	át ló roá	את לא רואה
that this is	šezé	שזה
the Mugrabi Theater?	kolnóa múgrabi?	קולנוע מוגרבי?
see	roá (f.s.pres.)	רואה

MRS. WILLIAMS

Ma'am,	gvirtí.	גברתי,
speak a little	dabrí kcát	דברי קצת
slower.	yotér leát.	יותר לאט.
I'm new	aní xadašá	אני חדשה
in the country	baárec.	בארץ.
new	xadašá (f.s.)	חדשה
I come	aní báa	אני באה
from America.	meamérika.	מאמריקה.
come	báa (f.s.pres.)	באה

PASSERBY

Oh, you're new in the country.	á- át xadašá baárec?	אה, את חדשה בארץ?
That's something else.	zé davár axér.	זה דבר אחר.
So why didn't	áz láma ló	אז למה לא
you tell me	amárt lí	אמרת לי
before?	kódem.	קודם?

MRS. WILLIAMS

When before?	matáy kódem?	מתי קודם?
You didn't give me	ló natát lí	לא נתת לי
a chance to speak.	hizdamnút ledabér.	הזדמנות לדבר.

7.3 Vocabulary Drills

A. Substitution Drill

Excuse me, I don't understand.

tisláx lí. aní ló mevín.	תסלח לי, אני לא מבין.
tislexí	תסלחי
tislexú	תסלחו
tisláxna	תסלחנה

(Women students should substitute /aní ló meviná/.)

B. Substitution - Agreement Drill   /tislǽx ~tislexí/

     Excuse me, Moshe, I have to run.

<u>tislǽx li, mošé.</u>   aní muxrǽx larúc.   .תסלח לי משה, אני מוכרח לרוץ

     xána – gvirtí – már káspi – miryám   חנה – גברתי – מר כספי – מרים
     avígdor – adoní – gvéret kóhen – davíd   אביגדור – אדוני – גברת כהן – דוד

(Women students should substitute /aní muxraxá/.)

C. Substitution - Agreement Drill   /amárti/ "I said"   אמרתי

     The instructor gives the underlined portion of the following sentences,
and the student responds with the entire sentence. The instructor may vary
the first person sentences, depending on the composition of the class,
/aní gára, ánu garót/.

     I told Moshe that <u>I live in Tel Aviv.</u>

     amárti lemošé <u>šeaní gár betél aviv.</u>   אמרתי למשה שאני גר בתל אביב
     amárnu lemošé <u>šeánu garím betél avív.</u>   אמרנו למשה שאנו גרים בתל אביב
     amárt lemošé <u>šeát gára betél avív.</u>   אמרת למשה שאנו גרים בתל א.יב
     amártem lemošé <u>šeatém garím betél avív.</u>   אמרתם למשה שאנו גרים בתל אביב
     amárta lemošé <u>šeatá gár betél avív.</u>   אמרת למשה שאנו גרים בתל אביב
     amárten lemošé <u>šeatén garót betél avív.</u>   אמרתן למשה שאנו גרים בתל אביב

D. Substitution- Agreement Drill

     I didn't give David the books.

<u>ló natáti ledavíd et hasfarím.</u>   .לא נתתי לדוד את הספרים

     atá – ánu – át – aní   אתה – אנו – את – אני
     atém – atén – atá – át   אתם – אתן – אתה – את

GRAMMAR NOTES

7.4 <u>Gender and Number - Present Tense Verbs and Adjectives</u>

Examine the underlined forms in the following sentences:

1. atá <u>medabér</u> ivrít mamáš kmó israelí.   אתה מדבר עברית ממש כמו ישראלי.
    át <u>medabéret</u> ivrít mamáš kmó israelít.   את מדברת עברית ממש כמו ישראלית.

2. aní ló <u>yodéa</u>.   אני לא יודע.
    aní ló <u>yodáat</u>.   אני לא יודעת.

3. atá <u>nimcá</u> axšáv al yád kolnóa múgrabi.   אתה נמצא עכשיו על יד קולנוע מוגרבי.
    át <u>nimcét</u> axšáv al yád kolnóa múgrabi.   את נמצאת עכשיו על יד קולנוע מוגרבי.

4. aní <u>rocé</u> lehagía lemisrád hatayarút.   אני רוצה להגיע למשרד התיירות.
    aní <u>rocá</u> lehagía lemisrád hatayarút.   אני רוצה להגיע למשרד התיירות.

5. aní <u>muxráx</u> larúc.   אני מוכרח לרוץ.
    aní <u>muxraxá</u> larúc.   אני מוכרחה לרוץ.

6. aní <u>gár</u> beynatáim bemalón dán.   אני גר בינתיים במלון דן.
    aní <u>gára</u> beynatáim bemalón dan.   אני גרה בינתיים במלון דן.

7. éyx aní <u>yaxól</u> lehagía ladóar hamerkazí.   איך אני יכול להגיע לדואר המרכזי.
    éyx aní <u>yexolá</u> lehagía ladóar hamerkazí.   איך אני יכולה להגיע לדואר המרכזי.

You will note here that, in contrast to the past tense verb forms, there is
no pronoun suffix to the verb itself. Instead the independent form of the
pronoun is used. Further, the verb form indicates the gender of the subject
with the first person, also. The pattern is similar to the noun-adjective
sentence pattern:

         aní xadáš baárec.   אני חדש בארץ.
         aní xadašá baárec.   אני חדשה בארץ.

The similarity extends to the plurals.

         ánu garím bexáyfa.   אנו גרים בחיפה.
         ánu garót bexáyfa.   אנו גרות בחיפה.

The present tense of verbs has just these four forms - masculine singular
and plural and feminine singular and plural - and person is indicated by an
independent subject.
    Plurals of present tense verb forms and of adjectives are all alike in that
the masculine plural has the suffix /-ím/ and the feminine plural has the suffix
/-ót/.

[Note: Some masculine plural <u>nouns</u> end in /-ót/ and some feminine plural
<u>nouns</u> in /-ím/. The present tense verbs and adjectives for these plurals,
however, end in /-ím/ and /-ót/ respectively.]

The feminine singular forms are of two major types - those that have a
suffix ending in /-t/ and those that have the suffix /-a/. The forms which
have thus far occurred are:

/-t/ feminines	/-a/ feminines
medabéret	muxraxá
oméret	meviná
xošévet	yexolá
mitkonénet	gára
yodáat	rišoná
mocét	báa
nimcét	xadašá
amerikáit	smexá
	mekavá
	rocá
	roá
	yafá

The variations of these two major types will be described and drilled in turn.

7.5 /t/ - Suffix Feminine Forms

a) Present Tense of Verbs with Stem Pattern /-éC/

Examine the verb forms in the following sentences:

    atá medabér ivrít.
    át medabéret ivrít.

In this pattern the masculine singular ends in /-éC/. The feminine is the same as the masculine but with an added unstressed /-et/. In the plurals the final stem vowel /-e-/ is dropped, unless a three-consonant cluster would result or two similar consonants would be juxtaposed.

    atém medabrím ivrít.
    atén medabrót ivrít.

    atém mitkonením lagúr berámat gán.
    atén mitkonenót lagúr berámat gán.

The adjective /axér/ is also of this pattern. The forms are:

    m.s. /axér/   m.pl. /axerím/
    f.s. /axéret/   f.pl. /axerót/

There are some other minor variations of this pattern in the plurals, and these will be described as they occur in the text.

The following drills are substitution-agreement drills. The last substitution cue given in each drill will result in the model sentence. Each drill should be done a number of times in continuous succession until correct entire sentences are given without hesitation as responses.

Substitutions for the first person may be masculine or feminine, depending on the class situation.

A. You speak Hebrew very well.

    atá medabér tóv meód ivrít.   . אתה מדבר טוב מאד עברית

    át - hém - már Williams - xána   אַת - הם - מר ווילַיאמס - חנה
    atén - hú - atém - ánu - atá   אתן - הוא - אתם - אנו - אתה

B. Moshe says that it's very late.

<u>mošé omér šekvár meuxár meód.</u>   מֹשֶׁה אוֹמר שֶׁכְּבר מאוחר מאד.

aní - hú - ánu - miryám - hém   אני - הוא - אנו - מרים - הם
gvéret káspi - hén - atén - mošé   גברת כספי - הן - אתן - משה

C. What do you think - is it far from here?

<u>má atá xošév - zé raxók mikán?</u>   מה אתה חושֵׁב - זה רחוק מכאן?

hí - atém - át - atén   היא - אתם - את - אתן
hém - hú - hén - atá   הם - הוא - הן - אתה

D. I plan to live in Savyon.

<u>aní mitkonén laqúr besavyón.</u>   אני מתכונן לגור בסביון.

hém - avígdor - iští veaní - hí   הם - אביגדור - אשתי ואני - היא
ánu - hén - hú - atára - aní   אנו - הן - הוא - עטרה - אני

E. In this drill some noun plurals are introduced. The instructor should
correct the student by giving the correct noun-adjective sequence rather
than by discussing gender per se.

He sees something else.

<u>hú roé davár axér.</u>   הוא רואה דבר אחר.

oniá - namál - sfarím - báit   אוניה - נמל - ספרים - כית
melonót - oniót - binyán - délet   מלונות - אוניות - כנין - רלת
šagrirút - misradím - mišpaxót - davár   שגרירות - משרדים - משפחות - דכר

b) <u>Present Tense of Verbs with Stem Pattern /-éa(x)/</u>

This is the pattern of /yodéa/ 'know'. The four forms are:

m.s. yodéa	f.s. yodáat	יורעת	יורע
m.pl. yod'ím	f.pl. yod'ót	יורעות	יורעים

Note that in the plurals an internal open juncture functions as a third
root consonant. Verbs in which the masculine singular ends in /-éax/ have a
similar pattern. The four forms have the following endings:

m.s. -éax   f.s. -áxat
m.pl. -xím   f.pl. -xót

[There is a close correspondence with written Hebrew in that all such words
are spelled with ע or ה and not with א or כ .]

F. He knows I'm new in the country.

<u>hú yodéa šeaní xadáš baárec.</u>   הוא יורע שׁאני חדש בארץ.

atá - ištó - hén - gvéret kóhen   אתה - אשתו - הן - גברת כהן
atén - át - davíd - atém - hú   אתן - את - רור - אתם - הוא

G.   I think he knows how to speak Hebrew.

ani xošév šehú yodéa ledabér ivrít.   אני חושב שהוא יודע לדבר עברית .

šehí - šeatá - šehém - šeištexá   שהיא - שאתה - שהם - שאשתך
šebaaléx - šehén - šedóv vemošé - šehú   שכעלך - שהן - שדכ ומשה - שהוא

c)   Present Tense Pattern /mocé ~mocét/

This pattern is characterized by the singular ending in /-é ~-ét/ and by
an internal open juncture functioning as a third root consonant in the plural
/-'ím ~ -'ót/. The full present of /mocé/ is:

      m.s. mocé   m.pl. moc'ím
      f.s. mocét   f.pl. moc'ót

In the plurals this pattern is similar to that of /yod'ím/ in Section b.
The student should be sure to practice the singulars of any such plural that he
may learn in order not to confuse the two types. There are pairs of verbs
whose only distinction is in this respect. The writing system reflects this
difference in that verbs of the /mocé ~ mocét/ pattern are spelled with א
and not with ע - the reverse of verbs like /yodéa/.

H.   I like the country.

haárec mócet xén beeynáy.   הארץ מוצאת חן בעיני .

habáit - hašagrirút - hasfarím - haavirón   הבית-השגרירות-הספרים-האוירון
haoniót - hém - atén - harexovót - haárec   האניות-הם-אתן-הרחובות-הארץ

I.   He finds that the house is very nice.

hú mocé šehabáit yafé meód.   הוא מוצא שהבית יפה מאד .

aní - már zahávi - ištexá - hém   אני - מר זהבי - אשתך - הם
atén - ánu - ištó veiští - hú   אתן - אנו - אשתו ואשתי - הוא

d)   Present Tense Pattern /nimcá ~ nimcét/

This pattern is a minor variation of a pattern which will be discussed later.
The plural suffixes are added to the masculine singular, and the feminine
singular has the suffix /-t/ with the vowel change. The student should simply
learn this particular verb at this time. The full present is:

      m.s. nimcá   f.s. nimcét
      m.pl. nimcaím
      f.pl. nimcaót

Some speakers use the pronunciation /nimceím, nimceót/ in the plural.
This particular pattern is similar to that of /mocé/ in that such verbs are
always spelled with א . In fact, /mocé/ and /nimcá/ are different conjugations
of the same verb root - /mocé/ 'finds', /nimcá/ 'is found' - but this point
will be discussed in detail further on.

J.   The Embassy is located in Tel Aviv.

hašagrirút nimcét betél avív.   השגרירות נמצאת בתל אביב .

habáit šelí - már Williams - ištó vehú   הבית שלי - מר וויליאמס - אשתו והוא
hén kulám - ištó - ištexa xána veléa   הן - כולם - אשתו - אשתך - חנה ולאה
hašagrirút   השגרירות

e. Derived   Adjectives with /-i/

Adjectives are often derived from other parts of speech by the addition
of /-i/, in certain cases with other changes in the form. Examples from our
text so far are:

/memšaltí/ derived from /memšalá/ 'government'
/amerikái/ derived from /amérika/ 'America'
/merkazí/ derived from /merkáz/ 'center'

The endings for these adjectives are of the following pattern:
       m.s.   /-í/   f.s.   /-ít/
       m.pl. /-iím/   f.pl. /-iót/

In some adjectives the stress is on a non final syllable as in /amerikái,
amerikáit/.

The above pattern occurs in derived __adjectives.__ There are also derived
__nouns,__ which have similar patterns.

For example:
       m.s. yisraeli   f.s. yisraelít
       m.pl. yisraelím   f.pl. yisraeliót

Note that a distinction is made in the following case:

       noun: /yisraelím/ 'Israelis'
       adjective: /avironím yisraeliím/ 'Israeli airplanes'

K. Where is the Government office?

__heyxán hamisrád hamemšaltí.__

       habinyán - hamisradím - hayoéc
       habinyaním - hayoacím - hamísrád

L. Where is the American Embassy?

__eyfó hašagrirút haamerikáit.__

       hayoéc - haoniá - habinyaním
       haoniót - hakolnóa - hašagrirút

היכן המשרד הממשלתי?

הבנין – המשרדים – היועץ
הבנינים – היועצים – המשרד

איפה השגרירות האמריקאית?

היועץ – האוניה – הבנינים
האוניות – הקולנוע – השגרירות

61

REVIEW CONVERSATIONS

A: šalom mošé. láma atá rác.   א. שלום משה. למה אתה רץ?

B: šalóm miryám. aní muxráx larúc lemisrád hatayarút.   ב. שלום מרים. אני מוכרח לרוץ למשרד התיירות.

A: leéyze misrád tayarút.   א. לאיזה משרד תיירות?

B: lemisrád hatayarút hamemšaltí.   ב. למשרד התיירות הממשלתי.

C: aní nimcá axšáv al yád kolnóa múgrabi. naxón?   ג. אני נמצא עכשיו על יד קולנוע מוגרבי. נכון?

D: kén. naxón. veatá rocé lehagía lisfát hayám?   ד. כן. נכון. ואתה רוצה להגיע לשפת הים?

C: ken. haim ze raxók mikán?   ג. כן. האם זה רחוק מכאן?

D: ló. zé ló raxók . léx yašár berexóv álenbi ád lesfát hayám.   ד. לא.זה לא רחוק. לך ישר ברחוב אלנבי עד לשפת הים.

E: adoní. dabér kcat yotér leát.   ה. אדוני, דבר קצת יותר לאט.

F: atá ló mevín ivrít?   ו. אתה לא מבין עברית?

E: kcát. aní xadáš baárec.   ה. קצת. אני חדש בארץ.

F: atá xadáš baárec? zé davár axér.   ו. אתה חדש בארץ? זה דבר אחר.

E: aní bá meamérika.   ה. אני בא מאמריקה.

8.1 Wandering through Tel Aviv (cont'd.)

PASSERBY

All right.	nú tóv.	נו טוב.
So you say	áz amárta	אז אמרת
you want to get	šeatá rocé lehagía	שאתה רוצה להגיע
to the tourist office,	lemisrád hatayarút.	למשרד התיירות,
right?	naxon?	נכון?

MR. WILLIAMS

Yes, that's right.	kén. naxón.	כן. נכון.

PASSERBY

Listen.	šmá.	שמע.
Are you in a hurry?	atá memahér?	אתה ממהר?
listen, hear	šmá (m.s.imv.)	שמע
hurry (verb)	memahér (m.s.pres.)	ממהר

MR. WILLIAMS

Not really.	ló kol káx.	לא כל כך.
I want to walk around	aní rocé letayél	אני רוצה לטייל
and see the city.	velir'ót et haír.	ולראות את העיד.
to stroll, hike	letayél	לטייל
to see	lir'ót	לראות
city	ír (f)	עיר
cities	arím (f.pl.)	ערים

PASSERBY

If so,	ím káx,	אם כן,
go straight	léx yašár	לך ישר
on Allenby Road	berexóv álenbi	ברחוב אלנבי
towards the seashore.	lekivún sfát hayám.	לכיוון שפת הים.
if	ím	אם
direction	kivún (m)	כיוון
shore, language, lip	safá (f)	שפה
sea	yám (m)	ים
seashore	sfát yám	שפת ים

MR. WILLIAMS

In this direction?	bakivún hazé?	בכיוון הזה?

PASSERBY

Yes. You'll pass	kén. taavór et	כן. תעבור את
the Brooklyn Bar.	brúklin bár.	ברוקלין בר.

MR. WILLIAMS

The what?	et má?	את מה?

PASSERBY

The Brooklyn Bar.	et brúklin bar.	את ברוקלין בר.
Do you know	atá yodéa	אתה יודע
where the Brooklyn Bar is?	éyfo šebrúklin bar?	איפה שברוקלין בר?

MR. WILLIAMS

No, I don't know.	16. aní 16 yodéa.	לא. אני לא יודע.
Haven't I told you	haréy amárti lexá	הרי אמרתי לך
that I'm new in the country.	šeaní xadáš baárec.	שאני חדש בארץ.
(interjection)	haréy	הרי

8.2 Wandering through Tel Aviv (cont'd.)

PASSERBY

All right.	nú tóv.	נו טוב.
So you say	áz amárt	אז אמרת
you want to get	šeát rocá lehagía	שאת רוצה להגיע
to the tourist office,	lemisrád hatayarút.	למשרד התיירות,
right?	naxón?	נכון?

MRS. WILLIAMS

Yes, that's right.	kén. naxón.	כן. נכון.

PASSERBY

Listen.	šim'í.	שמעי.
Are you in a hurry?	át memahéret?	את ממהרת?

MRS. WILLIAMS

Not really.	16 kol káx.	לא כל כך.
I want to walk around	aní rocá letayél	אני רוצה לטייל
and see the city.	velir'ót et haír.	ולדאות את העיר.

PASSERBY

If so,	ím káx,	אם כך,
go straight	lexí yašár	לכי ישר
on Allenby Road	berexóv álenbi	ברחוב אלנבי
towards the seashore.	lekivún sfát hayám.	לכיוון שפת הים.

MRS. WILLIAMS

In this direction?	bakivún hazé?	בכיוון הזה?

PASSERBY

Yes. You'll pass	kén. taavrí et	כן. תעברי את
the Brooklyn Bar.	brúklin bár.	ברוקלין בר.

MRS. WILLIAMS

The what?	et má?	את מה?

PASSERBY

The Brooklyn Bar.	et brúklin bár.	.אֶת ברוקלין בר
Do you know	át yodáat	אַת יודעת
where the Brooklyn Bar is?	éyfo šebrúklin bár?	?איפה שברוקלין בר

MRS. WILLIAMS

No, I don't know.	ló. aní ló yodáat.	.לא. אני לא יודעת
Haven't I told you	haréy amárti láx	הרי אמרתי לך
that I'm new in the country?	šeaní xadašá baárec.	.שאני חדשה בארץ

8.3 Vocabulary Drill

Present tense plurals of verbs in which the middle root consonant is
/h/ such as /memahér/ vary slightly from the pattern described in Section 7.5a.
The vowel /e/ is replaced by /a/ instead of being dropped. The present tense
forms of /memahér/ are:

m.s.	memahér	m.pl.	memaharím
f.s.	memahéret	f.pl.	memaharót

In normal speech intervocalic /-h-/ is often replaced by a smooth
transition between the vowels when the stress does not immediately follow
the /h/. Thus, one frequently hears /memaarím/ and /memaarót/.

A. Substitution - Agreement Drill

I'm hurrying to the movies.

aní memahér lakolnóa.   .אני ממהר לקולנוע

hí - már kóhen - már kóhen veištó   היא - מר כהן - מר כהן ואשתו
hén - gvéret Williams - atém - aní   הן - גב' וויל:אמס - אתם - אני

GRAMMAR NOTES

8.4 á-Suffix Feminine Forms

a. Present Tense of /lámed héy/ Verbs

A frequent pattern is illustrated by the following:

aní <u>rocé</u> lehagía lemisrád hatayarút.
aní <u>rocá</u> lehagía lemisrád hatayarút.

In the plurals the suffixes /-ím/ and /-ót/ are substituted.

hém <u>rocím</u> lehagía lemisrád hatayarút.
hén <u>rocót</u> lehagía lemisrád hatayarút.

This pattern occurs in a number of adjectives such as /yafé ~ yafá/.

[In traditional Hebrew grammars, which deal mainly with the written
language, verbs are classified according to the letters which comprise the
"roots". Verbs of the pattern described in this section are called "/lámed
héy/" verbs since the third letter of the root in the writing system is ה
/héy/. This designation may remain abstruse for the time being until the
student learns to read, but there is little to be gained by coining a new
term for these verbs. All /lámed héy/ verbs exhibit certain similarities
regardless of the conjugation or consonants of the root. With the exception
of one conjugation, this is true of the present tense. The exception will be
described later on.]

The following drills are substitution-agreement drills and should be done
as the drills in the previous unit.

A. He wants to get to the Eden Theater.

<u>hú rocé lehagía lekolnóa éden.</u>   הוא רוצה להגיע לקולנוע עדן.

hí - ánu - át - hén - dóv   היא – אנו – את – הן – רב
atém - sára - aní - hú   אחם – שרה – אני – הוא

B. He hopes to speak Hebrew in Israel.

<u>hú mekavé ledabér ivrít beisraél.</u>   הוא מקווה לדבר עברית בישראל.

aní - már Williams - gvéret Williams   אני – מר ויליאמס – גב' ויליאמס
iští veaní - hén - át - ánu - hú   אשתי ואני – הן – את – אנו – הוא

C. He sees the office.

<u>hú roé et hamisrád.</u>   הוא רואה את המשרד.

hém - atára - aní - xána veléa   הם – עטרה – אני – חנה ולאה
ánu - hí - hayoéc veištó - hú   אנו – היא – היועץ ואשתו – הוא

66

D.   I heard that the house is very nice.

   <u>Šamáti šehabáit yafé meód.</u>   .שמעתי שהבית יפה מאד

   Šehaárec - Šemiryám - Šehamisradím   שהארץ – שמרים – שהמשרדים
   Šehaoniót - Šehanamál - Šehasfarím   שהאניות – שהנמל – שהספרים
   Šesára veatára - Šezé   Šehabáit   ששרה ועטרה – שזה – שהבית

b.   <u>Common Adjective Pattern</u>

   The pattern illustrated in the following pairs of sentences is very
frequent in adjectives and occurs in certain conjugations of verbs.

         aní <u>xadáš</u> baárec. (man speaking)
         aní <u>xadašá</u> baárec. (woman speaking)

         aní <u>muxráx</u> larúc. (man speaking)
         aní <u>muxraxá</u> larúc. (woman speaking)

   In the plurals the suffixes /-ím/ and /-ót/ are substituted where the
feminine singular has /-á/.

         ánu <u>muxraxím</u> larúc.
         ánu <u>muxraxót</u> larúc.

   When the masculine singular is a monosyllabic verb then the stress is on
the first syllable in the feminine singular.

         aní <u>gára</u> bemalón dán.
         aní <u>báa</u> meamérika.

   When the masculine singular form has the consonant-vowel pattern /CaCV̂C/
e.g. /xadíš, gadól, yašár/, then the pattern of the feminine and plurals is
phonologically a bit more complicated.

   The /-a-/ of the masculine singular is dropped when the suffixes for the
feminine and plurals are added.

         m.s.   gadól   karóv
         f.s.   gdolá   krová
         m.pl. gdolím   krovím
         f.pl. gdolót   krovót

   If a phonologically impossible cluster would result from dropping the
/-a-/, then the vowel /e/ occurs between the first two consonants in the pattern
/CeCVCá/. Bear in mind that there are many clusters which are quite possible
in Hebrew, but which the student will be tempted to break up by inserting a
vowel as in /gdolá/ above.

         m.s.   raxók   yašár

         f.s.   rexoká   yešará
         m.pl. rexokím   yešarím
         f.pl. rexokót   yešarót

If the first consonant is /x/, /'/, or /h/, then the vowel /a/ is inserted to break up the resulting cluster. The net effect is that the feminine and plural suffixes are added without change.

m.s.	xadáš	xadíš	f.s.	xadašá	xadišá
			m.pl.	xadaším	xadiším
			f.pl.	xadašót	xadišót

The consonants /h/ and /'/ are often dropped between vowels. Vowels which break up clusters containing these consonants are retained even when the consonants are dropped. In this text the transcription usually reflects the informal spoken pronunciation, especially when /'/ is elided.

m.s.	naím	(for /na'ím/)	f.s.	neimá	(for /ne'imá/)
			m.pl.	neimím	(for /ne'imím/)
			f.pl.	neimót	(for /ne'imót/)

E. He has to live near the office.

<u>hú muxráx lagúr karóv lamisrád.</u>

הוא מוכרח לגור קרוב למשרד.

át - ánu - hayoéc - hém
atén - gvéret kóhen - aní - hú

אח - אנו - היועץ - הם
אחן - גב' כהן - אני - הוא

F. Moshe lives on Allenby Road.

<u>mošé gár berexóv álenbi.</u>

משה גר ברחוב אלנבי.

hém - aní - atára - ánu
davíd veištó - hén - mošé

הם - אני - עטרה - אנו
דוד ואשתו - הן - משה

G. I'm coming to see Mr. Zahavi.

<u>aní bá lir'ót et már zahávi.</u>

אני בא לראות את מר זהבי.

ánu - hí - gvéret kármi - hém
atén - avígdor - hén - aní

אנו - היא - גב' כרמי - הם
אתן - אביגדור - הן - אני

H. The Lydda airport is new and beautiful.

<u>nemál hateufá lúd xadáš veyafé.</u>

נמל התעופה לוד חדש ויפה.

malón dán - haoniót - kolnóa múgrabi
haavironím - hašagrirút - nemál hateufá

מלון דן - האוניות - קולנוע מוגרבי
האווירונים - השגרירות
נמל התעופה

I. The tourist office is very large.

<u>misrád hatayarút gadól meód.</u>

משרד התיירות גדול מאד.

malón dán - haoniót - hakolnóa
haavironím - hašagrirút - misrád hatayarút

מלון דן - האוניות - הקולנוע
האווירונים - השגרירות
משרד התיירות

J. The ships are very far from the port.

<u>haoniót rexokót meód mehanamál.</u>

האוניות רחוקות מאד מהנמל.

hašagrirút - habatím - misrád hatayarút
haavironím - malón dán - haoniót

השגרירות - הבתים - משרד התיירות
האווירונים - מלון דן - האוניות

K. The plane is very close to the port.

<u>haavirón karóv meód lanamál.</u>   .האווירון קרוב מאד לנמל

habatím - haoniót - misrád hatayarút   משרד החיירות – האוניות – הכחים
malón dán - kolnóa múgrabi - haavirón   מוגרבי קולנוע – דן מלון
                                                 האווירון

L. Moshe's family is very pleasant.

<u>hamišpaxá šel mošé neimá meód.</u>   .המשפחה של משה נעימה מאד

ištexá - atá - hém - atén - atém   אחם – אחן – הם – אחה – אשתך
gvéret zahávi - már kóhen - hamišpaxá šel mošé   כהן מר – זהבי גב'
                                                 משה של המשפחה

M. Mr. Williams is honest and good.

<u>már Williams yašár vetóv.</u>   .מר ווילייאמס ישר וטוב

hén - hú - atára - ánu   אנו – עטרה – הוא – הן
mošé - atá vedavíd - már Williams   ווילייאמס מר – ודוד אחה – משה

N. You can't see the ship.

<u>atá ló yaxól lir'ót et haoniá.</u>   .אחה לא יכול לדאות את האוניה

atém - hén - aní - hú   הוא – אני – הן – אחם
gvéret kármi - ánu - hí - atá   אחה – היא – אנו – כרמי גב'

c. <u>Adjectives ending in /-√ax/</u>

A variation of the above patterns is that of /saméax/ 'happy'. In this
adjective pattern the masculine singular ends in /-√ax/.

            m.s. saméax   f.s. smexá
                                m.pl. smexím
                                f.pl. smexót

[There is a close correspondence with written Hebrew in that all such
words are spelled with ח , and not with כ .   Compare Section 7.5b.]

o. I'm very happy to see Mr. Carmi.

<u>aní saméax meód lir'ót et már kármi.</u>   .אני שמח מאד לדאות את מר כרמי

ánu - hí - atém - sára veléa   ולאה שרה – אחם – היא – אנו
kulám - baalá - ištó - aní   אני – אשתו – בעלה – כולם

69

REVIEW CONVERSATIONS

A: amárt šeát rocá lehagía
lemalón dán. naxón?

       א: אמרת שאת רוצה להגיע
       למלון דן, נכון?

B: ló. amárti šeaní rocá lehagía
lemisrád hatayarut.

       ב: לא. אמרתי שאני רוצה להגיע
       למשרד התיירות.

A: slixá. ló šamáti otáx.

       א: סליחה. לא שמעתי אותך.

C: šim'í. át memahéret?

       ג: שמעי, את ממהרת?

D: ló kol káx. veatá?

       ד: לא כל כך. ואתה?

C: gám aní ló memahér.

       ג: גם אני לא ממהר.

E: át rocá glída?

       ה: את רוצה גלידה?

F: ken. éyfo brúklin bar?

       ו: כן. איפה ברוקלין בר?

E: berexóv álenbi bekivún sfát hayám.

       ה: ברחוב אלנבי בכיוון שפת הים.

F: haglída šám tová meód.

       ו: הגלידה שם טובה מאוד.

E: kén, aní yodéa.

       ה: כן, אני יודע.

G: atá yodéa éyfo šebrúklin bár?

       ז: אתה יודע איפה שברוקלין בר?

H: ló. aní ló yodéa.

       ח: לא. אני לא יודע.

G: atá ló tél avívi?

       ז: אתה לא תל אביבי?

H: ló. aní xadáš baárec.

       ח: לא. אני חדש בארץ.

I: atá rocé laléxet lemisrád hatayarút?

       ט: אתה רוצה ללכת למשרד התיירות?

J: kén. lemisrád hatayarút hamemšaltí.

       י: כן. למשרד התיירות הממשלתי.

I: im káx, léx yašár birxóv álenbi.

       ט: אם כך, לך ישר ברחוב אלנבי.

J: rexóv álenbi hú bakivún hazé?

       י: רחוב אלנבי הוא בכיוון הזה?

I: kén.

       ט: כן.

K: atá yodéa éyfo nimcét hašagrirút?

       כ: אתה יודע איפה נמצאת השגרירות?

L: ló, aní ló yodéa. aní xadáš betél avív.

       ל: לא, אני לא יודע. אני חדש בתל אביב.

K: tóv. áz tamšíx yašár barexóv hazé.

       כ: טוב. אז תמשיך ישר ברחוב הזה.

L: todá rabá.

       ל: תודה רבה.

M: át memahéret, gvirtí?   ?מ: את ממהרת, גברתי

N: ló. aní ló memahéret. aní rocá   נ: לא. אני לא ממהרת. אני רוצה
   letayél velir'ót et haír.   לטייל ולראות את העיר.

M: áz lexí lemisrád hatayarút.   מ: אז לכי למשרד התיירות.

N: aní ló yodáat éyfo šemisrád hatayarút.   נ: אני לא יודעת איפה שמשרד התיירות.

M: kán bapiná harišoná.   מ: כאן בפינה הראשונה.

O: láma atá memahér, adoní?   ?ס: למה אתה ממהר, אדוני

P: kvár meuxár veaní rocé   ע: כבר מאוחר, ואני רוצה
   lehagía lekolnóa múgrabi.   להגיע לקולנוע מוגרבי.

O: zé ló raxók mikán.   ס: זה לא רחוק מכאן.

P: kén. aní yodéa šezé ló raxók.   ע: כן. אני יודע שזה לא רחוק.

O: áz láma atá memahér?   ?ס: אז למה אתה ממהר

P: amárti lexá šekvár meuxár.   ע: אמרתי לך שכבר מאוחר.

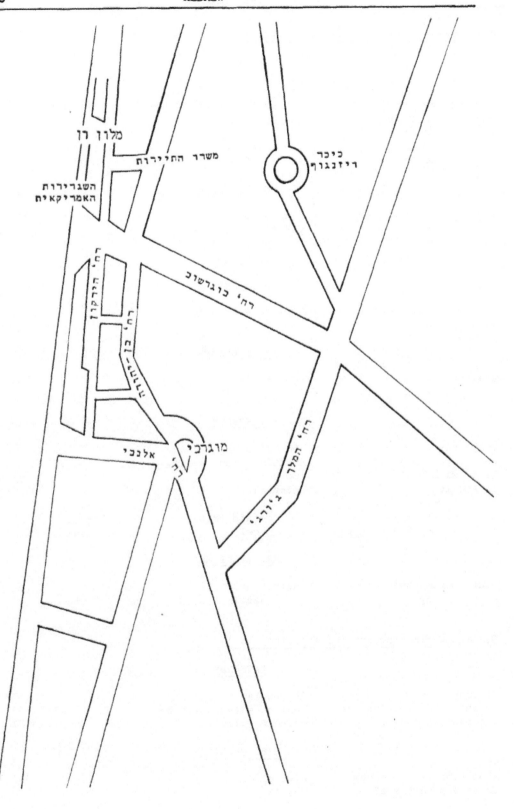

72

9.1 Wandering through Tel Aviv (cont'd.)

PASSERBY

You can	atá yaxól	אתה יכול
go into the Brooklyn Bar	lehikanés lebrúklin bár	להכנס לברוקלין בר
and eat ice cream.	veleexól glída.	ולאכול גלידה.
to enter	lehikanés	להכנס
to eat	leexól	לאכול
ice cream	glída, glidá (f)	גלידה

MR. WILLIAMS

What kind of ice cream	éyzo glída	איזו גלידה
do they have there?	yéš šám.	יש שם?
which	éyzo (f)	איזו
there is	yéš	יש

PASSERBY

The ice cream there	haglidá šám	הגלידה שם
is very good.	tová meód.	טובה מאד.

MR. WILLIAMS

Really?	beemét?	באמת?
truth	emét (f)	אמת

PASSERBY

They even	hém afílu	הם אפילו
make a banana split	mexiním banána splít	מכינים בננה ספליט
like [with you]	kmó eclexém	כמו אצלכם
in America.	beamérika.	באמריקה.
even	afílu	אפילו
prepare	mexín (m.s.)	מכין
at (French chez)	écel	אצל

MR. WILLIAMS

What do you say!	má atá sáx!	מה אתה שח!
say	sáx (m.s.pres.)	שח

9.2 Wandering through Tel Aviv (cont'd.)

PASSERBY

You can	át yexolá	את יכולה
go into the Brooklyn Bar	lehikanés lebrúklin bár	להכנס לברוקלין בר
and eat ice cream.	veleexól glída.	ולאכול גלידה.

MRS. WILLIAMS

What kind of ice cream	éyzo glída	איזו גלידה
do they have there?	yéš šám.	יש שם?

PASSERBY

| The ice cream there
is very good. | haglída šám
tová meód. | הגלידה שם
טובה מאד. |

MRS. WILLIAMS

| Really? | beemét? | באמת? |

PASSERBY

| They even
make a banana split
like [with you]
in America. | hém afílu
mexiním banána splít
kmó eclexém
beamérika. | הם אפילו
מכינים בננה סֿפּליט
כמו אצלכם
באמֿדיקה. |

MRS. WILLIAMS

| What do you say! | má át sáxa! | מה את שֿחה! |

9.3   Vocabulary Drills

    A.   They are preparing the ice cream.

      hém mexiním et haglída.   הם מכינים את הגלידה.

        hí - ánu - atén - davíd   היא - אנו - אתן - דוד
        atára - xána veiští - hú - hém   עטרה - חנה ואשתי - הוא - הם

The preposition /écel/ is difficult to translate succinctly. It is
roughly comparable to the French <u>chez</u> and means "at the home, place, office
of, by, with", etc.
    The preposition has the alternate form /ecl-/ before pronominal suffixes.
It is used with the singular set.
    Many speakers have the following variant forms with some of the suffixes.

      2 f.s. /ecláx/   for   /ecléx/
      3 m.pl. /eclahém/   for   /eclám/
      3 f.pl. /eclahén/   for   /eclán/

    B.   Substitution Drill

      The book is at my house.

      haséfer nimcá eclí babáit.   הספר נמצא אצלי כבית.
             eclexá   אצלך
             ecléx   אצלך
             ecló   אצלו
             eclá   אצלה
             eclénu   אצלנו
             eclexém   אצלכם
             eclexén   אצלכן
             eclám   אצלם
             eclán   אצל ן

GRAMMAR NOTES

9.4 The Construct State of Nouns

a. Examine the underlined noun phrases in the following sentences:

1. lúd hú nemál teufá yafé vexadíš.
2. beéyze bet séfer lamádeta.

In each of these phrases a noun is modified by another noun. In Sentence 1, for example, the noun /namál/ (in the alternate form /nemál/) is modified by /teufá/. This construction is comparable to the English in which one noun modifies another, except that in English the first noun modifies the second, while in Hebrew the reverse is true.

/namál/	"port"
/teufá/	"flight"
/nemál teufá/	(lit.) "flight port"

In sentence 2 the noun /báit/ (in the alternate form /bét/) is modified by /séfer/

/báit/	"house"
/séfer/	"book"
/bet séfer/	"school" (lit.) "book house"

The first noun in such a sequence is said to be in the <u>construct state.</u>

b. As noted in Grammar Section 3.4 some nouns have an alternate form when occurring as the first noun in this construction. It is hard to predict the alternate forms, but as patterns occur in this text they will be pointedd out. If not otherwise noted it may be at least temporarily assumed that there is no alternate construct state form.

(1) Masculine singular nouns of the pattern /CaCVC/ have a construct form without the /-a-/ unless the first consonant is /x-/.
/šalóm/ - /šlóm ištexá/
/namál/ - /nemál teufá/ (with /-e-/ because /nm-/ is a non-permissible initial cluster)
This pattern is very similar to the pattern of masculine-feminine adjectives described in Grammar Section 8.4b
(2) Feminine singular nouns ending in /-á/ have a construct form ending in /-át/, sometimes with other changes.
/safá/ - /sfát yám/ "seashore"
(3) Alternates forms of other nouns in this text so far are:
/báit/ "house" - /bét/ or /béyt/
/išá/ "wife" - /éšet/
/áin/ "eye" - /éyn/
/mišpaxá/ "family" - /mišpáxat/

c. The main stress in the comparable noun-noun constructions in English is on the first noun; in Hebrew it is on the second. In this text the primary stress of each word is indicated, but a comparatively louder stress will be heard on the second noun - /nemàl teufá/. When the stresses are on contiguous syllables the first may become unstressed - /bet séfer/, but /bét haséfer/.

d. The definite article /ha-/ is prefixed only to the <u>second</u> noun in the construct state sequence. The first noun, however, is still treated as definite.

/yoéc hašagrirút/	"the Embassy counsellor"	יועץ השגרירות
/misrád haxúc/	"the foreign office"	משרד החוץ
/binyán hadóar/	"the post office building"	בנין הדואר
/misrád hatayarút/	"the tourism office"	משרד התיירות

e. Adjectives modifying the first noun of a construct state sequence follow the entire construction.
/nemál teufá yafé vexadíš/ "a beautiful and modern airport"
Note that the adjectives /yafé vexadíš/ modify /nemál/ and are, therefore, masculine.

f. Three nouns may occur in a construct state sequence.
/kivún sfát hayám/ "the direction of the seashore"
Sequences of four nouns occur but they are rare and are often paraphrased.

g. Hebrew construct state sequences are not always translatable as English noun-noun constructions. They are sometimes translated as prepositional phrase constructions, usually with the preposition "of".
/kivún hayám/ "the direction of the sea"
/šagrirút yisraél/ "the Embassy of Israel" or "the Israel Embassy"

Some sequences are translatable as possessives.
/šlóm hamišpaxá/ "the family's welfare"

On the other hand, English noun-noun constructions are not necessarily translated as construct state sequences in Hebrew.
/misrád hatayarút <u>hamemšaltí</u>/ "the <u>government</u> tourist office"
Here the Hebrew has an adjective /memšaltí/ modifying /misrád/ while English has the noun "government" modifying "office".

A. Completion Drill - The instructor gives the sentence and then the noun in parentheses. The student responds by giving the sentence with a construct state sequence using the noun.

Instructor: He is in an office. (the hotel)
Student: He is in the hotel office.

1.	hú nimcá bemisrád. (hamalon).	הוא נמצא במשרד. (המלון).
	hú nimcá bemisrád hamalón.	הוא נמצא במשרד המלון.
2.	hú nimcá bebinyán. (hašagrirút).	הוא נמצא בבנין. (השגרירות).
	hú nimcá bebinyán hašagrirút.	הוא נמצא בבנין השגרירות.
3.	namál nimcá belúd. (teufá).	נמל נמצא בלוד. (תעופה).
	nemál teufá nimcá belúd.	נמל תעופה נמצא בלוד.
4.	mišpaxá tagía letél avív. (zahávi).	משפחה תגיע לתל אביב. (זהכי).
	mišpáxat zahávi tagía letél avív.	משפחת זהבי תגיע לתל אביב.
5.	raínu báit berexóv álenbi. (kolnóa)	ראינו בית בו חוב אלנבי. (קולנוע).
	raínu bét kolnóa berexóv álenbi.	ראינו בית קולנוע ברחוב אלנבי.
6.	hamšéx ád lepiná. (rexóv álenbi).	המשך עד לפינה. (רחוב אלנכי).
	hamšéx ád lepinát rexóv álenbi.	המשך עד לפינת רחוב אלנכי.

B. Transformation Drill - Indefinite to Definite

    Instructor: You saw a movie house.
    Student: You saw the movie house.

1. raítem bét kolnóa.
    raítem et bét hakolnóa.

    ראיתם בית קולנוע.
    ראיתם את בית הקולנוע.

2. higát etmól lenemál teufá.
    higát etmól lenemál hateufá.

    הגעת אתמול לנמל תעופה.
    הגעת אתמול לנמל התעופה.

3. már Williams hú yoéc šagrirút.
    már Williams hú yoéc hašagrirút.

    מר ווילאמס הוא יועץ שגרירות.
    מר ווילאמס הוא יועץ השגרירות.

4. lamádeti ivrít bebét séfer.
    lamádeti ivrít bebét haséfer.

    למדתי עברית בבית ספר.
    למדתי עברית בבית הספר.

5. misrád dóar nimcá kán bapiná.
    misrád hadóar nimcá kán bapina.

    משרד דאר נמצא כאן בפינה.
    משרד הדואר נמצא כאן בפינה.

6. hém rocím lir'ót sfát yám.
    hém rocím lir'ót et sfát hayám.

    הם רוצים לראות שפת ים.
    הם רוצים לראות את שפת הים.

9.5 Definite Article /ha-/ Prefixed to Adjectives

Examine the following underlined forms:

    (1) már Williams hú yoéc <u>hašagrirút haamerikáit.</u>

    (2) pné kán <u>bapiná harišoná yemína.</u>

    (3) <u>bakivún hazé?</u>

    Note that both the noun and the adjective modifying it are preceded by the definite article /ha-/. Whenever a noun is definite all adjectives modifying it in the same phrase are preceded by /ha-/. It does not matter how the noun is made definite. (Cf. Grammar Section 2.5)

    Examples of nouns made definite in other ways are:

    a. Nouns with a pronoun suffix: /ištó hayafá/ "his pretty wife"
    b. Proper names: /tél avív haxadišá/ "modern Tel Aviv"
    c. The first noun of a definite construct state sequence (see
        Grammar Section 9.4d): /misrád hatayarút hamemšaltí/
Note that the adjective /memšaltí/ modifies /misrád/ and is, therefore, masculine. On the other hand, in Sentence (1) above, the adjective /amerikáit/ modifies /šagrirút/ and is feminine.
    Ambiguities may occasionally arise when both nouns are of the same gender and either may reasonably be modified by the adjective, but context or paraphrasing usually settles the matter.
    When the adjective is not part of the same noun phrase it is not preceded by /ha-/. Thus, the following contrast may occur:
    (a) /habáit hagadól/ "the big house"
    (b) /habáit gadól/ "The house is big."

In the first example /hagadól/ modifies /habáit/ in the same noun phrase. In the other example /gadól/ modifies /habáit/, but it is in the second half of an equational sentence and, therefore, is not prefixed by /ha-/.

Demonstratives such as /zé/ "this" are prefixed with /ha-/ when they modify nouns as adjectives.

/bakivún hazé/ "in this direction"

In this example, as in Sentences 2 and 3 above, the /ha-/ preceding the noun is contracted into /ba-/. See Grammar Note 6.7.

A. Transformation Drill - Indefinite to Definite

    Instructor: I came in a big airplane.
    Student: I came in the big airplane.

1. báti beavirón gadól   ‎‏.1 ‏באתי באוירון גדול.
    báti baavirón hagadól.   ‎באתי באוירון הגדול.
2. raínu báit yafé.   ‎‏.2 ‏ראינו בית יפה.
    raínu et habáit hayafé.   ‎ראינו את הבית היפה.
3. hamšíxi yašár ád rexóv gadól.   ‎‏.3 ‏המשיכי ישר עד רחוב גדול.
    hamšíxi yašár ád harexóv hagadól.   ‎המשיכי ישר עד הרחוב הגדול.
4. haím zé binyán xadíš?   ‎‏.4 ‏האם זה בנין חדש?
    haím zé habinyán haxadíš?   ‎האם זה הבנין החדש?
5. oniá xadašá nimcét banamál.   ‎‏.5 ‏אוניה חדשה נמצאת בנמל.
    haoniá haxadašá nimcét banamál.   ‎האוניה החדשה נמצאת בנמל.
6. šamáti šezé misrád memšaltí.   ‎‏.6 ‏שמעתי שזה משרד ממשלתי.
    šamáti šezé hamisrád hamemšaltí.   ‎שמעתי שזה המשרד הממשלתי.

B. Transformation Drill - Definite to Indefinite

    Repeat Drill A in reverse.

C. Transformation Drill - Indefinite to Definite

    Instructor: I was impressed by a new government office.
    Student: I was impressed by the new government office.

1. hitrašámti mimisrád memšaltí xadáš.   ‎‏.1 ‏התרשמתי ממשרד ממשלתי חדש.
    hitrašámti mehamisrád hamemšaltí haxadáš.   ‎התרשמתי מהמשרד הממשלתי החדש.
2. hí gára bebáit gadól veyafé.   ‎‏.2 ‏היא גרה בבית גדול ויפה.
    hí gára babáit hagadól vehayafé.   ‎היא גרה בבית הגדול והיפה.
3. hém baím beoniót gdolót vexadišót.   ‎‏.3 ‏הם באים באוניות גדולות וחדישות.
    hém baím baoniót hagdolót vehaxadišót.   ‎הם באים באוניות הגדולות והחדישות.
4. šamáti šezé malón gadól venaím.   ‎‏.4 ‏שמעתי שזה מלון גדול ונעים.
    šamáti šezé hamalón hagadól vehanaím.   ‎שמעתי שזה המלון הגדול והנעים.

D. Transformation Drill - Definite to Indefinite

    Repeat Drill C in reverse.

E. Transformation Drill - Indefinite to Definite

    Instructor: Where is a government tourist office?
    Student: Where is the government tourist office?

1. éyfo misrád tayarút memšaltí.
    éyfo misrád hatayarút hamemšaltí.

    איפה משרד תיירות ממשלתי? .1
    איפה משרד התיירות הממשלתי?

2. már Williams hú yoéc šagrirút xadáš.
    már Williams hú yoéc hašagrirút haxadáš.

    מר ויליאמס הוא יועץ שגרירות חדש. .2
    מר ויליאמס הוא יועץ השגרירות החדש.

3. raíti misrád dóar gadól.
    raíti et misrád hadóar hagadól.

    ראיתי משרד דואר גדול. .3
    ראיתי את משרד הדואר הגדול.

4. zé bet séfer tóv.
    zé bét haséfer hatóv.

    זה בית ספר טוב. .4
    זה בית הספר הטוב.

5. higáta lenemál teufá xadíš.
    higáta lenemál hateufá haxadíš.

    הגעת לנמל תעופה חדיש. .5
    הגעת לנמל התעופה החדיש.

6. raíti otó bebét kolnóa karóv.
    raíti otó bebét hakolnóa hakaróv.

    ראיתי אותו בבית קולנוע קרוב. .6
    ראיתי אותו בבית הקולנוע הקרוב.

7. aní roé binyán šagrirút gadól.
    aní roé et binyán hašagrirút hagadól.

    אני רואה בנין שגרירות גדול. .7
    אני רואה את בנין השגרירות הגדול.

F. Transformation Drill - Definite to Indefinite

    Repeat Drill E in reverse.

G. Transformation Drill

    Instructor: I saw his wife. She is pretty.
    Student: I saw his pretty wife.

1. raíti et ištó. hí yafá.
    raíti et ištó hayafá.

    ראיתי את אשתו. היא יפה. .1
    ראיתי את אשתו היפה.

2. raíti et baalá. hú báal tóv.
    raíti et baalá hatóv.

    ראיתי את בעלה. הוא בעל טוב. .2
    ראיתי את בעלה הטוב.

3. raíti et eynéha. hén gdolót.
    raíti et eynéha hagdolót.

    ראיתי את עיניה. הן גדולות. .3
    ראיתי את עיניה הגדולות.

4. raíti et misradxá. hú xadáš.
    raíti et misradxá haxadáš.

    ראיתי את משרדך. הוא חדש. .4
    ראיתי את משרדך החדש.

5. raíti et arcexém. hí yafá.
    raíti et arcexém hayafá.

    ראיתי את ארצכם. היא יפה. .5
    ראיתי את ארצכם היפה.

    The instructor may vary this drill by changing /raíti/ to /aní rocé lir'ót/.

H. Transformation Drill

    Instructor: We saw Israel. It's modern.
    Student: We saw the modern Israel.

1. raínu et yisraél. hí xadišá.
    raínu et yisraél haxadišá.

    ראינו את ישראל. היא חדישה. .1
    ראינו את ישראל החדישה.

2. raínu et atára. hí yafá.
    raínu et atára hayafá.

    ראינו את עטרה. היא יפה. .2
    ראינו את עטרה היפה.

3. raínu et davíd. hú gadól.
    raínu et davíd hagadól.

    ראינו את דוד. הוא גדול. .3
    ראינו את דוד הגדול.

4. raínu et avígdor. hú saméax.
    raínu et avígdor hasaméax.

    ראינו את אביגדור. הוא שמח. .4
    ראינו את אביגדור השמח.

5. raínu et dóv. hú tóv.
    raínu et dóv hatóv.

    ראינו את דוב. הוא טוב. .5
    ראינו את דוב הטוב.

6. raínu et sára vexána. hén amerikáiot.
    raínu et sára vexána haamerikáiot.

    ראינו את שרה וחנה. הן אמריקאיות. .6
    ראינו את שרה וחנה האמריקאיות.

REVIEW CONVERSATIONS

A: éyfo nimcá haséfer.   א: איפה נמצא הספר?

B: haséfer nimcá eclexá babáit.   ב: הספר נמצא אצלך בבית.

A: beemét?   א: באמת?

B: kén. natáti lexá et haséfer habóker.   ב: כן. נתתי לך את הספר הבוקר.

C: atá roé et bét hakolnóa hagadól?   ג: אתה רואה את בית הקולנוע הגדול?

D: ló. éyfo.   ד: לא. איפה?

C: kán bapiná.   ג: כאן בפינה.

D: O, kén.   ד: אה, כן.

E: mexiním banána splít bebrúklin bár.   ה: מכינים בננה ספליט בברוקלין בר.

F: má atá sáx !   ו: מה אתה שח !

E: kén. kmó beamérika.   ה: כן. כמו באמריקה.

G: ráinu et misrád hatayarút haxadáš.   ז: ראינו את משרד התיירות החדש.

H: babáit hagadól?   ח: בבית הגדול?

G: kén. babáit hagadól vehaxadíš.   ז: כן. בבית הגדול והחדיש.

I: šamáti šehabáit šel dóv gadól veyafé.   ט: שמעתי שהבית של דב גדול ויפה.

J: kén. raíti et habáit etmól.   י: כן. ראיתי את הבית אתמול.

I: éyfo? berámat gán?   ט: איפה? ברמת גן?

J: ló. hém garím bexulón.   י: לא. הם גרים בחולון.

10.1 Wandering through Tel Aviv (concluded)

PASSERBY

After	axaréy še-	אחרי ש–
you finish the ice cream	tigmór et haglída	תגמור את הגלידה
continue straight	tamšíx yašár	תמשיך ישר
towards the seashore.	lekivún hayám.	לכיוון הים.
after, behind	axaréy	אחרי
you will finish	tigmór (m.s.)	תגמור

MR. WILLIAMS

Yes-	ken-	כן –

PASSERBY

When you get	kšetagía	כשתגיע
to Hayarkon Street	lerexóv hayarkón,	לרחוב הירקון,
turn right	tifné yemína	תפנה ימינה,
and go straight	veteléx yašár	ותלך ישר
to Mendele Street.	ád rexóv méndele.	עד רחוב מנדלי.
when (conjunction)	kšé-	כש–
you will arrive	tagía (m.s.)	תגיע

MR. WILLIAMS

That is to say,	zót oméret še-	זאת אומרת ש–
the tourist office	misrád hatayarút	משרד התיירות
is located on Hayarkon St.	nimcá berexóv hayarkón	נמצא ברחוב הירקון
at the corner of Mendele?	pinát méndele?	פינת מנדלי?

PASSERBY

Not exactly	ló bediyúk	לא בדיוק
on the corner.	bapiná.	בפינה.
exactly	bediyúk	בדיוק
Turn right there	šám tifné yemína	שם תפנה ימינה
and go on to	veteléx ád	ותלך עד
the tourist office.	misrád hatayarút.	משרד התיירות.

MR. WILLIAMS

Is it possible	haím efšár	האם אפשר
to go by way of	laléxet dérex	ללכת דרך
Ben-Yehuda Street?	rexóv bén yehúda?	רחוב בן־יהודה?
possible	efšár	אפשר
to go	laléxet	ללכת
way, path, through	dérex (f)	דרך

PASSERBY

Yes, of course.	kén. behexlét.	כן. בהחלט.
definitely	behexlét	בהחלט

MR. WILLIAMS

Thank you,	todá rabá lexá,	תודה רבה לך,
Sir. Goodbye.	adoní. šalom.	אדוני, שלום.

PASSERBY

It was nothing.	al ló davár.	.על לא דבר
Goodbye and good luck.	šalóm uvraxá.	.שלום וברכה
blessing	braxá (f)	ברכה

10.2 Wandering through Tel Aviv (concluded)

PASSERBY

After	axaréy še-	–אחרי ש
you finish the ice cream	tigmerí et haglída	תגמרי את הגלידה
continue straight	tamšíxi yašár	תמשיכי ישר
towards the seashore.	lekivún hayám.	.לכיוון הים

MRS. WILLIAMS

| Yes– | kén– | – כן |

PASSERBY

When you get	kšetagíi	כשתגיעי
to Hayarkon Street	lerexóv hayarkón	לרחוב הירקון
turn right	tifní yamína	תפני ימינה
and go straight	vetelxí yašár	ותלכי ישר
to Mendele Street.	ád rexóv méndele.	.עד רחוב מנדלי

MRS. WILLIAMS

That is to say,	zót oméret še–	–זאת אומרת ש
that the tourist office	misrád hatayarút	משרד התיירות
is located on Hayarkon St.	nimcá berexóv heyarkón	נמצא ברחוב הירקון
at the corner of Mendele?	pinát méndele?	?פינת מנדלי

PASSERBY

Not exactly	ló bediyúk	לא בדיוק
on the corner.	bapiná.	.בפינה
Turn right there	šam tifní yamína	שם תפני ימינה
and go to	vetelxí ád	ותלכי עד
the tourist office.	misrád hatayarút.	.משרד הֿתיירות

MRS. WILLIAMS

Is it possible	haím efšár	האם אפשר
to go by way of	laléxet dérex	ללכת דרך
Ben-Yehuda street?	rexóv bén yehúda?	?רחוב בן־יהודה

PASSERBY

| Yes, of course. | kén. behexlét. | .כן. בהחלט |

MRS. WILLIAMS

| Thank you, | todá rabá láx | , תודה רבה לך |
| ma'am. Goodbye. | gvirtí. šalóm. | .גברֿי, שלום |

PASSERBY

| It was nothing. | ál ló davár. | על לא דבר. |
| Goodbye and good luck. | šalóm uvraxá. | שלום וברכה. |

10.3 Vocabulary Drill

A variation of the stark and gentle imperative is the pattern of /tagía/.
In this pattern the masculine singular ends in /-CV̆a/ and the feminine plural
ends in /-Cána/. The forms of /tagía/ are:

| m.s. /tagía/ | m.pl. /tagíu/ |
| f.s. /tagíi/ | f.pl. /tagána/ |

[In the Basic Sentences of this unit the verb is used as a second person
future.]

A. Substitution-Agreement Drill - Use the underlined words as cues.

When you get to the intersection turn left.

kšetagía lahictalvút tifné smóla.	כשתגיע להצטלבות תפנה שמאלה.
kšetagíu lahictalvút tifnú smóla.	כשתגיעו להצטלבות תפנו שמאלה.
kšetagíi lahictalvút tifní smóla.	כשתגיעי להצטלבות תפני שמאלה.
kšetagána lahictalvút tifnéna smóla.	כשתגענה להצטלבות תפנינה שמאלה.

כשתבנה ימינה...

83

GRAMMAR NOTES

10.4   The Relative Conjunction /še-/

a)   Whenever an equational sentence, or a declarative sentence containing
a verb, is included within another sentence, but not as a direct quotation,
then it is preceded by the conjunction /še-/.
   Examine the following sentences:

1.   habáit gadól veyafé.   "The house is big and beautiful."
     šamáti šehabáit gadól veyafé.   "I heard that the house is big
                                         and beautiful."
2.   arcénu mócet xén beeynéxa.   "You like our country."
     aní mekavé šearcénu mócet   "I hope you like our country."
        xén beeynéxa.

   Note that although the conjunction "that" is optional in English the
conjunction /še-/ is required in Hebrew.
b)   /še-/ is used when prepositions precede such included sentences:

3.   báta héna.   "You came here."
     lifnéy šebáta hena   "before you came here"
4.   tigmór et haglída.   "You will finish the ice cream."
     axaréy šetigmór et   "after you finish the
        haglída   the ice cream"

   The conjunction /kše-/ is a contraction of the prefixed preposition /ke-/
"as" and /še-/.

5.   tagía lerexóv hayarkon.   "You will get to Hayarkon Street."
     kšetagía lerexóv hayarkón   "when you get to Hayarkon Street"

c)   When the included sentence is a question beginning with an interrogative,
the /še-/ is optional, but after the interrogative.

6.   éyfo brúklin bár.   "Where is the Brooklyn Bar?"
     atá yodéa éyfo   "Do you know where
        šebrúklin bar?   the Brooklyn Bar is ?"
(or) atá yodéa éyfo
        brúklin bár?

7.   heyxán atá nimca.   "Where are you located?"
     atá ló yodéa heyxán   "You don't know where you are?"
        atá nimca?

d)   A sentence with an included sentence may in turn be included in a still
larger sentence.

8.   báta héna.   "You came here."
     lamádeta ivrít lifnéy   "You studied
        šebáta héna.   Hebrew before you came here."

      tóv meód asíta   "You did well
         šelamádeta ivrít lifnéy   to study Hebrew
         šebáta héna.   before you came here."

It cannot be repeated too often that the above description refers to the Hebrew sentences and <u>not</u> to the English translations. In sentences 4 and 5 the English verb form changes; in sentences 5, 6 and 7 the word order changes; and in Sentence 8 "you studied" changes to "to study". In the Hebrew, however, the included sentences remain intact except for intonation patterns. There are stylistic variations of word order in included sentences in Hebrew, but these are relatively minor.

[Note: This conjunction is always written in Hebrew as a prefix to the following word. asíta עשית lamádeta למדה báta באת

šeasíta שעשית šelamádeta שלמדה šebáta שבאת]

The following drills are expansion drills. The instructor gives a sentence, and the student responds with a larger sentence in which the instructor's sentence is included.

Instructor: tigmór et haglidá.   "You will finish the ice cream."
Student: aní rocé šetigmór   "I want you to
        et haglidá.   finish the ice cream."

A more literal translation would be "I want that you should finish the ice cream," but this is, of course, awkward English.

Instructor's sentences:

1. már Williams gár berámat gán.   .1 מר ווילאמס גר ברמת גן.
2. ištó medabéret ivrít.   .2 אשתו מדברת עברית.
3. miryám nimcét betél avív.   .3 מרים נמצאת בתל אביב.
4. lamádeta bevét haséfer lesafót.   .4 למדת בבית הספר לשפות.
5. hašagrirút nimcét al yád malón dán.   .5 השגרירות נמצאת על יד מלון דן.
6. habinyán xadíš.   .6 הבנין חדיש.
7. haárec yafá meód.   .7 הארץ יפה מאד.

Student adds:

A. aní xošév še-   -ש א. אני חושב
B. aní mekavé še-   -ש ב. אני מקוה
C. hú roé še-   -ש ג. הוא רואה
D. šamánu še-   -ש ד. שמענו
E. raíti še-   -ש ה. ראיתי

Instructor's Sentences:

8. lamádeta ivrít.   .8 למדת עברית.
9. šamáta mimár káspi.   .9 שמעת ממר כספי.
10. raínu et habáit šeló.   .10 ראינו את הבית שלו.
11. natáti lemiryám et hasfarím.   .11 נתתי למרים את הספרים.

Student adds:

F. higáta laárec lifnéy še-   -ש ו. הגעת לארץ לפני
G. higáta héna axaréy še-   -ש ז. הגעת הנה אחרי

Instructor's Sentences:

12. natáta ló et haséfer.   12. ‏נתת לו את הספר.‏

13. raíta et hamisrád.   13. ‏ראית את המשרד.‏

14. higáta lamalón.   14. ‏הגעת למלון.‏

Student adds:

H. má amárta ló kše-   ח . ‏מה אמרת לו כש-‏

I. má asíta kše-   ט . ‏מה עשית כש-‏

Additions H and I can be varied by changing /kše-/ to /axaréy še-/ or /lifnéy še-/.

10.5 Adjectives used to Modify Verbs

a. The masculine singular form of adjectives is used to modify verbs.

1. léx yašár berexóv álenbi.   "Go straight on Allenby Street."

2. át medabéret yafé meód.   "You speak very nicely."

3. tóv asíta šelamádeta ivrít.   "You did well to study Hebrew."

The following synonymous sentences illustrate the use of an adjective to modify a noun or a verb.

4. atá medabér ivrít yafá meód.   "You speak a very beautiful Hebrew."

5. atá medabér ivrít yafé meód.   "You speak Hebrew very nicely."

b. When there is no noun antecedent in the context the masculine singular form of the adjective is used.

6. kvár meuxár.   "It's late already."

7. naím lí meod lehakír otxá.   "I am very pleased to meet you."

Although the English translations have pronoun antecedents for "late" and "pleased" the Hebrew does not. In sentence 7 the form is /naím/ even when a woman is speaking. See Section 2.2.

REVIEW CONVERSATIONS

A: axaréy šetigmór leexól et haglída
teléx lemisrád hatayarút?

אחרי שתגמור לאכול את הגלידה : א
תלך למשרד התיירות?

B: ló. lašagrirút haamerikáit.

לא. לשגרירות האמריקאית. : ב

A: áz tamšíx lekivún sfát hayám.

אז תמשיך לכיוון שפת הים. : א

B: kén. aní yodéa.

כן. אני יודע. : ב

C: éyfo nimcá misrád hatayarút.

איפה נמצא משרד התיירות? : ג

D: kán. bapiná harišoná.

כאן. בפינה הראשונה. : ד

C: berexóv bén yehúda?

ברחוב בן יהודה? : ג

D: ló. berexóv méndele.

לא. ברחוב מנדלי. : ד

E: atá medabér ivrít yafé meód.

אתה מדבר עברית יפה מאוד. : ה

F: todá rabá.

תודה רבה. : ו

E: haím lamádeta ivrít lifnéy šebáta héna?

האם למדת עברית לפני שבאת הנה? : ה

F: ló. lamádeti ivrít axaréy šehigáti lekán.

לא. למדתי עברית אחרי שבאתי לכאן. : ו

E: matáy higáta.

מתי הגעת? : ה

F: lifnéy xodšáim.

לפני חודשיים. : ו

E: veatá medabér kvár kmo israelí.
aní xošév šezé tóv meód.

ואתה מדבר כבר כמו ישראלי. : ה
אני חושב שזה טוב מאוד.

G: raíta et habinyán haxadáš
šel misrád hatayarút?

ראית את הבניין החדש : ז
של משרד התיירות?

H: ló. áx šamáti šehú xadíš meód.

לא. אך שמעתי שהוא חדיש מאוד. : ח

G: kén. xadíš vegadól. hú méod móce
xén beeynáy.

כן. חדיש וגדול. הוא מאוד מוצא : ז
חן בעיני.

87

זו מסורת אצלנו בבית לאכול

בליל שישי דגים ממולאים...

11.1 Dinner Invitation

MR. CASPI

Mr. Williams,	már Williams.	מר ווילאמס,
what are you doing	má atém osím	מה אתם עושים
Friday evening? *	belél šiší.	בליל שישי?
do	osé (m.s.pres.)	עושה
night	láyla (m)	לילה
sixth	šiší (m.s.)	שישי

MR. WILLIAMS

This Friday evening?	belél šiší hakaróv?	בליל שישי הקרוב?

MR. CASPI

Yes.	kén.	כן.

MR. WILLIAMS

I think that	aní xošév še-	אני חושב ש–
we don't have	éyn lánu	אין לנו
any plans.	kól toxnít.	כל תוכנית.
there is not	éyn	**אין**
to us	lánu	**לנו**
plan, program	toxnít (f)	תוכנית

MR. CASPI

We want	ánu rocím	אנו רוצים
to invite you	lehazmín otxém	להזמין אתכם
for dinner.	learuxát érev.	לארוחת ערב.
to invite	lehazmín	להזמין
meal	aruxá (f)	ארוחה
evening	érev (m)	ערב

MR. WILLIAMS

Thank you.	todá rabá.	תודה רבה.
We will be very happy.	nismáx meód.	נשמח מאוד.
we will be happy	nismáx (1 pl. fut.)	נשמח

MR. CASPI

Is	haím	האם
seven-thirty	šéva ušloším	שבע ושלושים
all right?	mat'ím?	מתאים?
seven	šéva	שבע
thirty	šloším	שלושים
is suitable	mat'ím (m.s.pres.)	מתאים

MR. WILLIAMS

Yes. Give me	kén. tén lí	כן. תן לי
your address.	et haktóvet šelaxém.	את הכתובת שלכם.
give	tén (m.s.imv.)	תן
address	któvet (f)	כתובת

[*Many speakers insist that /lél šiší/ is properly Thursday night
and that Friday night is /lél šabát/.]

MR. CASPI

We live	ánu garím	אנו גרים
on Mozkin Street,	birxóv móckin	ברחוב מוצקין
number 3.	mispár šalóš.	מספר שלוש.
number	mispár (m) מספר	
three	šalóš שלוש	

MR. WILLIAMS

I think that	aní xošév še-	אני חושב ש-
we will find	nimcá	נמצא
the place	et hamakóm	את המקום
without difficulty.	leló kóši.	ללא קושי.
we will find	nimcá (1 pl. fut.) נמצא	
place	makóm (m) מקום	
difficulty	kóši (m) קושי	

11.2 ADDITIONAL VOCABULARY

What are you doing Sunday?	má atá osé beyóm rišón.	מה אתה עושה ביום ראשון?
What are you doing Monday?	má atá osé beyóm šení.	מה אתה עושה ביום שני?
What are you doing Tuesday?	má atá osé beyóm šliší.	מה אתה עושה ביום שלישי?
What are you doing Wednesday?	má atá osé beyóm revií.	מה אתה עושה ביום רביעי?
What are you doing Thursday?	má atá osé beyóm xamiší.	מה אתה עושה ביום חמישי?
What are you doing Friday?	má atá osé beyóm šiší.	מה אתה עושה ביום שישי?
What are you doing Saturday?	má atá osé bešabát.	מה אתה עושה בשבת?
What are you doing today?	má atá osé hayóm.	מה אתה עושה היום?

What are you doing	má át osá	מה את עושה
...Sunday evening?	..beyóm rišón baérev.	ביום ראשון בערב?
...Monday evening?	..beyóm šení baérev.	ביום שני בערב?
...Tuesday evening?	..beyóm šliší baérev.	ביום שלישי בערב?
...Wednesday evening?	..beyóm revií baérev.	ביום רביעי בערב?
...Thursday evening?	..beyóm xamiší baérev.	ביום חמישי בערב?
...Friday evening?	..beyóm šiší baérev.	ביום שישי בערב?
...Saturday evening?	..bemocaéy šabát.	במוצאי שבת?
...this evening?	..haérev.	הערב?
We have a plan.	yéš lánu toxnít.	יש לנו תוכנית.

I want to eat	aní rocé leexól.	אני רוצה לאכול ארוחת בוקר.
breakfast. (morning meal)	aruxát bóker.	
I want to eat	ani rocé leexól	אני רוצה לאכול ארוחת צהריים.
lunch. (noon meal)	aruxát cohoráim.	
I want to eat	aní rocé leexól	אני רוצה לאכול ארוחת עשר.
brunch. (10 a.m. snack)	aruxát éser.	

11.3 Vocabulary Drills

A. Substitution Drill

Please give me the book.

tén li, bevakašá, et haséfer.	תן לי, בבקשה, את הספר.
tní	תני
tnú	תנו
ténna	תנה

B. Underline: Substitution - Agreement Drill   The instructor gives the underlined forms
        as cues.

        Please give me your telephone number.

        תן לי, בבקשה, -

        tén li, bevakašá, et mispár hatélefon šelxá.   את מספר הטלפון שלך.
        tnú li, bevakašá, et mispár hatélefon šelaxém.   תנו את מספר הטלפון שלכם.
        tní li, bevakašá, et mispár hatélefon šeláx.   תני את מספר הטלפון שלך.
        tén li, bevakašá, et mispár hatélefon šelxá,   תן את מספר הטלפון שלך.
        ténna li, bevakašá, et mispár hatélefon šelaxén.   תנה את מספר הטלפון שלכן.
        tní li, bevakašá, et mispár hatélefon šelax.   תני את מספר הטלפון שלך.

C. Substitution Drill

        Don't give me any ice cream.

        ál titén li glidá.   אל תיתן לי גלידה.
            titní   תני
            titnú   תנו
            titénna   תתנה

D. Transformation Drill - Affirmative to Negative

            Instructor: Give her the books.
            Student: Don't give her the books.

    tén lá et hasfarím.   ál titén lá et hasfarím.   אל תיתן לה את הספרים.
    tnú lá et hasfarím.   ál titnú lá et hasfarím.   אל תתנו לה את הספרים.
    tní lá et hasfarím.   ál titní lá et hasfarím.   אל תתני לה את הספרים.
    ténna lá et hasfarím.   ál titénna lá et hasfarím.   אל תתנה לה את הספרים.
    tén lá et hasfarím.   ál titén lá et hasfarím.   אל תיתן לה את הספרים.
    tní lá et hasfarím.   ál titní lá et hasfarím.   אל תתני לה את הספרים.
    tnú lá et hasfarím.   ál titnú lá et hasfarím.   אל תתנו לה את הספרים.

E. Transformation Drill - Negative to Affirmative

        Repeat Drill D in reverse.

F. Substitution Drill

        Let me walk around and see the city.

        tén lí letayél velir'ót et haír.   תן לי לטייל ולראות את העיר.
            tní   תני
            ténna   תנה
            tnú   תנו

91

11.4   Cardinal Numbers

a)   The situation with respect to the cardinal numbers can be described as complicated. There are historically two sets of numbers - masculine and feminine.
However, the alternation of the forms is the opposite of what one would expect;
that is, the masculine appear to be feminine forms, and vice versa.

> For example: šalóš (feminine) šlošá (masculine)
> Compare: karóv (masculine) krová (feminine)

b)   In formal speech masculine numbers (i.e., those with the apparent
feminine shape) are used with masculine nouns, and feminine numbers with
feminine nouns. This usage is preferable at all levels of speech.

c)   In counting and in reading off numerals the feminine form is used.

> /axát, štáim, šalóš, arbá./   "One, two, three, four."
> /rexóv móckin, mispár šalóš./   "Mozkin Street, number 3."

d)   In informal speech the two sets are often used interchangeably, with the
feminine numbers being the more frequent choice. One often hears hybrid forms
such as /šnéymesre/ 'twelve' from /šnéymasar/ and /štéymesre/. To complicate
matters a bit more, occasional new distinctions have developed in modern
Hebrew such as /arbá/ 'four' (masculine) and /árba/ (feminine).

zero (name of numeral only)   éfes (m)

	Feminine	Masculine	זכר	נקבה
one	axát	exád	אחד	אחת
two	štáim	šnáim	שנים	שתים
three	šalóš	šlošá	שלושה	שלוש
four	arbá	arbaá	ארבעה	ארבע
five	xaméš	xamišá	חמשה	חמש
six	šéš	šišá	שישה	שש
seven	šéva	šiv'á	שבעה	שבע
eight	šmóne	šmoná	שמונה	שמונה
nine	téša	tiš'á	תשעה	תשע
ten	éser	asará	עשרה	עשר
eleven	axát'esre	axád'asar	אחד-עשר	אחת-עשרה
twelve	štéym'esre	snéym'asar	שנים עשר	שתים-עשרה
thirteen	šlóš'esre	šlošáasar	שלושה-עשר	שלוש-עשרה
fourteen	arbáesre	arbáasar	או בע-עשר	ארבע-עשרה
fifteen	xaméš'esre	xamišáasar	חמשה-עשר	חמש-עשרה
sixteen	šéš'esre	šišáasar	ישה-עשר	שש-עשרה
seventeen	šváesre	šiv'áasar	שבעה-עשר	שבע-עשרה
eighteen	šmonéesre	šmonáasar	שמונה-עשר	שמונה-עשרה
nineteen	tšáesre	tiš'áasar	תשעה-עשר	תשע-עשרה
twenty	esrím	esrím	עשרים	עשרים

A.   Count to twenty.

B.   Recite the masculine numbers one to twenty.

C.   Read off the following numerals.

1. 3 - 0 - 1	7. 0 - 8 - 15
2. 5 - 8 - 8	8. 4 - 7 - 7 - 4
3. 4 - 1 - 8 - 2	9. 7 - 3 - 7
4. 2 - 0 - 2	10. 8 - 7 - 5 - 0
5. 8 - 2 - 9	11. 3 - 5 - 1
6. 5 - 3 - 3 - 6	12. 1 - 1 - 0 -

GRAMMAR NOTES

11.5 Contraction of Initial Syllables

Compare the following underlined forms:

léx yašár berexóv álenbi.
ánu garím birxóv móckin.

When the prefix /be-/ precedes a form beginning with the pattern
/CeCV-/ (with unstressed /e/) the two syllables may be contracted to
/biCCV-/.
This contraction, interestingly enough, is characteristic of the formal
style, but it is often heard in informal speech, also.
A similar contraction is made with the prefixes /le-/ 'to' and /ke-/ 'as'.

11.6 /yéš lí/, /éyn lí/

a)   A special grammatical construction is used to indicate possession.
Examine the following sentence:
      yéš lánu toxnít.   "We have a plan."

b)   The construction consists of the form /yéš/ "there is, there are" plus
the preposition /le-/ "to". (In the example above the preposition has a
pronominal suffix.) This construction translates the present tense forms of
the English verb "have" with the meaning "possess".
      The negative of this construction consists of /éyn/ plus /le-/.
      éyn lánu toxnít.   "We don't have a plan."

c)   Though, strictly speaking, neither /yéš/ nor /éyn/ is a verb, the direct
object preposition /et/ is used before definite nouns which are "possessed".
      yéš lánu séfer.   "We have a book."
      yéš lánu et haséfer.   "We have the book."

d)   The word order of the construction may be inverted for emphasis or style
reasons. This inversion is frequent when a name follows the preposition.
      ledavíd yéš glidá.   "David has ice cream."
or   yéš ledavíd glidá.

e)   The preposition /le-/ occurs with the singular set of pronominal suffixes,
with the same variations that occur with /šel/: /láx, lánu, laxém, laxén,
lahém, lahén/.

A. Substitution Drill

    I have a house in Ramat Gan.

    yéš lí báit berámat gán.   .יש לי בית ברמת גן
         lexá   לך
         láx   לך
         ló   לו
         lá   לה
         lánu   לנו
         laxém   לכם
         laxén   לכן
         lahém   להם
         lahén   להן

93

B. Substitution Drill - Repeat Drill A in the negative.

I don't have a house in Ramat Gan.

éyn lí báit berámat gán.   אין לי בית ברמת גן.

C. Transformation Drill - Affirmative to Negative

Instructor: I have Miriam's phone number.
Student: I don't have Miriam's phone number.

yéš li et mispár hatélefon šel miryám.   יש לי את מספר הטלפון של מרים.
éyn lí...   אין לי...
yéš lánu et mispár hatélefon šel miryám.   יש לנו את מספר הטלפון של מרים.
éyn lánu ...   אין לנו...
yéš láx et mispár hatélefon šel miryám.   יש לך את מספר הטלפון של מרים.
éyn láx ...   אין לך...
yéš ló et mispár hatélefon šel miryám.   יש לו את מספר הטלפון של מרים.
éyn ló ...   אין לו...
yéš laxém et mispár hatélefon šel miryám.   יש לכם את מספר הטלפון של מרים.
éyn laxém ...   אין לכם...
yéš lá et mispár hatélefon šel miryám.   יש לה את מספר הטלפון של מרים.
éyn lá ...   אין לה...
yéš lexá et mispár hatélefon šel miryám.   יש לך את מספר הטלפון של מרים.
éyn lexá ...   אין לך...
yéš lahém et mispár hatélefon šel miryám.   יש להם את מספר הטלפון של מרים.
éyn lahém ...   אין להם...

D. Transformation Drill - Negative to Affirmative

Repeat Drill C in reverse.

E. Response Drill

Instructor: Student:
Where do you live?   We have a house in Savyon.

éyfo atém garím.   yeš lánu báit besavyón.   איפה אתם גרים?
éyfo hú gár.   yeš ló báit besavyón.   איפה הוא גר?
éyfo hém garím.   yeš lahém báit besavyón.   איפה הם גרים?
éyfo át gára.   yeš lí báit besavyón.   איפה את גרה?
éyfo gár mošé.   yeš ló báit besavyón.   איפה גר משה?
éyfo atá gár.   yeš lí báit besavyón.   איפה איזה גר?
éyfo gára léa.   yeš lá báit besavyón.   איפה גרה לאה?

F. Transformation Drill

Instructor: The books are at my place.
Student: I have the books.

hasfarím nimcaím eclí.   yéš lí et hasfarím.   הספרים נמצאים אצלי.
hasfarím nimcaím ecló.   yéš ló et hasfarím.   הספרים נמצאים אצלו.
hasfarím nimcaím eclá.   yéš lá et hasfarím.   הספרים נמצאים אצלה.
hasfarím nimcaím écel dóv. yéš ledóv et hasfarím. הספרים נמצאים אצל דב.
hasfarím nimcaím eclénu. yéš lánu et hasfarím.   הספרים נמצאים אצלנו.
hasfarím nimcaím eclám.   yéš lahém et hasfarím.   הספרים נמצאים אצלם.
hasfarím nimcaím eclexá. yéš lexá et hasfarím.   הספרים נמצאים אצלך.
hasfarím nimcaím ecléx.   yéš láx et hasfarím.   הספרים נמצאים אצלך.
hasfarím nimcaím eclaxém. yéš laxém et hasfarím. הספרים נמצאים אצלכם.

G.   Transformation Drill

     Instructor: He doesn't speak Hebrew.
     Student: He doesn't have a chance to speak Hebrew.

hú ló medabér ivrít.   הוא לא מדבר עברית.
     éyn ló hizdamnút ledabér ivrít.   אין לו הזדמנות לדבר עברית.
hém ló medabrím ivrít.   הם לא מדברים עברית.
     eyn lahém hizdamnút ledabér ivrít.   אין להם הזדמנות לדבר עברית.
aní ló medabér ivrít.   אני לא מדבר עברית.
     éyn lí hizdamnút ledabér ivrít.   אין לי הזדמנות לדבר עברית.
atá ló medabér ivrít.   אתה לא מדבר עברית.
     éyn lexá hizdamnút ledabér ivrít.   אין לך הזדמנות לדבר עברית.
ánu ló medabrím ivrít.   אנו לא מדברים עברית.
     éyn lánu hizdamnút ledabér ivrít.   אין לנו הזדמנות לדבר עברית.
atém ló medabrím ivrít.   אתם לא מדברים עברית.
     éyn laxém hizdamnút ledabér ivrít.   אין לכם הזדמנות לדבר עברית.
ištó ló medabéret ivrít.   אשתו לא מדברת עברית.
     éyn leištó hizdamnút ledabér ivrít.   אין לאשתו הזדמנות לדבר עברית.
hí ló medabéret ivrít.   היא לא מדברת עברית.
     éyn lá hizdamnút ledabér ivrít.   אין לה הזדמנות לדבר עברית.
át ló medabéret ivrít.   את לא מדברת עברית.
     éyn láx hizdamnút ledabér ivrít.   אין לך הזדמנות לדבר עברית.
atén ló medabrót ivrít.   אתן לא מדברות עברית.
     éyn laxén hizdamnút ledabér ivrít.   אין לכן הזדמנות לדבר עברית.
hén ló medabrót ivrít.   הן לא מדברות עברית.
     éyn lahén hizdamnút ledabér ivrít.   אין להן הזדמנות לדבר עברית.

REVIEW CONVERSATIONS

A: má atém osím maxár.   א: מה אתם עושים מחר?

B: aní ló yodéa. aní xošév   ב: אני לא יודע. אני חושב
     šeéyn lánu toxnít.   שאין לנו תוכנית.

A: ánu rocím lehazmín otxém   א: אנו רוצים להזמין אתכם
     lebrúklin bár.   לברוקלין בר.

B: todá rabá. nismáx meód.   ב: תודה רבה. נשמח מאד.

A: haím šéš mat'ím?   א: האם שש מתאים?

B: kén. behexlét.   ב: כן. בהחלט.

C.   tén li bevakašá, et hasfarím hagdolím.   ג: תן לי, בבקשה, את הספרים הגדולים.

D: natáti lexá otám etmól.   ד: נתתי לך אותם אתמול.

C: ló. ló natáta et hasfarím lí.   ג: לא. לא נתת את הספרים לי.
     natáta otám lemiryám.   נתת אותם למרים.

D: lemiryám éyn et hasfarím.   ד: למרים אין את הספרים.

C: kén. yéš lá et hasfarím eclá babáit.   ג: כן. יש לה את הספרים אצלה בבית.

E:　eyfó atém garím.　　　　　　　　　　　　　　　ה: איפה אתם גרים?

F:　yéš lánu báit betél avív.　　　　　　　　　　ו: יש לנו בית בתל אביב.

E:　tnú lí bevakašá, et mispár　　　　　　　　　ה: תנו לי, בבקשה, את מספר
　　hatélefon šelaxém.　　　　　　　　　　　　　　　הטלפון שלכם.

F:　éyn lánu adáin télefon.　　　　　　　　　　　ו: אין לנו עדיין טלפון.

E:　áz tnú lí et haktóvet šelaxém.　　　　　　　ה: אז תנו לי את הכתובת שלכם.

G:　atá yodéa éyfo šemisrád hatayarút?　　　　ז: אתה יודע איפה שמשרד התיירות?

H:　zé axaréy habinyán hagadól hazé.　　　　　ח: זה אחרי הבנין הגדול הזה.

G:　todá.　aní xošév šenimcá et hamakóm　　　　ז: תודה. אני חושב שנמצא את המקום
　　leló kóši.　　　　　　　　　　　　　　　　　　　ללא קושי.

I:　éyn lánu toxnít lelél šiší.　　　　　　　　　ט: אין לנו תוכנית לליל שישי.
　　má atém osím.　　　　　　　　　　　　　　　　　מה אתם עושים?

J:　ánu rocím laléxet lir'ót　　　　　　　　　　י: אנו רוצים ללכת לראות
　　et már Williams.　　　　　　　　　　　　　　　את מר ווילימס.

I:　haím már Williams gár adáin　　　　　　　　　ט: האם מר ווילימס גר עדיין
　　bemalón dán?　　　　　　　　　　　　　　　　　　במלון דן?

J:　ló.　yéš ló báit berámat gán.　　　　　　　י: לא. יש לו בית ברמת גן.

I:　atá yodéa et haktóvet šeló?　　　　　　　　ט: אתה יודע את הכתובת שלו?

J:　kén.　yéš li et haktóvet bamisrád.　　　　י: כן. יש לי את הכתובת במשרד.

12.1 Friday Evening Dinner

MRS. CASPI

Hello, Mrs. Williams.	šalóm gvéret Williams.	שלום, גברת וויל`יאמס.
Hello, Mr. Williams.	šalóm már Williams.	שלום, מר וויל`יאמס.
How are you?	má šlomxém.	מה שלומכם?

MR. WILLIAMS

| Hello. Good Sabbath. | šalóm. šabát šalóm. | שלום. שבת שלום. |
| (Greeting used from sunset Friday to sunset Saturday) | šabát šalóm | שבת שלום |

MRS. CASPI

| I'm very happy | aní smexá meód | אני שמחה מאד |
| that you came. | šebátem. | שבאתם. |

MRS. WILLIAMS

How could we	éyx yaxólnu	איך יכולנו
refuse?	lesarév.	לסרב?
we were able	yaxólnu	יכולנו
to refuse	lesarév	לסרב

MRS. CASPI

Let's go	háva nigáš	הַכָה נִיגַש
to the table	lašulxán.	לְשֻלחן.
let's	háva	הכה
we will approach	nigáš (1.pl.fut.)	ניגש
table	šulxán (m)	שולחן

Moshe,	mošé.	מַשה,
please pour	mezóg bevakašá	מזוג בבקשה
the wine	et hayáin	את היין
for Kiddush.	lekidúš.	לקידוש.
pour	mezóg (m.s.imv.)	מזוג
wine	yáin (m)	יין
(Sabbath ceremony)	kidúš (m)	קידוש

12.2 ADDITIONAL VOCABULARY

Good evening.	érev tóv.	ערב טוב.
Good morning.	bóker tóv.	בוקר טוב.
Good night.	láyla tóv.	לילה טוב.

The above Hebrew expressions are almost identical to the English in usage. /érev/ 'evening' begins at sunset. In the afternoon /šalóm/ is used.

| Happy holiday. | xág saméax. | חג שמח. |

This greeting is used on holidays, similarly to /šabát šalóm/.

Happy New Year.	šaná tová.	שנה טובה.
Congratulations.	mazál tóv.	מזל טוב.
luck	mazál (m)	מזל

12.3　Vocabulary Drills

A.　Transformation Drill

>　Instructor:　We didn't come yesterday.
>　Student:　We couldn't get here.

ló bánu etmól.	ló yaxólnu lehagía.	לא באנו אתמול.
ló bátem etmól.	ló yaxóltem lehagía.	לא באתם אתמול.
ló báti etmól.	ló yaxólti lehagía.	לא באתי אתמול.
ló báta etmól.	ló yaxólta lehagía.	לא באת אתמול.
ló bát etmól.	ló yaxólt lehagía.	לא באת אתמול.
ló báten etmól.	ló yaxólten lehagía.	לא באתן אתמול.

B.　Substitution Drill

>　Please pour the wine.

mezóg bevakašá et hayáin.	מזוג בבקשה את היין.
mizgí	מזגי
mizgú	מזגו
mezógna	מזוגנה

GRAMMAR NOTES

12.4 Cardinal Numbers with Nouns

a)   Note in the following example that the number precedes the noun that is
quantified.

lexí kearbaá rexovót.   "Go about four blocks."

    With the exception of /exád, axát/ "one" which follow the noun, the
cardinal numbers precede the noun.

/yóm exád/   "one day"
/šlošá yamím/   "three days"

b)   The number /šnáim, štáim/ "two" has the alternate forms /šnéy, štey/
when preceding the quantified noun.

/šnéy avironím/   "two airplanes"
/štéy oniót/   "two ships"

    Compare, on the other hand, the following:

/lí yéš šnéy sfarím,   "I have a book,
vegám ló yéš šnáim./   and he has two, also."

c)   In certain stereotyped expressions the singular form of the noun is
          used after numbers higher than ten.

/éser šaním/   "ten years"
/esrím šaná/   "twenty years"

d)   When the noun is definite the preceding number is treated as a construct
state noun itself. The masculine numbers "three" to "ten" have the alternate
forms listed below.
Compare then:
/
/šlošá batím/   "three houses"
/šlóšet habatím/   "the three houses"

    Some feminine numbers have alternate forms in formal speech, but
otherwise they do not. However, many speakers use the alternate, construct-
state form of the masculine numbers before feminine nouns which are definite.

/šalóš oniót/   "three ships"
/šlóšet haoniót/   "the three ships"

    It should be remembered that there is wide variation in the use of
numbers.

            the three...   /šlóšet ha-/
            the four...   /arbáat ha-/
            the five...   /xaméšet ha-/
            the six...   /šéšet ha-/
            the seven...   /šiv'át ha-/
            the eight...   /šmonát ha-/
            the nine...   /tiš'át ha-/
            the ten...   /aséret ha-/

In the following drills some new plurals are introduced.

Note that some masculine plural nouns end in /-ót/ and some feminine plural nouns in /-ím/.

A. Transformation Drill - Student adds one.

>   Instructor: I have one table.
>   Student: I have two tables.

yéš lí šulxán exád.	yéš lí šnéy šulxanót.	‏יש לי שולחן אחר.‏
yéš lí šnéy šulxanót.	yéš lí šlošá šulxanót.	‏יש לי שני שולחנות.‏
yéš lí šlošá šulxanót.	yéš lí arbaá šulxanót.	‏יש לי שלושה שולחנות.‏
yéš lí arbaá šulxanót.	yéš lí xamišá šulxanót.	‏יש לי ארבעה שולחנות.‏
yéš lí xamišá šulxanót.	yéš lí šišá šulxanót.	‏יש לי חמשה שולחנות.‏
yéš lí šišá šulxanót.	yéš lí šiv'á šulxanót.	‏יש לי ששה שולחנות.‏
yéš lí šiv'á šulxanót.	yéš lí šmoná šulxanót.	‏יש לי שבעה שולחנות.‏
yéš lí šmoná šulxanót.	yéš lí tiš'á šulxanót.	‏יש לי שמונה שולחנות.‏
yéš lí tiš'á šulxanót.	yéš lí asará šulxanót.	‏יש לי תשעה שולחנות.‏

B. Transformation Drill - Repeat Drill A in reverse. Student subtracts one.

>   Instructor: yéš lí asará šulxanót.
>   Student: yéš lí tiš'á šulxanót.

‏מורה: יש לי עשרה שולחנות.‏
‏תלמיד: יש לי תשעה שולחנות.‏

The instructor may vary Drills A and B by selecting numbers at random.

C. Transformation Drill - Student adds one.

>   Instructor: We want to see one big city.
>   Student: We want to see two big cities.

ánu rocím lir'ót ír axát gdolá.
        ánu rocím lir'ót štéy arím gdolót.
ánu rocím lir'ót štéy arím gdolót.
        ánu rocím lir'ót šalóš arím gdolót.
ánu rocím lir'ót šalóš arím gdolót.
        ánu rocím lir'ót árba arím gdolót.
ánu rocím lir'ót árba arím gdolót.
        ánu rocím lir'ót xaméš arím gdolót.
ánu rocím lir'ót xaméš arím gdolót.
        ánu rocím lir'ót šéš arím gdolót.
ánu rocím lir'ót šéš arím gdolót.
        ánu rocím lir'ót šéva arím gdolót.
ánu rocím lir'ót šéva arím gdolót.
        ánu rocím lir'ót šmóne arím gdolót.
ánu rocím lir'ót šmóne arím gdolót.
        ánu rocím lir'ót téša arím gdolót.
ánu rocím lir'ót téša arím gdolót.
        ánu rocím lir'ót éser arím gdolót.

‏אנו רוצים לראות עיר אחת גדולה.‏
‏אנו רוצים לראות שתי ערים גדולות.‏
‏אנו רוצים לראות שלוש ערים גדולות.‏
‏אנו רוצים לראות ארבע ערים גדולות.‏
‏אנו רוצים לראות חמש ערים גדולות.‏
‏אנו רוצים לראות שש ערים גדולות.‏
‏אנו רוצים לראות שבע ערים גדולות.‏
‏אנו רוצים לראות שמונה ערים גדולות.‏
‏אנו רוצים לראות תשע ערים גדולות.‏

D. Transformation Drill - Repeat Drill C in reverse. Student subtracts one.

      Instructor: ánu rocím lir'ót éser arím gdolót.
      Student: ánu rocím lir'ót téša arím gdolót.

The instructor may vary Drills C and D by selecting numbers at random.

E. Transformation Drill - Student totals numbers.

      Instructor: I have four books, and he has seven.
      Student: We have eleven books.

lí yéš arbaá sfarím, veló yéš šiv'á.   לי יש ארבעה ספרים, ולו יש שבעה.
    yéš lánu axádasár sfarím.   יש לנו אחד-עשר ספרים.
lí yéš šmoná sfarím, veló yéš arbaá.   לי יש שמונה ספרים, ולו יש ארבעה.
    yéš lánu snéymasar sfarím.   יש לנו שנים-עשר ספרים.
lí yéš asará sfarim, veló yéš šlošá.   לי יש עשרה ספרים, ולו יש שלושה.
    yéš lánu šlošáasar sfarím.   יש לנו שלושה-עשר ספרים.
lí yéš šmoná sfarím, veló yéš šišá.   לי יש שמונה ספרים, ולו יש ששה.
    yéš lánu arbáasar sfarím.   יש לנו ארבעה-עשר ספרים.
lí yéš séfer exád, veló yéš arbáasar.   לי יש ספר אחד, ולו יש ארבעה-עשר.
    yéš lánu xamišáasar sfarím.   יש לנו חמשה-עשר ספרים.
lí yéš tiš'á sfarím, veló yéš šiv'á.   לי יש תשעה ספרים, ולו יש שבעה.
    yéš lánu šišáasar sfarím.   יש לנו ששה-עשר ספרים.
lí yéš šmoná sfarím, veló yéš tiš'á.   לי יש שמונה ספרים, ולו יש תשעה.
    yéš lánu šiváasar sfarím.   יש לנו שבעה-עשר ספרים.
lí yéš asará sfarím, veló yéš šmoná.   לי יש עשרה ספרים, ולו יש שמונה.
    yéš lánu šmonáasar sfarím.   יש לנו שמונה-עשר ספרים.
lí yéš axádasar sfarím, veló yéš šmoná.   לי יש אחד-עשר ספרים, ולו יש שמונה.
    yéš lánu tišáasar sfarím.   יש לנו תשעה-עשר ספרים.
lí yéš šlošáasár sfarím veló yéš šiv'á.   לי יש שלושה-עשר ספרים, ולו יש שבעה.
    yéš lánu esrím sfarím.   יש לנו עשרים ספרים.

F. Transformation Drill - Student total numbers.

      Instructor: I saw four women speaking Hebrew,
               and you saw seven.
      Student We saw eleven women speaking Hebrew.

aní raíti árba naším medabrót ivrít,   אני ראיתי ארבע נשים מדברות עברית,
           veatá raíta šéva.   ואתה ראית שבע.
  raínu axát'esre naším medabrót ivrít.   (אחת-עשרה)
aní raíti šmóne naším medabrót ivrit,   אני ראיתי שמונה נשים מדברות עברית,
           veatá raíta árba.   ואתה ראית ארבע.
  raínu štéym'esre naším medabrót ivrit.   (שתים-עשרה)
aní raíti išá axát medabéret ivrít,   אני ראיתי אשה אחת מדברת עברית,
           veatá raíta štéym'esre.   ואתה ראית שתים-עשרה.
  raínu šlóš'esre naším medabrót ivrít.   (שלוש-עשרה)
aní raíti xaméš naším medabrót ivrít,   אני ראיתי חמש נשים מדברות עברית,
           veatá raíta téša.   ואתה ראית תשע.
  raínu arbá'esre naším medabrót ivrít.   (ארבע-עשרה)
aní raíti éser naším medabrót ivrít,   אני ראיתי עשר נשים מדברות עברית,
           veatá raíta xaméš.   ואתה ראית חמש.
  raínu xaméš'esre naším medabrót ivrít.   (חמש-עשרה)
aní raíti xaméš'esre naším medabrót ivrít,   אני ראיתי חמש-עשרה נשים מדברות עברית,
           veatá raíta axát.   ואתה ראית אחת.
  raínu šéš'esre naším medabrót ivrít.   (שש-עשרה)

aní raíti téša naším medabrót ivrít,
    veatá raíta šmoné.
  raínu šváesre naším medabrót ivrít.
aní raíti šmóne naším medabrót ivrít,
    veatá raíta éser.
  raínu šmonáesre naším medabrót ivrít.
aní raíti šlóšesre naším medabrót ivrít,
    veatá raíti šéš.
  raínu tšáesre naším medabrót ivrít.
aní raíti šváesré naším medabrót ivrít,
    veatá raíta šalóš.
  raínu esrím naším medabrót ivrít.

אני ראיתי תשע נשים מדברות עברית,
  ואתה ראית שמונה.
  (שבע-עשרה)
אני ראיתי שמונה נשים מדברות עברית,
  ואתה ראית עשר.
  (שמונה-עשרה)
אני ראיתי שלוש-עשרה נשים מדברות עברית,
  ואתה ראית שש.
  (תשע-עשרה)
אני ראיתי שבע-עשרה נשים מדברות עברית,
  ואתה ראית שלוש.
  (עשרים)

G. Transformation Drill

Instructor: We have two books.
Student: Give us the two books.

מורה: יש לנו שני ספרים.
תלמיד: תנו לנו את שני הספרים.

yéš lánu šnéy sfarím.
  tnú lánu et šnéy hasfarím.
yéš lánu šlošá sfarím.
  tnú lánu et šlóšet hasfarím.
yéš lánu arbaá sfarím.
  tnú lánu et arbáat hasfarím.
yéš lánu xamišá sfarím.
  tnú lánu et xaméšet hasfarím.
yéš lánu šišá sfarím.
  tnú lánu et šéšet hasfarím.
yéš lánu šiv'á sfarím.
  tnú lánu et šiv'át hasfarím.
yés lánu šmoná sfarím.
  tnú lánu et šmonát hasfarím.
yéš lánu tiš'á sfarím.
  tnú lánu et tiš'át hasfarím.
yéš lánu asará sfarím.
  tnú lánu et aséret hasfarím.

יש לנו שני ספרים.
תנו לנו את שני הספרים.
יש לנו שלושה ספרים.
תנו לנו את שלושת הספרים.
יש לנו ארבעה ספרים.
תנו לנו את ארבעת הספרים.
יש לנו חמשה ספרים.
תנו לנו את חמשת הספרים.
יש לנו ששה ספרים.
תנו לנו את ששת הספרים.
יש לנו שבעה ספרים.
תנו לנו את שבעת הספרים.
יש לנו שמונה ספרים.
תנו לנו את שמונת הספרים.
יש לנו תשעה ספרים.
תנו לנו את תשעת הספרים.
יש לנו עשרה ספרים.
תנו לנו את עשרת הספרים.

H. Transformation Drill

Instructor: Yesterday I saw two ships.
Student: Where did you see the two ships?

etmól raíti štéy oniót.
  éyfo raíta et štéy haoniót.
etmól raíti šalóš oniót.
  éyfo raíta et šlóšet haoniót.
etmól raíti árba oniót.
  éyfo raíta et arbáat haoniót.
etmól raíti xaméš oniót.
  éyfo raíta et xaméšet haoniót.
etmól raíti šéš oniót.
  éyfo raíta et šéšet haoniót.
etmól raíti šéva oniót.
  éyfo raíta et šiv'át haoniót.
etmól raíti šmóne oniót.
  éyfo raíta et šmonát haoniót.
etmól raíti téša oniot.
  éyfo raíta et tiš'át haoniót.
etmól raíti éser oniót.
  éyfo raíta et aséret haoniót.

אתמול ראיתי שתי אוניות.
איפה ראית את שתי האוניות?
אתמול ראיתי שלוש אוניות.
איפה ראית את שלושת האוניות?
אתמול ראיתי ארבע אוניות.
איפה ראית את ארבעת האוניות?
אתמול ראיתי חמש אוניות.
איפה ראית את חמשת האוניות?
אתמול ראיתי שש אוניות.
איפה ראית את ששת האוניות?
אתמול ראיתי שבע אוניות.
איפה ראית את שבעת האוניות?
אתמול ראיתי שמונה אוניות.
איפה ראית את שמונת האוניות?
אתמול ראיתי תשע אוניות.
איפה ראית את תשעת האוניות?
אתמול ראיתי עשר אוניות.
איפה ראית את עשרת האוניות?

12.5 Ordinal Numbers

a) The ordinal numbers are adjectives. The numbers from "second" to
"tenth" have forms resembling the corresponding cardinal numbers.
Ordinal numbers "eleventh" and higher are identical in form to the
corresponding cardinal numbers, but they follow the noun as adjectives.

	Masculine	Feminine	זכר	נקבה
first	rišón	rišoná	ראשון	ראשונה
second	šení	šniá	שני	שניה
third	šliší	šlišít	שלישי	שלישית
fourth	revií	reviít	רביעי	רביעית
fifth	xamiší	xamišít	חמישי	חמישית
sixth	šiší	šišít	שישי	שישית
seventh	švií	šviít	שביעי	שביעית
eighth	šminí	šminít	שמיני	שמינית
ninth	tšií	tšiít	תשיעי	תשיעית
tenth	asirí	asirít	עשירי	עשירית
eleventh	axád'asar	axát'esre	אחד-עשר	אחת עשרה
twelfth	šnéym'asar	štéym'esre	שנים-עשר	שתים עשרה
etc.				

b) The names of the days of the week are proper nouns. Thus, the following
distinction is made.

/beyóm rišón/   "on Sunday"
/bayóm harišón/   "on the first day"

     The ordinal number may be used with the name of the day.

/beyóm rišón harišón/   "on the first Sunday"

     /šabát/ often has the definite article when modified.

/hašabát harišoná/   "the first Saturday"

A. Transformation Drill

          Instructor: Go four blocks.
          Student: Turn right at the fourth street.

léx arbaá rexovót.	barexóv harevií pné yamína.	לך ארבעה רחובות.
léx šnéy rexovót.	barexóv hašení pné yamína.	לך שני רחובות.
léx šlošá rexovót.	barexóv hašliší pné yamína.	לך שלושה רחובות.
léx šišá rexovót.	barexóv hašiší pné yamína.	לך שישה רחובות.
léx šmoná rexovót.	barexóv hašminí pné yamína.	לך שמונה רחובות.
léx asará rexovót.	barexóv haasirí pné yamína.	לך עשרה רחובות.
léx xamišá rexovót.	barexóv haxamiší pné yamína.	לך חמישה רחובות.
léx šiv'á rexovót.	barexóv hašvií pné yamína.	לך שבעה רחובות.
léx tiš'á rexovót.	barexóv hatšií pné yamína.	לך תשעה רחובות.

     This drill may be varied by making it an expansion drill.

          Instructor: léx arbaá rexovót.   לך ארבעה רחובות,
          Student: léx arbaá rexovót, ubarexóv   לך ארבעה רחובות וברחוב
               harevií pné yemína.   הרביעי פנה ימינה.

B. Transformation Drill

> Instructor: Go four blocks.
> Student: Turn left at the fourth corner.

lexí arbaá rexovót.	bapiná hareviít pní smóla.	לכי ארבעה רחובות.
lexí asará rexovót.	bapiná haasirít pní smóla.	לכי עשרה רחובות.
lexí šnéy rexovót.	bapiná hašniá pní smóla.	לכי שני רחובות.
lexí šlošá rexovót.	bapiná hašlišít pní smóla.	לכי שלושה חובות.
lexí xamišá rexovót.	bapiná haxamišít pní smóla.	לכי חמישה רחובות.
lexí šmoná rexovót.	bapiná hašminít pní smóla.	לכי שמונה רחובות.
lexí šišá rexovót.	bapiná hašišít pní smóla.	לכי שישה חובות.
lexí šiv'á rexovót.	bapiná hašviít pní smóla.	לכי שבעה חובות.
lexí tiš'á rexovót.	bapiná hatšiít pní smóla.	לכי תשעה וחובות.

This drill may be varied by may be varied by making it an expansion drill.

> Instructor: lexí arbaá rexovót.
> Student: lexí arbaá rexovót, ubapiná hareviít
>   pní smóla.

C. Transformation Drill

> Instructor: He lives eleven blocks from here.
> Student: Go up to the eleventh street.

hú gár axád'asar rexovót mikán.	הוא גר אחד-עשר רחובות מכאן.
léx ád harexóv haaxád'asar.	לך עד הרחוב האחד-עשר.
hú gár šnéym'asar rexovót mikán.	הוא גר שנים-עשר רחובות מכאן.
léx ád harexóv hašnéym'asar.	לך עד הרחוב השנים עשר.
hú gár šlošáasar rexovót mikán.	הוא גר שלושה עשר רחובות מכאן.
léx ád harexóv hašlošáasar.	לך עד הרחוב השלושה-עשר.
hú gár arbáasar rexovót mikán.	הוא גר ארבעה-עשר חובות מכאן.
léx ád harexóv haarbáasar.	לך עד הרחוב הארבעה-עשר.
hú gár xamišáasar rexovót mikán.	הוא גר חמישה-עשר רחובות מכאן.
léx ád harexóv haxamišáasar.	לך עד הרחוב החמישה-עשר.
hú gár šišáasar rexovót mikán.	הוא גר שישה-עשר רחובות מכאן.
léx ád harexóv hašišáasar.	לך עד הרחוב הישישה-עשר.
hú gár šiváasar rexovót mikán.	הוא גר שבעה-עשר רחובות מכאן.
léx ád harexóv hašiváasar.	לך עד הרחוב השבעה-עשר.
hú gár šmonáasar rexovót mikán.	הוא גר שמונה-עשר חובות מכאן.
léx ád harexóv hašmonáasar.	לך עד הרחוב השמונה-עשר.
hú gár tišáasar rexovót mikán.	הוא גר תשעה-עשר חובות מכאן.
léx ád harexóv hatišáasar.	לך עד הרחוב התשעה-עשר.
hú gár esrím rexovót mikán.	הוא גר עשרים רחונות מכאן.
léx ád harexóv haesrím.	לך עד הרחוב העשרים.

D. Expansion Drill

Instructor: <u>Yesterday I saw ten ships.</u>

Student: Yesterday I saw ten ships
and today I saw the eleventh ship.

etmól raíti éser oniót.   .אתמול ראיתי עשר אוניות 1.
  vehayóm raíti et haoniá haaxát'esre.   .והיום ראיתי את האוניה האחת-עשרה
etmól raíti axát'esre oniót.   .אתמול ראיתי אחת-עשרה אוניות 2.
  vehayóm raíti et haoniá haštéym'esre.   .והיום ראיתי את האוניה השתים עשרה
etmól raíti štéym'esre oniót.   .אתמול ראיתי שתים-עשרה אוניות 3.
  vehayóm raíti et haoniá hašlóš'esre.   .והיום ראיתי את האוניה השלוש-עשרה
etmól raíti šlóš'esre oniót.   .אתמול ראיתי שלוש-עשרה אוניות 4.
  vehayóm raíti et haoniá haarbá'esre.   .והיום ראיתי את האוניה הארבע-עשרה
etmól raíti arbá'esre oniót.   .אתמול ראיתי ארבע-עשרה אוניות 5.
  vehayóm raíti et haoniá haxaméš'esre.   .והיום ראיתי את האוניה החמש-עשרה
etmól raíti xaméš'esre oniót.   .אתמול ראיתי חמש-עשרה אוניות 6.
  vehayóm raíti et haoniá hašéš'esre.   .והיום ראיתי את האוניה השש-עשרה
etmól raíti šéš'esre oniót.   .אתמול ראיתי שש-עשרה אוניות 7.
  vehayóm raíti et haoniá hašvá'esre.   .והיום ראיתי את האוניה השבע-עשרה
etmól raíti švá'esre oniót.   .אתמול ראיתי שבע-עשרה אוניות 8.
  vehayóm raíti et haoniá hašmóne'esre. .והיום ראיתי את האוניה השמונה-עשרה
etmól raíti šmóne'esre oniót.   .אתמול ראיתי שמונה עשרה אוניות 9.
  vehayóm raíti et haoniá hatšá'esre.   .והיום ראיתי את האוניה התשע-עשרה
etmól raíti tšá'esre oniót.   .אתמול ראיתי תשע-עשרה אוניות 10.
  vehayóm raíti et haoniá haesrím.   .והיום ראיתי את האוניה העשרים

E. Expansion Drill

Instructor: I live in the second house from
the corner.

Student: I live in the second house from
the corner, and Hanna lives in
the third house.

aní gár babáit hašení mehapiná.   .אני גר בבית השני מהפינה 1.
  vexána gára babáit hašliši.   .וחנה גרה בבית השלישי
aní gár babáit harevií mehapiná.   .אני גר בבית הרביעי מהפינה 2.
  vexána gára babáit haxamiší.   .וחנה גרה בבית החמישי
aní gár babáit hašiší mehapiná.   .אני גר בבית הששי מהפינה 3.
  vexána gára babáit hašvií.   .וחנה גרה בבית השביעי
aní gár babáit hašmini mehapiná.   .אני גר בבית השמיני מהפינה 4.
  vexána gára babáit hatšií.   .וחנה גרה בבית התשיעי
aní gár babáit haasirí mehapiná.   .אני גר בבית העשירי מהפינה 5.
  vexána gára babáit haaxádasar.   .וחנה גרה בבית האחד-עשר

REVIEW CONVERSATIONS

A: šalóm avígdor. matáy higátem letél avív.   א: שלום אביגדור. מתי הגעתם לתל אביב?

B: higánu beyóm rišón.   ב: הגענו ביום ראשון.

A: ánu rocím lehazmín otxém learuxát   א: אנו רוצים להזמין אתכם לארוחת
   cohoráim.   צהריים.

B: nismáx meód. lematáy?   ב: נשמח מאוד. למתי?

A: lehayóm. haím štéymesre mat'ím?   א: להיום. האם שתים־עשרה מתאים?

B: kén. behexlét.   ב: כן, בהחלט.

C: háva nigáš lašulxán.   ג: הבה ניגש לשולחן.

D: ló, todá. kvár meuxár.   ד: לא, תודה. כבר מאוחר.

C: éyx atém yexolím lesarév?   ג: איך אתם יכולים לסרב?

D: slixá. ánu muxraxím larúc.   ד: סליחה, אנו מוכרחים לרוץ.

E: šim'í, miryám. át memahéret?   ה: שמעי, מרים, את ממהרת?

F: ló. ló kol káx.   ו: לא. לא כל כך.

E: háva nigáš lebrúklin bár.   ה: הבה ניגש לברוקלין בר.

F: tóv. haglída šám tová.   ו: טוב. הגלידה שם טובה.

13.1 Friday Evening Dinner (cont'd)

MRS. WILLIAMS

The fish	hadagím	הדגים
is wonderful,	nehedarím,	נהדרים,
and so is the <u>chalah</u>.	vexén haxalá.	וכן החלה.
fish	dág (m)	דג
wonderful	nehedár (m.s.)	נהדר
and so	vexén	וכן
<u>chalah</u> (twist bread)	xalá (f)	חלה

MRS. CASPI

Thank you very much.	todá rabá.	תודה רבה.

MRS. WILLIAMS

Mrs. Caspi,	gvéret káspi,	גברת כספי,
you must	át muxraxá	את מוכרחה
give me	latét lí	לתת לי
the recipe	et hamiršám	את המרשם
for the fish.	ladagím.	לדגים.
to give	latét	לתת
recipe	miršám (m)	מרשם

MRS. CASPI

Gladly.	beracón	ברצון
I'll give you	etén láx	אתן לך
the recipe,	et hamiršám,	את המרשם,
Mrs. Williams.	gvéret Williams.	גברת וויליאמס.
desire,	racón (m)	רצון
willingly	beracón	ברצון
I will give	etén (1 s.)	אתן

It's a tradition	zú masóret	זו מסורת
in our homes	eclénu babáit,	אצלנו בבית
to eat	leexól	לאכול
on Friday evening	belél šiší	בליל שישי
<u>gefilte fish</u>.	dagím memulaím.	דגים ממולאים.
it, this	zú (f)	זו
tradition	masóret (f)	מסורת
filled	memulá	ממולא

MRS. WILLIAMS

Mrs. Caspi,	gvéret káspi.	גברת כספי,
please,	bevakašá	בבקשה
don't give me	ál titní li	אל תתני לי
any more to eat.	yotér óxel.	יותר אוכל.
more	yotér	יותר
food	óxel (m)	אוכל

MRS. CASPI

But	haréy	הרי
you haven't eaten	ló axáltem	לא אכלתם
anything.	klúm.	כלום.
I ate	axálti	אכלתי
nothing	ló...klúm	לא...כלום

MRS. WILLIAMS

I'm on a diet.	aní bediéta.	אני בדיאטה.
diet	diéta (f)	דיאטה

The food was	haóxel hayá	האוכל היה
very delicious.	taím meód.	טעים מאד.
was	hayá (3 m.s.)	היה
delicious, tasty	taím (m.s.)	טעים

MRS. CASPI

Thank you.	todá rabá.	תודה רבה.

MRS. WILLIAMS

I'll start	atxíl	אתחיל
on my diet	badiéta šelí	בדיאטה שלי
tomorrow.	maxár.	מחר.
I will begin	atxíl (1 s.)	אתחיל

13.2 ADDITIONAL VOCABULARY

He will give her	hú yitén lá	הוא יתן לה את המירשם.
the recipe.	et hamiršám.	
She will give her	hí titén lá	היא תתן לה את המידשם.
the recipe.	et hamiršám.	
We will give her	nitén lá	ניתן לה את המירשם.
the recipe.	et hamiršám.	
They (m) will give her	hém yitnú lá	הם יתנו לה את המירשם.
the recipe.	et hamiršám.	
They (f) will give here	hén titénna lá	הן תיתנה לה את המירשם.
the recipe.	et hamiršám.	

The meal was	haaruxá haytá	הארוחה היחה טעימה מאד.
very delicious.	teíma meód.	

The fish was	hadagím hayú	הדגים היו טעימים מאד.
very tasty.	teimím meód.	

The chalahs were	haxalót hayú	החלות היו טעימות מאד.
very tasty.	teimót meód.	

13.3 <u>Vocabulary Drills</u>

The adjective /memulá/ is similar to /nimcá/ "is found" in the pattern of its forms.

m.s.	memulá	f.s.	memulét	ממולאת	ממולא
m.pl.	memulaím				ממולאים
f.pl.	memulaót				ממולאות

Note that in the Hebrew spelling the third root consonant is א , as in /nimcá/ נמצא.

The adjective /nehedár/ is also similar to /nimcá/. The feminine singular has a /-t/ suffix with change of vowel.

m.s.	nehedár	f.s.	nehedéret	נהדרת	נהדר
m.pl.	nehedarím				נהדרים
f.pl.	nehedarót				נהדרות

A. Substitution Drill - Masculine Singular

The house is wonderful.

habáit nehedár.	הבית נהדר.
hamalón	המלון
hayám	הים
binyán hadóar	בנין הדואר
atá	אתה
hú	הוא
nemál hateufá	נמל התעופה

B. Substitution Drill - Feminine Singular

The <u>chalah</u> is wonderful.

haxalá nehedéret.	החלה נהדרת.
haárec	הארץ
haglidá	הגלידה
rámat gán	רמת גן
hí	היא
miryám	מרים
dálya	דליה
sfát hayám	שפת הים
haaruxá	הארוחה

C. Substitution Drill - Masculine Plural

The fish is wonderful.

hadagím nehedarím.	הדגים נהדרים.
atém	אתם
harexovót	הרחובות
hayeynót	היינות
habatím	הבתים
hašulxanót	השולחנות
kulám	כולם
hayamím	הימים

D.   Substitution Drill - Feminine Plural

      The <u>chalahs</u> are wonderful.

haxalót nehedarót.	. החלות נהדרות
hatocaót	התוצאות
atén	אתן
haaracót	הארצות
hanaším	הנשים
hamišpaxót	המשפחות
haglidót	הגלידות

E.   Substitution - Agreement Drill - /nehedár/

      The country is wonderful.

<u>haárec nehedéret.</u>	. <u>הארץ נהדרת</u>
hamisrád	המשרד
haxalá	החלה
hadagím	הדגים
hayáin	היין
atém	אתם
hatocaót	התוצאות
hamišpaxá	המשפחה
haanaším	האנשים
hamisradím	המשרדים
habatím	הבתים
haoniót	האוניות
hamlonót	המלונות
haaruxót	הארוחות

F.   Substitution - Agreement Drill - /axálti/ "I ate"

      I haven't eaten breakfast yet.

<u>adáin 16 axálti aruxát bóker.</u>	. עדיין לא אכלתי ארוחת בוקר
áta - át - ánu - atém	אתה - את - אנו - אתם
aní veiští - atén - aní	אני ואשתי - אתן - אני

GRAMMAR NOTES

13.4 Consonant Alternation /k ~ x/

The consonant /k/ often alternates with /x/ when not initial in the word.

/kén/   'so, yes'
/vexén/   'and so'

This alternation occurs in a number of forms and is characteristic of roots in certain verb patterns. In other cases it is optional, with the /x/-form usually the more formal in style.

/lekán ~ lexán/   "to here"

This alternation is similar to that of /b ~ v/ described in Grammar Note 5.6. The alternation is always spelled in Hebrew with the ambiguous letter כ , and not with ק and ח .

13.5 Formation of the Future Tense

As has been noted in the description of the gentle imperative, Grammar Section 6.5, the second person future forms of verbs have a prefix of the pattern /tV-/.

Examples are:

/tifné/ "you will turn"   /teléx/ "you will go"
/tigmór/ "you will finish" /tedabér/ "you will speak"

/tamšíx/ "you will continue"/tomár/ "you will say"
/taavór/ "you will pass"

(Some verbs have /u/ as the prefix vowel, though none have occurred in this text so far.)

Compare now the first person plural forms which have occurred so far:
nimcá et hamakóm leló kóši.
háva nigáš lašulxán.
nitén lá et hamiršám.

Note that these all begin with a prefix of the pattern /nV-/. (By coincidence the vowel of the prefix in the three examples is /-i-/.) Thus it may be seen that the future tense of verbs consists of a stem plus prefixes to distinguish person, gender, and number. Some of the forms have suffixes, also.

/titén/   "you (m.s.) will give"
/titní/   "you (f.s.) will give"
/titnú/   "you (m.pl.) will give"
/titénna/ "you (f.pl.) will give"

These second person forms have been described in the section on the gentle imperatives. The forms of the entire future tense of this verb are shown in the following table:

1 s.	etén	1 pl.	nitén
2 m.s.	titén	2 m.pl.	titnú
2 f.s.	titní	2 f.pl.	titénna
3 m.s.	yitén	3 m.pl.	yitnú
3 f.s.	titén	3 f.pl.	titénna

Extracting the stem /tén/, the pattern of prefixes and suffixes in the future tense is as follows:

[Note: The stem appears as /-tn-/ before the suffixes /-í, -ú/. See Grammar Note 6.9.]

1.s.	e_____	1 pl.	ni_____
2 m.s.	ti_____	2 m.pl.	ti_____ú
2 f.s.	ti___í	2 f.pl.	ti_____na
3 m.s.	yi_____	3 m.pl.	yi_____ú
3 f.s.	ti_____	3 f.pl.	ti_____na

The following observations may be made which are characteristic of the future tense of all verbs:

a. There is no gender distinction in the first person. (This is true of the past tense forms, also. See Grammar Note 5.4)

b. The 2 m.s. and the 3 f.s. are identical in form.

c. The 2 f.pl. and the 3 f.pl. are identical in form. In some patterns these two forms have a different stem vowel from that in the other future tense forms - /tamšíxi, tamšéxna/; /tagíi, tagána/. See Vocabulary Drill, Section 10.3.

The following are general comments about the future tense:

d. The first person singular prefix is simply a vowel. In some verb patterns it is the same vowel as in the other prefixes. This is always so when the vowel is /o/ or /u/.
    In other verb patterns the vowel of the first person singular is different from that of the other prefixes. At this point the student will have to drill the verbs in order to memorize which ones have a different vowel. Verbs showing possible alternations have occurred in the text. Examples are:

Alternation	1 s.	2 m.s.
/e- ~ ti-/	egmór	tigmór
/ee- ~ taa-/	eevór	taavór
/a- ~ te-/	adabér	tedabér

112

Nevertheless, one frequently hears these first person singular forms with the same prefix vowel as in the rest of the future tense - e.g., /edabér/ as well as /adabér/.

When the first person singular prefix has a different vowel it will be noted in the drills.

e. The suffixes /-i, -u/ are not stressed in the following cases:
   1. When the stem vowel is /-í/: /tamšíxi, tamšíxu, yamšíxu/
   2. When the stem has the pattern /CúC/: /taqúri, taqúru, yaqúru/ "will reside"
   3. In a small list of other verbs. Example: /tavói, tavóu, yavóu/ "will come"

f. Verbs such as /nimcá/ "we will find" have an internal open juncture as a third root consonant. At the end of a word it is, of course, not pronounced.   Before the suffixes /-í, -ú/ it creates a three-consonant cluster which is broken up by the insertion of /-e-/.

   /timcá/   "you (m.s.) will find"
   /timce'í/   "you (f.s.) will find"
   /timce'ú/   "you (m.pl.) will find"
   /yimce'ú/   "they (m) will find"

The juncture is usually replaced by a smooth transition in ordinary speech. /timceí/, etc.

g. Some verbs have a more complicated future tense pattern, but these have been described generally in the note on the gentle imperative. The full set of future tense forms may be derived from the gentle imperative by substitution of prefixes.

Example:
   From 2 m.s. /tagía/ the following may be derived /agía, yagía, nagía/.
   The 3 f.s. /tagía/ is identical in form with the 2 m.s.
   From 2 m.pl. /tagíu/ the 3 m.pl. /yagíu/ may be derived.
   The 3 f.pl. /tagána/ is identical to the 2 f.pl., as in all verbs.

13.6 Use of the Future Tense

a. The future tense is used to indicate an occurrence later in time than the present moment. This often corresponds to the English construction "will_____".

   1. hamišpaxá šelí tagía   "My family will arrive
      beód kexódeš yamím.   in about a month."

In an included sentence it often corresponds to the simple English verb.

   2. axaréy šetigmór et haglidá,   "After you finish the ice cream
      tamšíx yašar lekivún hayám.   continue towards the sea."

Other sentences which illustrate its use and the corresponding English are:

   3. amárta lí šeatxíl maxár.   "You said that I would begin
                           tomorrow."

4.   amárnu ló šeyedabér   'We told him that <u>he should speak</u>
       ivrít beisraél.   Hebrew in Israel."

b.   The third person forms generally occur with an independent subject
unless one is stated in a closely preceding context.

     <u>hú yitén</u> lá et hamiršám.
     amartí <u>ló šeyitén</u> lá et hamiršám.

Independent pronoun subjects may be used with the first and second person
forms for emphasis, contrast, etc. Compare this with the similar use of
independent pronouns with past tense forms. See Grammar Note 5.4.

     aní eléx maxár,   "I'll go tomorrow,
     veatá teléx beyóm šení.   and you'll go on Monday."

c.   The negative of the future tense is formed by using /ló/ before the
verb. In the second person this will contrast with the negative
imperative in which /ál/ is used.

     ló telxí hayóm.   "You won't go today."
     ál telxí hayóm.   "Don't go today."

A.   Substitution Drill - /e- ~ ti-/

I'll give the recipe to Miriam.

aní etén et hamiršám lemiryám.	אני אתן את המירשם למרים.
atá titén	אתה תיתן
át titní	את תיתני
dóv yitén	דוב יתן
léa titén	לאה תיתן
ánu nitén	אנו ניתן
atém titnú	אתם תיתנו
atén titénna	אתן תיתנה
hém yitnú	הם יתנו
hén titénna	הן תיתנה

B.   Substitution - Agreement Drill

I won't let him speak English.

<u>aní ló etén ló ledabér anglít.</u>   <u>אני לא אתן לו לדבר אנגלית.</u>

atá - ánu - yoéc hašagrirút - hí	אתה - אנו - יועץ השגרירות - היא
hén - atén - yaakóv vedóv - atém	הן - אתן - יעקב ודוב - אתם
iští veaní - át - aní	אשתי ואני - את - אני

C.   Substitution Drill - /e- ~ ti-/

I will finish the meal.

ani egmór et haaruxá.	אני אגמור את הארוחה.
atá tigmór	אתה תגמור
át tigmerí	את תגמרי
hú yigmór	הוא יגמור
hí tigmór	היא תגמור
ánu nigmór	אנו נגמור
atém tigmerú	אתם תגמרו
atén tigmórna	אתן תגמורנה
hém yigmerú	הם יגמרו
hén tigmórna	הן תגמורנה

D. Substitution - Agreement Drill

I'll finish the book by tomorrow.

<u>egmór et haséfer ád maxár.</u>   . אגמור את הספר עד מחר

    atém - már kóhen - ánu - hí   היא – אנו – מר כהן – אתם
    atén - hém - át - hén   הן – את – הם – אתן
    ištexá - atá - baaléx - aní   אני – בעלך – אתה – אשתך

E. Substitution Drill - /e- ~ ti-/

I'll find the place without difficulty.

    emcá et hamakóm leló kóši.   . אמצא את המקום ללא קושי
    timcá   תמצא
    timceí   תמצאי
    hú yimcá   הוא ימצא
    hí timcá   היא תמצא
    nimcá   נמצא
    timceú   תמצאו
    timcána   תמצאנה
    hém yimceú   הם ימצאו
    hén timcána   הן תמצאנה

F. Substitution-Agreement Drill

You'll find Moshe in the office.

<u>timcá et mošé bamisrád.</u>   . תמצא את משה במשרד

    át - hém - atém - hú   הוא – אתם – הם – את
    aní - ánu - atén - hén   הן – אתן – אנו – אני
    hí - át - atém - atá   אתה – אתם – את – היא

G. Substitution Drill - /e- ~ ti-/

I'll go to the Brooklyn Bar to have ice cream.

    egáš lebrúklin bár leexól glidá.   . אגש לברוקלין בר לאכול גלידה
    tigáš   תיגש
    tigší   תיגשי
    davíd yigáš   דוד יגש
    atára tigáš   עטרה תיגש
    nigáš   ניגש
    tigšú   תגשו
    tigášna   תגשנה
    hém yigšú   הם יגשו
    hanaším tigášna   הנשים תגשנה

H.   Substitution Agreement Drill

We'll go see Mr. Williams.

<u>niqáš lir'ót et már Williams.</u>   <u>.ניגש לראות את מר וויליאמס</u>

   aní - át - atén - mošé   אני - את - אתן - משה
   baaléx - ištó - atá - hén   בעלך - אשתו - אתה - הן
   atém ~ dóv veištó - ánu   אתם - דוב ואשתו - אנו

I.   Substitution Drill - /e- ~ ti-/

I'll be very happy to see them.

   esmáx meód lir'ót otám.   .אשמח מאד לראות אותם
   tismáx   תשמח
   tismexí   תשמחי
   hú yismáx   הוא ישמח
   hí tismáx   היא תשמח
   nismáx   נשמח
   tismexú   תשמחו
   tismáxna   תשמחנה
   hém yismexú   הם ישמחו
   hén tismáxna   הן תשמחנה

J.   Substitution - Agreement Drill

She'll be happy to live there.

<u>hí tismáx laqúr šám.</u>   <u>.היא תשמח לגור שם</u>

   atá - ánu - hayoéc haxadáš   אתה - אנו - היועץ החדש
   atém - hú veištó - atén - át   אתם - הוא ואשתו - אתן - את
   aní - hamišpaxá - hén - hí   אני - המשפחה - הן - היא

K.   Substitution Drill - /e- ~ ti-/

I'll turn at this corner.

   aní efné bapiná hazót.   .אני אפנה בפינה הזאת
   atá tifné   אתה תפנה
   át tifní   את תפני
   hú yifné   הוא יפנה
   hí tifné   היא תפנה
   ánu nifné   אנו נפנה
   atém tifnú   אם, תפנו
   atén tifnéna   אתן תפנינה
   hém yifnú   הם יפנו
   hén tifnéna   הן תפנינה

L. Substitution - Agreement Drill

We'll address Mr. Cohen in Hebrew.

<u>nifné lemár kóhen beivrít.</u>   <u>נפנה למר כהן בעברית.</u>

  hú - aní - atén - gvéret kármi   הוא - אני - אתן - גברת כרמי
  atém - hém - hén - atá   אתם - הם - הן - אתה
  már Williams - át - ánu   מר וויל= אמס - את - אנו

M. Substitution Drill - /e- ~ ti-/

I'll open the door.

  eftáx et hadélet.   אפתח את הדלת.
  tiftáx   תפתח
  tiftexí   תפתחי
  dóv yiftáx   דוב יפתח
  xána tiftáx   חנה תפתח
  niftáx   נפתח
  atém tiftexú   אתם תפתחו
  atén tiftáxna   אתן תפתחנה
  hém yiftexú   הם יפתחו
  hén tiftáxna   הן תפתחנה

N. Substitution - Agreement Drill

Mr. Zahavi will open the office this morning.

<u>már zahávi yiftáx et hamisrád habóker.</u> מר זהבי יפתח את המשרד הבוקר.

  aní - miryám vedóv - gvéret kóhen.   אני - מרים ודוב - גברת כהן
  atém - sára veléa - atén - ánu   אתם - שרה ולאה - אתן - אנו
  át - atá - már zahávi   את - אתה - מר זהבי

O. Substitution Drill - /e- ~ ti-/

I'll close the door.

  aní esgór et hadélet.   אני אסגור את הדלת.
  atá tisgór   אתה תסגור
  át tisgerí   את תסגרי
  dóv yisgór   דוב יסגור
  léa tisgór   לאה תסגור
  ánu nisgór   אנו נסגור
  atém tisgerú   אתם תסגרו
  atén tisgórna   אתן תסגורנה
  hém yisgerú   הם יסגרו
  hén tisgórna   הן תסגורנה

P. Substitution - Agreement Drill

I'll close the office this evening.

<u>aní esgór et hamisrád haérev.</u>   אני אסגור את המשרד הערב.

  david - atá - atára - át   דוד - אתה - עטרה - את
  atém - mošé veaní - hén   אתם - משה ואני - הן
  hém - atén - aní   הם - אתן - אני

Q. Substitution Drill - /ee- ˜ taa-/

I'll pass the embassy.

eevór et hašagrirút.	אעבור את השגרירות.
taavór	תעבור
taavrí	תעברי
hú yaavór	הוא יעבור
hí taavór	היא תעבור
naavór	נעבור
taavrú	תעברו
taavórna	תעבורנה
hém yaavrú	הם יעברו
hén taavórna	הן תעבורנה

R. Substitution - Agreement Drill

We'll go past their house.

<u>naavór al yád habáit šelahém.</u>   <u>נעבור על יד הבית שלהם.</u>

mošé - sára - atá veištexá - aní	משה - שרה - אתה ואשתך - אני
atén - át - hí veiští - hí vebaalá	אתן - את - היא ואשתי - היא ובעלה
atá - ánu	אתה - אנו

S. Substitution Drill - /a- ˜ te-/

I'll speak Hebrew, too.

gám aní adabér ivrít.	גם אני אדבר עברית.
atá tedabér	אתה תדבר
át tedabrí	את תדברי
hú yedabér	הוא ידבר
hi tedabér	היא תדבר
ánu nedabér	אנו נדבר
atém tedabrú	אתם תדברו
atén tedabérna	אתן תדברנה
hém yedabrú	הם ידברו
hén tedabérna	הן תדברנה

T. Substitution - Agreement Drill

I think you'll speak Hebrew on the phone.

<u>aní xošév šeatá tedabér ivrít batélefon.</u>   אני חושב שאתה תדבר עברית בטלפון.

šehém - šehayoéc haxadáš - šeaní	שהם - שהיועץ החדש - שאני
šehí - šeatém - šehén - šeánu	שהיא - שאתם - שהן - שאנו
šeát vemiryám - šeát - šeatá	שאת ומרים - שאת - שאתה

U. Substitution Drill

I'll go to the Eden Theater this evening.

eléx lekolnóa éden haérev.	אלך לקולנוע עדן הערב.
teléx	תלך
telxí	תלכי
mošé yeléx	משה ילך
sára teléx	שרה תלך
ánu neléx	אנו נלך
telxú	תלכו
teléxna	תלכנה
kulám yelxú	כולם ילכו
hén teléxna	הן תלכנה

V. Substitution - Agreement Drill

I'll go as far as the hotel and no further.

<u>eléx ád lamalón veló yotér.</u>	<u>אלך עד למלון ולא יותר.</u>
ánu - hú - hí - atá	אנו - הוא - היא - אתה
át - atém - hém - hén	את - אתם - הם - הן
atén - aní	אתן - אני

W. Substitution Drill

I'll sit in the office until 5:00.

ešév bamisrád ád xaméš.	אשב במשרד עד חמש.
tešév	תשב
tešví	תשבי
hú yešév	הוא ישב
sára tešév	שרה תשב
nešév	נשב
tešvú	תשבו
tešévna	תשבנה
hém yešvú	הם ישבו
hén tešévna	הן תשבנה

X. Substitution - Agreement Drill

We'll sit here until he arrives.

<u>nešév kán ád šehú yagía.</u>	<u>נשב כאן עד שהוא יגיע.</u>
aní - atá - át - ištó	אני - אתה - את - אשתו
kulám - hén - ánu - atén	כולם - הן - אנו - אתן
avígdor - atém - ánu	אביגדור - אתם - אנו

Y.   Substitution Drill

What shall I say to Moshe?

má omár lemošé.	מה אומר למשה?
tomár	תאמר
tomrí	תאמרי
hú yomár	הוא יאמר
hí tomár	היא תאמר
nomár	נאמר
tomrú	תאמרו
tomárna	תאמרנה
hém yomrú	הם יאמרו
hén tomárna	הן תאמרנה

Z.   Substitution - Agreement Drill

She won't tell Moshe anything.

<u>hí 16 tomár klúm lemošé.</u>   <u>היא לא תאמר כלום למשה.</u>

aní - xána - ánu - atá	אני - חנה - אנו - אתה
baaléx - atém - hém - aní	בעלך - אתם - הם - אני
atén - davíd - hén - hi	אתן - דוד - הן - היא

AA.   Substitution Drill

I'll start eating before 6:00.

	atxíl leexól lifnéy šéš.		אתחיל לאכול לפני שש.
	tatxíl		תתחיל.
	tatxíli		תתחילי
moše	yatxíl	משה	יתחיל
xána	tatxíl	חנה	תתחיל.
	natxíl		נתחיל
	tatxílu		תתחילו
atén	tatxélna	אתן	תתחלנה.
hú veištó yatxilu		הוא ואשתו יתחילו	
hén	tatxélna	הן	תתחלנה

BB.   Substitution - Agreement Drill

I'll start strolling after lunch.

<u>atxíl letayél axaréy aruxát hacohoráim.</u>   אתחיל לטייל אחרי ארוחת הצהריים.

ánu - atá - kulám - davíd	אנו - אתה - כולם - דוד
gvéret alón - át - atén - hén	גברת אלון - את - אתן - הן
atém - iští veaní - sára - aní	אתם - אשתי ואני - שרה - אני

120

CC. Substitution Drill

I'll arrive in Haifa on Tuesday.

agía lexáyfa beyóm šliší.	אגיע לחיפה ביום שלישי.
tagía	תגיע
tagíi	תגיעי
már Williams yagía	מר ווילאמס יגיע
ištó tagía	אשתו תגיע
nagía	נגיע
tagíu	תגיעו
atén tagána	אתן תגענה
hém yagíu	הם יגיעו
hén tagána	הן תגענה

DD. Substitution - Agreement Drill

I'll arrive in Tel Aviv tomorrow.

<u>agía maxár letél avív.</u>   <u>אגיע מחר לתל אביב.</u>

már kóhen - atá - hamišpaxá	מר כהן - אתה - המשפחה
át - át vebaaléx - hú veaní	את - את ובעלך - הוא ואני
hém - gverét zahávi - atén - hén - aní	הם - גברת זהבי - אתן - הן - אני

EE. Substitution Drill

I'll continue straight on this street.

amšíx yašár barexóv hazé.	אמשיך ישר ברחוב הזה.
tamšíx	תמשיך
tamšíxi	תמשיכי
hú yamšíx	הוא ימשיך
hí tamšíx	היא תמשיך
namšíx	נמשיך
tamšíxu	תמשיכו
tamšéxna	תמשכנה
hém yamšíxu	הם ימשיכו
hén tamšéxna	הן תמשכנה

FF. Substitution - Agreement Drill

We'll keep going towards the harbor.

<u>namšíx laléxet lekivún hanamál.</u>   <u>נמשיך ללכת לכיוון הנמל.</u>

aní - át - hén - hú	אני - את - הן - הוא
hém - atá - hí - atém	הם - אתה - היא - אתם
atén - ánu	אתן - אנו

REVIEW CONVERSATIONS

A: haóxel hayá taím meód.   א: האוכל היה טעים מאוד.

B: todá rabá. 16 axált klúm.   כ: תודה רבה. לא אכלת כלום.

A: aní bediéta.   א: אני בדיאטה.

B: zé davár axér.   כ: זה דבר אחר.

C: zú masóret eclénu leexól   ג: זו מסורת אצלנו לאכול
     belél šiší dagím memulaím.   בליל שישי דגים ממולאים.

D: hadagím teimím meód.   ד: הדגים טעימים מאוד.

C: át rocá et hamiršám?   ג: את רוצה את המירשם?

D: kén. tní li bevakašá et hamiršám.   ר: כן. תני לי נבקשה את המירשם.

C: beracón.   ג: ברצון.

E: bevakašá. ál titní lánu yotér óxel.   ה: בבקשה. אל תתני לנו יותר אוכל.

F: láma? atém bediéta?   ר: למה? אתם בדיאטה?

E: kén.   ה: כן.

F: tatxílu badiéta maxár.   ו: תתחילו בדיאטה מחר.

G: atém rocím glidá?   ז: אתם רוצים גלידה?

H: 16 todá. ánu rocím yáin.   ח: לא תודה. אנו רוצים יין.

G: mošé. mezóg bevakašá yáin.   ז: משה. מזוג בבקשה יין.

H: mizgí át, miryám. hayáin al yadéx.   ח: מזגי את, מרים. היין על ידך.

I: dóv rocé lehazmín et már alón   ט: דוב רוצה להזמין את מר אלון
     learuxát érev. matáy hú yagía.   לארוחת ערב. מתי הוא יגיע?

J: hú yagía haérev.   י: הוא יגיע הערב.

I: gám gvéret alón tagía?   ט: גם גברת אלון תגיע?

J: ken. aní xošév káx.   י: כן. אני חושב כך.

K: háva nigáš lir'ót et miryám.   .כ: הבה ניגש לראות את מרים

L: yéš láx et haktóvet šelá?   ?ל: יש לך את הכתובת שלה

K: ló. tén lí et mispár hatélefon šelá.   .כ: לא. תן לי את מספר הטלפון שלה

L: éyn lí et mispár hatélefon.   .ל: אין לי את מספר הטלפון

K: aní xošévet šeemcá et hamakóm.   .כ: אני חושבת שאמצא את המקום

M: xána. matáy telxí letayél.   ?מ: חנה, מתי תלכי לטייל

N: axaréy šeegmór et haaruxá.   .נ: אחרי שאגמור את הארוחה

M: aní xošév šegám aní eléx.   .מ: אני חושב שגם אני אלך

N: tóv. neléx yáxad.   .נ: טוב. נלך יחד

O: miryám tigáš lir'ót et mošé haérev.   .ס: מרים תיגש לראות את משה הערב

P: beemét? mošé yismáx meód lir'ót otá.   .ע: באמת? משה ישמח מאוד לראות אותה

O: hém yismexú meód lehitraót.   .ס: הם ישמחו מאוד להתראות

Q: zú masóret eclénu leexól xalót belél šiší.   .פ: זו מסורת אצלנו לאכול חלות בליל שישי

R: zú masóret yafá meód. haxalót teimót.   .צ: זו מסורת יפה מאד. החלות טעימות

Q: todá rabá. atá rocé dagím?   ?פ: תודה רבה. אתה רוצה דגים

R: kén. éyx aní yaxól lesarév.   ?צ: כן. איך אני יכול לסרב

Q: amárta šeatá bediéta.   .פ: אמרת שאתה בדיאטה

R: adáin ló. atxíl maxár.   .צ: עדיין לא. אתחיל מחר

לא, תודה. זה הכל...

14.1 <u>At the Grocery Store</u> /bexanút makólet/   .נַחֲנוּת מכולת

STOREKEEPER /xenvaní/

Good morning, Mrs. Zahavi.	bóker tóv, gvéret zahávi.	בוקר טוב, גברת זהבי,
What can I	má aní yaxól	מה אני יכול
do for you?	laasót bišviléx.	לעשות בשבילך?
to do	laasót	לעשות
for	bišvíl	בשביל

MRS. ZAHAVI

Please give me	tén li bevakašá,	תן לי בבקשה,
200 grams	matáim grám	מאתיים גרם
of cheese.	gviná.	גבינה.
two hundred	matáim	מאתיים
gram	grám (m)	גרם
cheese	gviná (f)	גבינה

STOREKEEPER

Yellow cheese or	gviná cehubá, ó	גבינה צהובה או
white cheese?	gviná levaná.	גבינה לבנה?
yellow	cahóv (m.s.)	צהוב
white	laván (m.s.)	לבן

MRS. ZAHAVI

Yellow cheese.	gviná cehubá.	גבינה צהובה.
Are the eggs fresh?	habeycím triót?	הביצים טריות?
egg	beycá (f)	ביצה
fresh	tarí (m.s.)	טרי

STOREKEEPER

Yes.	kén.	כן.
I received them	kibálti otán	קבלתי אותן
this morning.	habóker.	הבוקר.
I received	kibálti	קבלתי

MRS. ZAHAVI

Then give me	áz tén li	אז תן לי
a dozen.	treysár.	תריסר.
dozen	treysár (m)	תריסר

STOREKEEPER

Do you need	át crixá	את צריכה
any vegetables?	yerakót?	ירקות?
Fruits?	peyrót?	פירות?
need, must, have to	caríx (m.s.)	צריך
vegetable	yérek (m)	ירק
fruit	prí (m)	פרי

MRS. ZAHAVĪ

No, thank you.	ló, todá.	לא, תודה.
That's all.	zé hakól.	זה הכל.
How much do I	káma aní	כמה אני
owe you?	xayévet lexá.	חייבת לך?
	everything	hakól	הכל
	how much, how many	káma	כמה
	owe	xayáv (m.s.)	חייב

STOREKEEPER

That will cost you	zé yaalé láx	זה יעלה לך
eighty-three	šmoním vešalóš	שמונים ושלוש
agorot.	agorót.	אגורות.
	will cost, go up	yaalé (3 m.s.)	יעלה
	eighty	šmoním	שמונים
	agora (1/100 lira)	agorá (f)	אגורה

MRS. ZAHAVI

Give me	tén li	תן לי
change from a lira.	ódef milíra.	עורף מלירה.
	surplus	ódef (m)	עורף
	Israeli pound	líra (f)	לירה

14.2 ADDITIONAL VOCABULARY

The vegetables are	hayerakót		הירקות
cheap today.	zolím hayóm.		זולים היום.
	cheap	zól (m.s.)	זול
The vegetables are	hayerakót		הירקות
expensive today.	yekarím hayóm.		יקרים היום.
	expensive, dear	yakár (m.s.)	יקר

[The names of vegetables and fruits in the following list are given in the singular or plural depending on how one asks for them in the question /bekáma.../ "How much is/are..."]

How much are the beans?	bekáma hašuít.	בכמה השעועית?

	beans	šeuít (f)	שעועית
	beet	sélek (m)	סלק
	cabbage	krúv (m)	כרוב
	carrot	gézer (m)	גזר
	cauliflower	kruvít (f)	כרובית
	corn	tíras (m)	תירס
	cucumbers	melafefoním (m.pl.)	מלפפונים
	dill	šamír (m)	שמיר
	eggplants	xacilím (m.pl.)	חצילים
	garlic	šúm (m)	שום
	kohlrabi	kolerábi (m)	קולרבי
	lettuce	xása (f)	חסה
	olives	zeytím (m.pl.)	זיתים
	onion	bacál (m)	בצל
	parsley	petruzília (f)	פטרוזיליה
	peas	afuná (f)	אפונה
	potatoes	tapuxéy adamá (m.pl.)	תפוחי אדמה

radishes	cnoniót (f.pl.)	צנוניות
scallion	bacál yarók (m)	בצל ירוק
spinach	téred (m)	תרד
squash	kišuím (m.pl.)	קשואים
tomatoes	agvaniót (f.pl.)	עגבניות
turnip	cnón (m)	צנון

I want	aní rocá		אני רוצה
to buy fruit.	liknót peyrót.		לקנות פירות.
to buy	liknót	לקנות	

How much are the apples?	bekáma hatapuxím.		בכמה התפוחים?
apple	tapúax (m)	תפוח	

bananas	banánot (f.pl.)	בננות
canteloupe	milón (m)	מילון
cherries	duvdevaním (m.pl.)	דובדבנים
dates	tmarím (m.pl.)	תמרים
figs	teením (f.pl.)	תאנים
fig	teená (f)	תאנה
grapefruits	eškoliót (f.pl.)	אשכוליות
grapes	anavím (m.pl.)	ענבים
lemons	limoním (m.pl.)	לימונים
oranges	tapuzím (m.pl.)	תפוזים
peaches	afarsekím (m.pl.)	אפרסקים
pears	agasím (m.pl.)	אגסים
plums	šezifím (m.pl.)	שזיפים
pomegranates	rimoním (m.pl.)	רימונים
watermelons	avatixím (m.pl.)	אבטיחים
watermelon	avatíax (m)	אבטיח

Give me two kilos	tén lí šnéy kílo		תן לי שני קילו
of flour.	kémax.		קמח.
flour	kémax (m)	קמח	
salt	mélax (m)	מלח	
sugar	sukár (m)	סוכר	

How much is	káma olé		כמה עולה
a bottle of milk?	bakbúk xaláv.		בקבוק חלב?
cost	olé (m.s.pres.)	עולה	
bottle	bakbúk (m)	בקבוק	
milk	xaláv (m)	חלב	
oil	šémen (m)		שמן
orange juice	míc tapuzím		מיץ תפוזים
juice	míc (m)		מיץ

How much is	káma olá		כמה עולה
a can of sardines?	kufsát sardínim.		קופסת סרדינים?
can, box	kufsá (f)	קופסה	
cans, boxes	kufsaót (f.pl.)	קופסאות	

How much is	káma olá		כמה עולה
a package of butter?	xavilát xem'á.		חבילת חמאה?
package	xavilá (f)	חבילה	
butter	xem'á (f)	חמאה	

How much is	káma olá	כמה עולה
a jar of sour cream?	cincénet šaménet.	צנצנת שמנת?
jar	cincénet (f) צנצנת	
sour cream	šaménet (f) שמנת	
jelly	ribá (f)	ריבה
mustard	xardál (m)	חרדל

Give me half a	tén lí xací	תן לי חצי
kilo of grapes.	kílo anavím.	קילו ענבים.
half	xéci (m) חצי	
half of	xací (construct) חצי	

14.3 Vocabulary Drills

A. Transformation Drill - /bišvíl/ "for"

> Instructor: I want ice cream.
> Student: I'll have ice cream. (lit. For me ice cream.)

aní rocé glida.	bišvili glidá.	בשבילי גלידה.	אני רוצה גלידה.
atá rocé yáin.	bišvilxá yáin.	בשבילך יין.	אתה רוצה יין.
át rocá xaláv.	bišviléx xaláv.	בשבילך חלב.	את רוצה חלב.
hú rocé míc.	bišviló míc.	בשבילו מיץ.	הוא רוצה מיץ.
hí rocá ribá.	bišvilá ribá.	בשבילה ריבה.	היא רוצה ריבה.
ánu rocím tapuzím.	bišvilénu tapuzím.	בשבילנו תפוזים.	אנו רוצים תפוזים.
atém rocím dagím.	bišvilxém dagím.	בשבילכם דגים.	אתם רוצים דגים.
atén rocót gviná.	bišvilxén gviná.	בשבילכן גבינה.	אתן רוצות גבינה.
hém rocím šaménet.	bišvilám šaménet.	בשבילם שמנת.	הם רוצים שמנת.
hén rocót kémax.	bišvilán kémax.	בשבילן קמח.	הן רוצות קמח.

B. Substitution - Agreement Drill /tarí/ "fresh"

Is the milk fresh?

haím haxaláv tarí?   ?האם החלב טרי

haagvaniót - haagvaniá - hasélek	העגבניות - העגבניה - הסלק
hapeyrót - hayerakót - haxása	הפירות - הירקות - החסה
hateením - habevcím - haxaláv	התאנים - הביצים - החלב

C. Substitution - Agreement Drill - /caríx/ "have to, need"

I have to buy chalahs for the Sabbath.

aní caríx liknót xalót lešabát.   .אני צריך לקנות חלות לשבת

| iští - hén - baalá - hí | אשתי - הן - בעלה - היא |
| ánu - hú - atém - aní | אנו - הוא - אתם - אני |

D. Substitution - Agreement Drill - /kibálti/ "I received"

    I received a bottle of wine from Dov.

    <u>kibálti bakbúk yáin midóv.</u>   .קבלתי בקבוק יין מדוב

    atém - át - ánu   אתם - את - אנו
    atá - atén - aní   אתה - אתן - אני

E. Substitution Drill - /ee- ~ taa-/ Endings are similar to /tifné/.

    I'll go up to the Embassy this morning.

    eelé lašagrirút habóker.   .אעלה לשגרירות הבוקר
    taalé   תעלה
    taalí   תעלי
    hú yaalé   הוא יעלה
    hi taalé   היא תעלה
    naalé   נעלה
    atém taalú   אתם תעלו
    atén taaléna   אתן תעלינה
    hém yaalú   הם יעלו
    hén taaléna   הן תעלינה

F. Substitution - Agreement Drill

    Let's go up to Miriam's this evening.

    <u>háva naalé lemiryám haérev.</u>   .הבה נעלה למרים הערב

    át - dóv veištó - atá veištexá   את - דוב ואשתו - אתה ואשתך
    aní - atá - xána - atén   אני - אתה - חנה - אתן
    avígdor - hén - háva   אביגדור - הן - הבה

14.4 <u>Cardinal Numbers, 20 - 1000</u>

    Numbers which are multiples of 10 do not show gender distinction.

20	esrím	עשרים
30	šloším	שלושים
40	arbaím	ארבעים
50	xamiším	חמישים
60	šiším	שישים
70	šiv'ím	שבעים
80	šmoním	שמונים
90	tiš'ím	תשעים

    The numbers 'one' to 'nine' follow the multiples of ten and are preceded
by /ve-/. These numbers show gender distinction.

    /šmoním vešalóš agorót/   "83 agorot"   שמונים ושלוש אגורות
    /esrím vexamišá sfarím/   "25 books"   עשרים וחמשה ספרים

    The form /meá/ "hundred" and its multiples are also used before both
masculine and feminine nouns.

100	meá	מאה
200	matáim	מאתיים

129

300	šlóš meót	שלוש מאות
400	arbá meót	ארבע מאות
500	xaméš meót	חמש מאות
600	šéš meót	שש מאות
700	švá meót	שבע מאות
800	šmóne meót	שמונה מאות
900	tšá meót	תשע מאות
1000	élef	אלף

Numbers are given with the highest digit first, as in English.

    1965   /élef tšámeot šiším vexaméš/

A. Read off the following numbers. Do not read the individual numerals.

1.	82	13.	217	
2.	73	14.	458	
3.	64	15.	336	
4.	55	16.	789	
5.	46	17.	265	
6.	37	18.	924	
7.	28	19.	593	
8.	19	20.	847	
9.	90	21.	670	
10.	101	22.	1040	

B. The instructor asks each student for the year of his/her birth.

In which year were you born?	beéyze šaná noládeta.	באיזה שנה נולדת?
you were born	noládeta	נולדת

I was born in (the year) 1948.	noládeti bišnát élef tšá meót arbaím vešmóne.	נולדתי בשנת אלף תשע מאות ארבעים ושמונה.

C. Conversational Response Drill

    Instructor: How much are beets?
    Student: 30 <u>agorot</u> a kilo.
    Instructor: Give me one and a half kilos.
    Student: That will be 45 agorot.

    Instructor: bekáma hasélek.   המורה: בכמה הסלק?
    Student: šloším agorót hakílo.   תלמיד: שלושים אגורות הקילו.
    Instructor: tén lí kílo vaxéci.   המורה: תן לי קילו וחצי.
    Student: zé yaalé lexá arbaím vexaméš agorót. תלמיד: זה יעלה לך ארבעים וחמש אגורות.

    The instructor and students may substitute other items, prices, and
quantities.

14.5 Colors   /cvaím/   צבעים

What is the color	má hacéva	מה הצבע
of the table?	šél hašulxán.	של השולחן?
color	céva (m)	צבע

The table is black.	hašulxán šaxór.	השולחן שחור.
The box is black.	hakufsá šxorá.	הקופסה שחורה.

The apple is red.	hatapúax adóm.	התפוח אדום.
The cherries are red.	haduvdevaním adumím.	הדובדבנים אדומים.

The carrot is orange.	hagézer katóm.	הגזר כתום.
The package is orange.	haxavilá ktumá.	החבילה כתומה.

The corn is yellow.	hatíras cahóv.	התירס צהוב.
The bananas are yellow.	habanánot cehubót.	הבננות צהובות.

The pear is green.	haagás yarók.	האגס ירוק.
The olives are green.	hazeytím yerukím.	הזיתים ירוקים.

The book is blue.	haséfer kaxól.	הספר כחול.
The sky is blue.	hašamáim kxulím.	השמים כחולים.
sky, heaven	šamáim (m.pl.)	שמים

The eggplant is purple.	haxacíl segól.	החציל סגול.
The grapes are purple.	haanavím sgulím.	הענבים סגולים.

The date is brown.	hatamár xúm.	התמר חום.
The figs are brown.	hateením xumót.	התאנים חומות.

GRAMMAR NOTES

14.6 /o ~ u/ Alternation in Related Forms

    Examine the following set of related forms:

m.s.	/yarók/	"green"	ירוק
f.s.	/yeruká/		ירוקה
m.pl.	/yerukím/		ירוקים
f.pl.	/yerukót/		ירוקות

    This pattern is similar to the pattern of /raxók ~ rexoká/ except that in the suffixed forms the vowel /u/ occurs instead of /o/. This alternation occurs in a limited but fairly frequently used set of forms. The student will have to memorize them since there are sets of related forms which have /o/ when suffixed, as /rexoká, gdolá/, and sets which have /u/ whether suffixed or not, as /xúm, xumá/ "brown".

    Now compare the following pair of forms.

m.s.	/cahóv/	"yellow"	צהוב
f.s.	/cehubá/		צהובה

    Forms which have this /o ~ u/ alternation will also have the /v ~ b/ alternation, with the /b/ occurring before the suffixes.

    Similarly, the alternation /f ~ p/ occurs in such forms, with /p/ occurring before the suffixes.

    The alternation /x ~ k/ may occur in related forms with the /o ~ u/ alternation, with /k/ occurring in the suffixed forms.

m.s.	/aróx/	"long"	ארוך
f.s.	/aruká/		ארוכה

    However, some forms have /k/ throughout, as /yarók/ "green". These latter forms are spelled with ק, while those which alternate /x ~ k/ are spelled with כ ~ ך.

A. Substitution - Agreement Drill

    The apples are red.

<u>hatapuxím adumím.</u>

    התפוחים אדומים.

haxavilót - hakufsá - haséfer	החבילות – הקופסה – הספר
habatím - hayáin - hacincénet	הבתים – היין – הצנצנת
hatapuxím	התפוחים

B. Progressive Substitution Drill

In this drill the instructor gives a substitution first from one column and then from the other.

The wine is red.

hayáin adóm.	היין אדום.
haagvaniá	העגבניה
yeruká	ירוקה
hatapúax	התפוח
cahóv	צהוב
habanánot	הבננות
xumót	חומות
haséfer	הספר
katóm	כתום
habakbukím	הבקבוקים
levaním	לבנים
habinyán	הבנין
adóm	אדום
hayáin	היין

C. Progressive Substitution Drill

The sky is blue.

hašamáim kxulím.	השמים כחולים.
hašezíf	השזיף
segól	סגול
haxacilím	החצילים
gdolím	גדולים
hacincénet	הצנצנת
xumá	חומה
habakbúk	הבקבוק
yarók	ירוק
hazáit	הזית
šaxór	שחור
hakufsaót	הקופסאות
kxulót	כחולות
hašamáim	השמים

14.7 Review of Negative Sentences

a. /ló/ precedes past, present, and future verb forms.

axálti et haglída.   "I ate the ice cream."
ló axálti et haglída. "I didn't eat the ice cream."

hí rocá liknót perót. "She wants to buy fruit."
hí ló rocá liknót   "She doesn't want to buy fruit."
  perót.

hú yagía maxár.   "He'll arrive tomorrow."
hú ló yagía maxár.   "He won't arrive tomorrow."

This corresponds to the negative, usually with -n't, of the verb auxiliary in English.

133

b.   /ló/ occurs between the main elements of an equational sentence.

hú amerikái.	"He's an American."	הוא אמריקאי.
hú ló amerikái.	"He's not an American."	הוא לא אמריקאי.

c.   /éyn/, usually with a pronoun suffix, may negate a present tense verb form or an equational sentence. The use of /éyn/ instead of /ló/ in these cases is more formal in style.

aní medabér ivrít.	"I speak Hebrew."	אני מדבר עברית.
eynéni medabér ivrít.	"I don't speak Hebrew."	אינני מדבר עברית.
aní xadáš baárec.	"I'm new in the country."	אני חדש בארץ.
eynéni xadáš baárec.	"I'm not new in the country."	אינני חדש בארץ.

Comparison of style:

aní ló yodéa.	(casual, informal)	אני לא יודע.
eynéni yodéa.	(less casual, formal)	אינני יודע.

The suffixed, or contracted forms of /éyn/ + the pronouns are:

éyn aní	eynéni	איני	אין אני
éyn atá	eynxá	אינך	אין אתה
éyn át	eynéx	אינך	אין את
éyn hú	eynénu, eynó	איננו, אינו	אין הוא
éyn hí	eynéna, eyná	איננה, אינה	אין היא
éyn ánu	eynénu	איננו	אין אנו
éyn atém	eynxém	אינכם	אין אתם
éyn atén	eynxén	אינכן	אין אתן
éyn hém	eynám	אינם	אין הם
éyn hén	eynán	אינן	אין הן

/éyn ánu/ is usually not contracted. The other sequences may be used in the uncontracted form, but this generally results in a very formal or stiff expression.

eynéni yodéa.	(less casual, formal)	אינני יודע.
éyn aní yodéa.	(formal, stiff)	אין אני יודע.

d.   /éyn/ is the negative of /yéš/ "there is."

yéš li gviná levaná.	"I have white cheese."	יש לי גבינה לבנה.
éyn li gviná levaná.	"I don't have white cheese."	אין לי גבינה לבנה.

e.   /ál/ negates the imperative.

tifné smóla.	"Turn left."	תפנה שמאלה.
ál tifné smóla.	"Don't turn left."	אל תפנה שמאלה.

A.   Transformation Drill - Affirmative to Negative

Instructor: I was very impressed by the house.
Student: I wasn't very impressed by the house.

1.   (16) hitrašámti meód mehabáit.   .1 (לא) הת שמחי מאוד מהבית.
2.   (16) axáltem et haxalá.   .2 (לא) אכלתם את החלה.
3.   (16) yaxólti lehagía bešéva.   .3 (לא) יכולתי להגיע בשבע.
4.   (16) kibálti et hapeyrót.   .4 (לא) קבלתי את הפירות.
5.   (16) natáta lí hizdamnút ledabér.   .5 (לא) נתח לי הזדמנות לדבר.
6.   (16) šamáti et hakól.   .6 (לא) שמעתי את הקול.
7.   atá (16) raíta et hamisrád šelánu.   .7 אתה (לא) ראית את המשרד שלנו.
8.   hadagím (16) hayú teimím.   .8 הדגים (לא) היו טעימים.

B.   Transformation Drill - Negative to Affirmative

Repeat Drill A in reverse.

C.   Transformation Drill - Affirmative to Negative

Instructor: I know where the Brooklyn Bar is.
Student: I don't know where the Brooklyn Bar is.

1.   aní (16) yodéa éyfo   brúklin bar.   .1 אני (לא) יורע איפה ברוקלין בר.
2.   gvéret zahávi (16) gára betél avív.   .2 גברח זהבי (לא) גרה כתל אביב.
3.   hén (16) medabrót ivrít.   .3 הן (לא) מדברות עבריו.
4.   hí (16) mexiná dagím memulaím.   .4 היא (לא) מכינה דגים ממולאים.
5.   haím haárec (16) mócet xén beeynéxa?   .5 האם הארץ (לא) מרצאת חן בעיניך?
6.   hú (16) rocé lehagía ladóar hamerkazí.   .6 הוא (לא) רוצה להגיע לדואר המרכזי.
7.   ánu (16) medabrím ivrít.   .7 אנו (לא) מדברים עברית.
8.   aní (16) caríx et hašulxán.   .8 אני (לא) צריך את השולחן.

D.   Transformation Drill - Negative to Affirmative

Repeat Drill D in reverse.

E.   Transformation Drill - Affirmative to Negative

Instructor: We'll go to the movies tonight.
Student: We won't go to the movies tonight.

1.   (16) neléx lakolnóa haérev.   .1 (לא) נלך לקולנוע הערב.
2.   (16) nigáš lexána hayóm.   .2 (לא) ניגש לחנה היום.
3.   hú (16) yaavór al yád habáit šelánu.   .3 הוא (לא) יעבור על יד הבית שלנו.
4.   hém (16) yisgerú et haxanút bešéš.   .4 הם (לא) יסגרו את החנות בשש.
5.   gvéret kármi (16) tiftáx et hamisrád.   .5 גברת כרמי (לא) חפתח את המשרד.
6.   sára vexána (16) tagána maxár.   .6 שרה וחנה (לא) חגענה מחר.
7.   ánu (16) natxíl leexól lifnéy šéš.   .7 אנו (לא) נחחיל לאכול לפני שש.
8.   (16) emcá otó bemisradó.   .8 (לא) אמצא אותו במשרדו.

F.   Transformation Drill - Negative to Affirmative

Repeat Drill E in reverse.

G.   Transformation Drill - Affirmative to Negative.

        Instructor: They're new in the country.
        Student: They're not new in the country.

1.   hém (16) xadaším baárec.   הם (לא) חדשים בארץ. .1
2.   iští (16) amerikáit.   אשתי (לא) אמריקאית. .2
3.   habáit šelahém (16) yafé.   הבית שלהם (לא) יפה. .3
4.   haglidá šehí mexiná (16) tová.   הגלידה שהיא מכינה (לא) טובה. .4
5.   nemál hateufá (16) raxók mehaír.   נמל התעופה (לא) רחוק מהעיר. .5
6.   haóxel (16) hayá taím.   האוכל (לא) היה טעים. .6

H.   Transformation Drill - Affirmative to Negative

        In this drill the sentences are negated by /éyn/.

1.   aní (eynéni) yodéa et haktóvet šelá.   אני (אינני) יודע את הכתובת שלה. .1
2.   atá (eynxá) gár karóv lašagrirút.   אתה (אינך) גר קרוב לשגרירות. .2
3.   át (eynéx) yodáat ledabér ivrít.   את (אינך) יודעת לדבר עברית. .3
4.   hú (eynénu) rocé lehazmín et miryám.   הוא (איננו) רוצה להזמין את מרים. .4
5.   hí (eynéna) rocá lehazmín otó.   היא (איננה) רוצה להזמין אותו. .5
6.   (éyn) ánu yod'ím éyfo šehém garím.   (אין) אנו יודעים איפה שהם גרים. .6
7.   atém (eynxém) xadaším baárec.   אתם (אינכם) חדשים בארץ. .7
8.   láma atén (eynxén) bediéta.   למה אתן (אינכן) בדיאטה? .8
9.   hém (eynám) xošvím šemeuxár.   הם (אינם) חושבים שמאוחר. .9
10. hén (eynán) crixót liknót dagím.   הן (אינן) צריכות לקנות דגים. .10

I.   Transformation Drill - Negative to Affirmative

        Repeat Drill H in reverse.

                    REVIEW CONVERSATIONS

A: má aní yaxól laasót bišviléx.   א: מה אני יכול לעשות בשבילך?

B: tén li bevakašá, gviná.   ב: תן לי, בבקשה, גבינה.

A: éyze gviná át rocá.   א: איזה גבינה את רוצה?

B: gviná levaná.   ב: גבינה לבנה.

C: habeycím triót?   ג: הביצים טריות?

D: kén, gvirtí. triót meód.   ד: כן, גברתי, טריות מאוד.

C: káma olé treysár?   ג: כמה עולה תריסר?

D: šiším agorót.   ד: שישים אגורות.

C: áz tén li šnéy treysár.   ג: אז תן לי שני תריסר.

                          136

E: át crixá yerakót, gvirtí?   ?ה: את צריכה ירקות, גברתי

F: kén. aní crixá melafefoním.   .ו: כן. אני צריכה מלפפונים

E: hamelafefoním zolím hayóm.   .ה: המלפפונים זולים היום

F: tóv meód. tén li kílo.   .ו: טוב מאוד. תן לי קילו

G: adoní, atá xayáv lí kílo agvaniót.   .ז: אדוני, אתה חייב לי קילו עגבניות

H. natáti láx et haagvaniót etmól.   .ח: נתתי לך את העגבניות אתמול

G: kén. áx hén ló hayú tovót.   .ז: כן. אך הן לא היו טובות

H: zé davár axér. etén láx axerót.   .ח: זה דבר אחר. אתן לך אחרות

I: matáy kibálta et hazeytím.   ?ט: מתי קבלת את הזיתים

J: kibálti otám etmól. át rocá zeytím?   ?י: קבלתי אותם אתמול. את רוצה זיתים

I: hém teimím?   ?ט: הם טעימים

J: kén. teimím meód.   .י: כן. טעימים מאוד

I: áz tén lí arbá meót grám.   .ט: אז תן לי ארבע מאות גרם

K: bekáma hakolerábi.   ?כ: בכמה הקולרבי

L: esrím agorót hakílo.   .ל: עשרים אגורות הקילו

K: zé yakár meód.   .כ: זה יקר מאוד

L: zé ló yakár. zé zól.   .ל: זה לא יקר. זה זול

M: bekáma hasélek.   ?מ: בכמה הסלק

N: xamiším agorót hakílo.   .נ: חמישים אגורות הקילו

M: tén lí šlošá kílo.   .מ: תן לי שלושה קילו

N: zé yaalé láx líra vaxéci.   .נ: זה יעלה לך לירה וחצי

Substitute other foods, prices, etc.

אתם רוצים עוגות?...

15.1 At a Coffee House /bebét kafé/

ATARA

Hello, David.	šalóm davíd.	שלום, דוד.
What's new?	má nišmá.	מה נשמע?
is heard	nišmá (m.s.)	נשמע

DAVID

Let's get	bói lištót	בואי לשתות
a cup of coffee,	kós kafé.	כוס קפה,
and I'll tell you	veasapér láx	ואספר לך
everything.	et hakól.	את הכל.
come	bó (m.s.imv.)	בוא
to drink	lištót	לשתות
drinking glass	kós (f)	כוס
coffee	kafé (m)	קפה
I will tell	asapér (1 s.fut.)	אספר

ATARA

Good idea.	rayón tóv.	רעיון טוב.
Where's the coffee house?	éyfo bét hakafé.	איפה בית הקפה?
idea	rayón (m)	רעיון

DAVID

Here on the corner.	pó bapiná.	פה בפינה.
here	pó	פה

(In the coffee house)

DAVID

Waiter,	melcár -	מלצר,
two	paamáim	פעמיים
coffees, please.	kafé bevakašá.	קפה, בבקשה.
waiter	melcár (m)	מלצר
waitress	melcarít (f)	מלצרית
time (occurrence)	páam (f)	פעם

WAITER

With or without milk?	ím o blí xaláv.	עם או בלי חלב?
with	ím	עם
or	ó	או
without	blí	בלי

ATARA

I'll have	bišvilí	בשבילי
espresso with milk.	espréso ím xaláv.	אספרסו עם חלב.

DAVID

And I'll have	vebišvilí	ובשבילי
café au lait.	kafé hafúx.	קפה הפוך.
reversed, inverted	hafúx (m.s.)	הפוך

139

WAITER

Do you want cakes?	atém rocím ugót?	?אתם רוצים עוגות
cake	ugá (f)	עוגה

ATARA

| What kind of cake | éyze ugót | איזה עוגות |
| do you have? | yéš laxém. | יש לכם? |

WAITER

We have	yéš lánu	יש לנו
apple cake	ugát tapuxím	עוגת תפוחים
and cheese cake.	veugát gviná.	ועוגת גבינה.

ATARA

| Apple cake, please. | ugát tapuxím, bevakašá. | עוגת תפוחים, בבקשה. |

DAVID

| For me, too. | gám bišvilí. | גם בשבילי. |

ATARA

The coffee is hot.	hakafé xám.	הקפה חם.
Be careful.	hizahér.	הזהר.
hot, warm	xam (m.s.)	חם
be careful	hizahér (m.s.imv.)	הזהר

DAVID

I'll wait a bit,	axaké kcát,	אחכה קצת,
and the coffee	vehakafé	והקפה
will cool down.	yitkarér.	יתקרר.
I will wait	axaké (l.s.fut.)	אחכה
it will cool	yitkarer (3 m.s.fut.)	יתקרר

15.2 ADDITIONAL VOCABULARY

Give me a glass of water.	tén li kós máim.	תן לי כוס מים.
water	máim (m.pl.)	מים
Give me a glass of seltzer.	tén li kós sóda.	תן לי כוס סודה.
club soda	sóda (f)	סודה

| The tea is hot. | hatéy xám. | התה חם. |
| The tea is cold. | hatéy kár. | התה קר. |

| The milk is sour. | haxaláv xamúc. | החלב חמוץ. |

| The coffee is bitter. | hakafé már. | הקפה מר. |

The tea is sweet.	hatéy matók.	התה מתוק.
The cake is sweet.	haugá metuká.	העוגה מתוקה.
Let's go to a restaurant.	bó neléx lemis'adá.	בוא נלך למסעדה.
restaurant	mis'adá (f)	מסעדה

15.3 Vocabulary Drills

A. Substitution Drill - /bó/ "come"

Come see our house.

bói lir'ót et habáit šelánu.   בּוֹאִי לִרְאוֹת אֶת הַבַּיִת שֶׁלָּנוּ.
bóu   בּוֹאוּ
bó   בּוֹא
bóna   בּוֹאנָה

B. Substitution Drill - /ál tavó/ "don't come"

Don't come in the afternoon.

ál tavó axaréy hacohoráim.   אַל תָּבוֹא אַחֲרֵי הַצָּהֳרַיִים.
    tavói   תָּבוֹאִי
    tavóu   תָּבוֹאוּ
    tavóna   תָּבוֹאנָה

C. Transformation Drill - Affirmative to Negative

    Instructor: Come with Tamar.
    Student: Don't come with Tamar.

bó im tamár.   ál tavó im tamár.   בּוֹא עִם תָּמָר. אַל תָּבוֹא עִם תָּמָר.
bóu im tamár.   ál tavóu im tamár.   בּוֹאוּ עִם תָּמָר. אַל תָּבוֹאוּ עִם תָּמָר.
bói im tamár.   ál tavói im tamár.   בּוֹאִי עִם תָּמָר. אַל תָּבוֹאִי עִם תָּמָר.
bóna im tamár.   ál tavóna im tamár.   בּוֹאנָה עִם תָּמָר. אַל תָּבוֹאנָה עִם תָּמָר.

D. Transformation Drill - Negative to Affirmative

    Repeat Drill C in reverse.

E. Substitution Drill - /avó/ "I will come"

    I'll come to her office tomorrow.

avó lemisradá maxár.   אָבוֹא לַמִּשְׂרָדָה מָחָר.
tavó   תָּבוֹא
tavói   תָּבוֹאִי
davíd yavó   דָּוִד יָבוֹא
sára tavó   שָׂרָה תָּבוֹא
navó   נָבוֹא
atém tavóu   אַתֶּם תָּבוֹאוּ
atén tavóna   אַתֶּן תָּבוֹאנָה
kulám yavóu   כֻּלָּם יָבוֹאוּ
hén tavóna   הֵן תָּבוֹאנָה

F. Substitution - Agreement Drill

    He'll come for dinner.

hú yavó learuxát érev.   הוּא יָבוֹא לַאֲרוּחַת עֶרֶב.

aní - hagvéret umár Williams   אֲנִי - הַגְּבֶרֶת וּמַר וִוילְיַאמְס
át veatára - hén - atém - ánu   אַתְּ וְעֲטָרָה - הֵן - אַתֶּם - אָנוּ
atá - ištó šel dóv - át - hú   אַתָּה - אִשְׁתּוֹ שֶׁל דּוֹב - אַתְּ - הוּא

G.   Substitution Drill - /a- ~ te-/

I'll tell Atara everything.

asapér leatára et hakól.	אספר לעטרה את הכל.
tesapér	תספר
tesaprí	תספרי
davíd yesapér	דור יספר
sára tesapér	שרה תספר
aní veiští nesapér	אני ואשתי נספר
atém tesaprú	אתם תספרו
atén tesapérna	אתן תספרנה
hém yesaprú	הם יספרו
hén tesapérna	הן תספרנה

H.   Substitution - Agreement Drill - /asapér/ "I will tell"

We'll tell them the good news.

<u>nesapér lahém et haxadašót hatovót.</u>   <u>נספר להם את החדשות הטובות.</u>

atém - atára vedavíd - hén - hú	אתם - עטרה ודוד - הן - הוא
aní - atén - sára - át	אני - אתן - שרה - את
atá - avígdor - hú - ánu	אתה - אביגדור - הוא - אנו

I.   Substitution Drill - /a- ~ te-/

I'll wait for Moshe till 5:00.

axaké lemošé ád xaméš.	אחכה למשה עד חמש.
texaké	תחכה
texakí	תחכי
dóv yexaké	דב יחכה
hí texaké	היא תחכה
ánu nexaké	אנו נחכה
atém texakú	אתם תחכו
atén texakéna	אתן תחכינה
hém yexakú	הם יחכו
hén texakéna	הן תחכינה

J.   Substitution - Agreement Drill - /axaké/ "I will wait"

(Use the forms of the verb /ešév/ "sit" as cues.)

I'll sit in the hotel and wait for him.

ešév bamalón veaxaké 16.		אשב במלון ואחכה לו.
nešév	(venexaké)	נשב (ונחכה)
tešvú	(vetexakú)	תשבו (ותחכו)
yešév	(veyexaké)	ישב (ויחכה)
tešév	(vetexaké)	תשב (ותחכה)
léa tešév	(vetexaké)	לאה תשב (ותחכה)
yešvú	(veyexakú)	ישבו (ויחכו)
hén tešévna	(vetexakéna)	הן תשבנה (ותחכינה)
tešví	(vetexakí)	תשבי (ותחכי)
atén tešévna	(vetexakéna)	אתן תשבנה (ותהכינה)

K. Substitution Drill - /hizahér/ "be careful"

Be careful; the cup is hot.

hizahér. hakós xamá.   .הזהר, הכוס חמה
hizaharí   הזהרי
hizaharú   הזהרו
hizahérna   הזהרנה

In Grammar Section 6.9 it was pointed out that the final stem vowel is
dropped in verb forms beginning with a stressed vowel. However, when the
second root consonant is h , as in /hizahér/, the sequence /-hr-/ results, and
the vowel /a/ is inserted.   The /-h-/ is often replaced by a smooth
transition in ordinary speech - /hizaarí, hizaarú/. Compare the forms of
/memahér/ "hurry" in Section 8.3.

In the following drills L to P the instructor supplies the verb form with
the noun substitution.

L. Substitution - Agreement Drill - /xám/ "hot"

The water was hot.

<u>hamáim hayú xamím.</u>   .המים היו חמים

haxalá haytá - haóxel hayá   החלה היתה - האוכל היה
habeycím hayú - haugá haytá   הביצים היו - העוגה היתה
hakafé hayá - hayerakót hayú   הקפה היה - הירקות היו
haagvaniót hayú - hamáim hayú   העגבניות היו - המים היו

M. Substitution - Agreement Drill - /kár/ "cold"

The milk was cold.

<u>haxaláv hayá kár.</u>   .החלב היה קר

haglída haytá - hadagím hayú   הגלידה היתה - הדגים היו
haeškoliót hayú - hamíc hayá   האשכוליות היו - המיץ היה
hagvinót hayú - haavatixím hayú   הגבינות היו - האבטיחים היו
hašaménet haytá - haxaláv hayá   השמנת היתה - החלב היה

N. Substitution - Agreement Drill - /már/ "bitter"

The coffee was bitter.

<u>hakafé hayá már.</u>   .הקפה היה מר

hateením hayú - hatéy hayá   התאנים היו - התה היה
hayeynót hayú - haribá haytá   היינות היו - הריבה היתה
haeškolít haytá - haanavím hayú   האשכולית היתה - הענבים היו
hagvinót hayú - hakafé hayá   הגבינות היו - הקפה היה

143

O. Substitution - Agreement Drill - /xamúc/   "sour"

The grapes were sour.

haanavím hayú xamucím.   .העובים היו חמוצים

        haxaláv hayá - hašaménet haytá   החלב היה - השמנת היתה
        hadagím hayú - hagviná haytá   הדגים היו - הגבינה היתה
        hayáin hayá - hateením hayú   היין היה - החאנים היו
        haugót hayú - haanavím hayú   העוגות היו - העובים היו

P. Substitution - Agreement Drill - /matók/   "sweet"

The plums were sweet.

hašezifím hayú metukím.   .השזיפים היו מתוקים

        hayáin hayá - haavatixím hayú   היין היה - האבטיחים היו
        haribá haytá - haeškoliót hayú   הריבה היתה - האשכוליות היו
        haxalót hayú - harimón hayá   החלות היו - הרימון היה
        haxalá haytá - hašezifím hayú   החלה היתה - השזיפים היו

    The instructor may vary the above drills by supplying only the noun
substitution, with the student making the necessary changes in the verb
/hayá, haytá, hayú/.

144

GRAMMAR NOTES

15.4 Roots

Examine the following sets of related forms and note that in each set
there is a sequence of consonants which recurs in all the forms:

1.	/ledabér/	"to speak"	לדבר
	/dabér/	"speak"	דבר
	/adabér/	"I will speak"	אדבר
	/medabér/	"speaks"	מדבר
2.	/saméax/	"happy"	שמח
	/nismáx/	"we will be happy"	נשמח
3.	/slixá/	"pardon" (noun)	סליחה
	/tisláx/	"you will pardon"	תסלח
4.	/séder/	"arrangement, order"	סדר
	/yesudár/	"it will be arranged"	יסודר

In group 1 the sequence /d-b-r/ recurs, with the basic meaning "speak";
in group 2 the sequence /s-m-x/ recurs, with the basic meaning "happy";
in group 3 the sequence /s-l-x/ recurs, with the basic meaning "pardon"; and
in group 4 the sequence /s-d-r/ recurs, with the basic meaning "arrange".
Such sequences, called roots, have been hinted at in the preceding units.
Hebrew roots generally consist of three consonants. Roots of four consonants,
such as /t-r-g-m/ in /targém/ "translate", are fairly common. Roots with only
one or two consonants, such as /b/ in /bá/ "come" and /r-c/ in /larúc/ "to run",
are less frequent. Roots of five consonants also occur, but infrequently, and
they are generally technical, or slang coinages, such as /letalgréf/ "to
telegraph".
These root consonants are often called radicals, and dictionaries list
verbs according to these radicals. Roots of less than three radicals are
"supplied" with additional radicals to make three for purposes of listing.
The particular consonant supplied is usually based on the Hebrew spelling of
one of the forms. The patterns are rather regular but complicated, and they
will be discussed as the opportunity presents itself.

15.5 Patterns Occurring with Roots

Examine the following groups of forms and note that in each group there is
a recurring sequence of vowels, and, in some of the groups, of consonants also:

5.	/xošév/	"thinks"	חושב
	/omér/	"says"	אומר
	/mocé/	"finds"	מוצא
	/rocé/	"wants"	רוצה
	/olé/	"costs"	עולה
	/osé/	"does"	עושה
	/roé/	"sees"	רואה
6.	/medabér/	"speaks"	מדבר
	/memahér/	"hurries"	ממהר
	/mekavé/	"hopes"	מקוה

7. /lamádeti/   "I studied"   למדתי
    /amárti/   "I said"   אמרתי
    /axálti/   "I ate"   אכלתי
    /šamáti/   "I heard"   שמעתי
    /natáti/   "I gave"   נתתי

8. /natxíl/   "we will begin"   נחחיל
    /namšíx/   "we will continue"   נמשיך

In group 5 the sequence /-o-é-/ indicates the present tense, while in
group 6 the sequence /me-a-é-/ carries this meaning.

In group 7 the sequence /-a-á-ti/ carries the general meaning "I _____
(past tense), with the root consonants indicating the basic verb meaning.

In group 8 the sequence /na--í-/ carries the meaning "we will _____",
and the radicals /t-x-l/ and /m-š-x/ indicate the basic verb meanings.

Thus it may be seen that the roots carry the basic meanings, and the
patterns of vowels, prefixes, and suffixes indicate the precise meanings of the
forms as they occur in sentences, such as present tense, etc.

Up to this point the emphasis in the grammatical drills has been on
prefixing, suffixing, and other changes which occur regardless of the pattern
occurring with the root. For example, the present tense verbs /xošév/ and
/medabér/ show similar changes for the feminine and plurals.

m.s.	/xošév/	/medabér/	מדבר	חושב
f.s.	/xošévet/	/medabéret/	מדברת	חושבת
m.pl.	/xošvím/	/medabrím/	מדברים	חושבים
f.pl.	/xošvót/	/medabrót/	מדברות	חושבות

However, though the /-o-é-/ and /me-a-é-/ patterns both indicate present
tense they are of different verb patterns and the other tenses will show
differences, also. The future tense forms of these verbs are, for example,
/taxšóv/ and /tedabér/.

If the student learns the various patterns with a few representative roots,
he will be able to derive all the forms of a new root by analogy from one or
two forms. For example, the following forms of the verb "to speak" have
occurred:

infinitive:	/ledabér/	"to speak"	לדבר
m.s.imv.	/dabér/	"speak"	דבר
f.s.imv.	/dabrí/	"speak"	דברי
1 s.fut.	/adabér/	"I will speak"	אדבר
3 m.pl.fut.	/yedabrú/	"they will speak"	ידברו
m.s.pres.	/medabér/	"speaks"	מדבר

Forms of two other roots with the same pattern have occurred so far:
/asapér/ "I will tell" and /letayél/ "to walk about". From these the matching
forms may be derived: (The derived forms are listed to the right.)

infinitive		/lesapér/	/letayél/	
m.s.imv.		/sapér/		/tayél/
f.s.imv.		/saprí/		/taylí/
1 s.fut.	/asapér/			/atayél/
3 m.pl.fut.	/yesaprú/			/yetaylú/
m.s.pres.		/mesapér/		/metayél/

As a further illustration, the root of /xošév/, xšv, occurs with the pattern of /dabér/ with the somewhat different meaning "to calculate" instead of "to think". The corresponding forms are:

infinitive	/lexašév/	"to calculate"	לחשב
m.s.imv.	/xašév/	"calculate"	חשב
f.s.imv.	/xašví/	"calculate"	חשבי
1 s.fut.	/axašév/	"I will calculate"	אחשב
3 m.pl.fut.	/yexašvú/	"they will calculate"	יחשבו
m.s.pres.	/mexašév/	"calculates"	מחשב

It is not all so simple as the above illustrations might make it appear. For one thing, even the simplest pattern with an unvarying root may have over twenty different forms of which the student must have automatic control. This requires a tremendous amount of drill, and the student should not be lulled into a feeling of confidence simply because he finds it easy to "encode" the correct form with some reflection.

Second, there are quite a few different verb patterns alone, not counting variations for phonological reasons. Mastery of these represents the major task for the beginning Hebrew student. In the following units a great deal of attention will be paid to it in the drills.

15.6 <u>Alternating Radicals</u>

Compare the related forms in the following groups:

1. /pné/   "turn"   פנה
    /tifné/   "you will turn'"   תפנה

2. /ptáx/   "open"   פתח
    /tiftáx/   "you will open"   תפתח

3. /bó/   "come"   בוא
    /tavó/   "you will come"   תבוא

The first member of each group has a root varying slightly from the apparent root of the second member. In the first two groups /p/ alternates with /f/, and in the third /b/ alternates with /v/. In addition, some roots have /k/ alternating with /x/ as one of the radicals.

These alternations have been mentioned before, and they are quite frequent in verbs. The patterns of alternation often depend on the pattern occurring with the root, but a few generalizations may be made at this point.
a) At the beginning of a word the alternants /p/, /b/, and /k/ occur:
      /pné/   "turn"   פנה
      /bó/   "come"   בוא
      /kén/   "yes, so"   כן

b) At the end of a word the alternants /f/, /v/, and /x/ occur:
      /cahóv/   "yellow"   צהוב
      /dérex/   "way"   דרך

c) After a stressed vowel the alternants /f/, /v/, and /x/ occur:
      /séfer/   "book"   ספר
      /šéva/   "seven"   שבע
      /óxel/   "food"   אוכל

d) As the second consonant of an initial two-consonant cluster the
alternants /f/, /v/, and /x/ occur:
          /sfarím/   "books"   סברים
          /švií/   "seventh"   שְׁבִיעִי

There is a close correspondence in the Hebrew spelling of radicals that
alternate and those which do not:
     /k/ alternating with /x/ is spelled   כ .
     /k/ not alternating with /x/ is spelled ק .
     /x/ not alternating with /k/ is spelled ח .

Thus, for example, initial /x/ will be spelled always with ח .
/xošév/   חושב
     Final /k/ will be spelled with ק .   /yarók/   ירוק

     /v/ alternating with /b/ is spelled ב .
     /v/ not alternating with /b/ is spelled ו .

In listing the roots p, b, and k will be used for the alternating radicals.
The student should learn these roots by drilling the forms. Attention to the
Hebrew spelling will be of help in roots with /k/ and /x/.
     Thus, the root of /séfer/ "book" will be listed as spr, the same as
for /sapér/ "tell".

15.7 Alternating Patterns

Patterns alternate in a number of ways, and some of these have been described
already. Alternations such as the /a/ in /memaharím/ m.pl.pres. "hurry"
depend on the particular consonants which comprise the root. Other pattern
alternations are the result of historical or phonological changes in Hebrew
which leave forms similar in one part of a pattern and different in other
parts. For example, the future of the roots /p-t-x/ "open" and /s-m-x/ "be
happy" are very similar - /eftáx/ "I will open" and /esmáx/ "I will be happy".
However, the present tense of the former is /potéax/ and the corresponding
form of the latter is /saméax/, which has been treated as an adjective.
     The student should not try to memorize a huge series of rules, but he
should drill the patterns as they occur and use the descriptions in the notes
as an aid. Summaries will be provided from time to time for further assistance.

15.8 Designation of Patterns

In previous units we have discussed patterns by using the symbols C for
"consonant" and V for "vowel". For ease in discussing patterns we will
designate them by using the arbitrary root p'l. The choice of this root is
dictated by Hebrew grammatical tradition. Other roots which are often used by
grammarians for this purpose are q t l and š m r.
     The choice of p'l has the disadvantage that the internal open juncture
/'/ is usually replaced by a smooth transition. The roots q t l (q is often
used as a symbol for the /k/ which never alternates with /x/) and šmr do not
have this disadvantage; their consonants do not vary. However, the use of
p'l will allow the student to be a bit conversant in the traditional Hebrew
description of Hebrew as taught in Israeli schools.

An advantage in using p'l is that the p will occur as /f/ in the patterns
where it is called for and give the student an additional aid in deriving forms.
     Thus, for example, the form /kibél/ will be said to be a pi'él form
(pronounced /pi'él/ or /piél/). The form /slixá/ will be said to be a p'ilá
form (pronounced /pe'ilá/ or /peilá/ since /p'/ is a non-permissible initial
cluster).
NOTE: This section and the following one are not grammatical explanations.
        They are explanations of grammatical terms used in this text.

15.9 Designation of Radicals

     The root p'l consists, in the Hebrew spelling, of the letters פ /péy/,
ע /áin/, and ל /lámed/   . Since most Hebrew roots consist of three
consonants or can be spelled with three letters when they consist of less,
the radicals are named after these letters. The first radical is called the
"/péy/" of the root, the second is called the "/áin/", and the third is called
the "/lámed/". We will use these traditional designations as well as C with
subscript numerals in discussion of roots and patterns.
     In Grammar Note 8.4a the term /lámed héy/ was used. This means that some
forms of these roots are spelled in Hebrew with the letter ה /héy/ as the
third consonant. Actually, there is no third consonant in their pronunciation.
The root consists of two consonants with the second always followed by a
vowel. The /héy/ is an instance of a third "consonant" being added to regularize
the designation.
     More specifically, the dictionary listing of the root is usually the third
person masculine singular past tense form of the verb. The verb "to be" would
be listed under the root hyh since the 3 m.s. past is /hayá/ היה . This
verb, also, is a lámed héy verb.
     Below is a partial list of the roots which have occurred in the text and
some representative forms illustrating the root. Note that the internal open
juncture /'/ may function as a radical.
     Verbs listed with h as the third radical may be assumed to be lámed héy
verbs. Verb roots in which the final radical is the consonantal aspirate /h/
are very few in number and will be specifically designated when they occur.
They are listed in dictionaries in their normal alphabetical order.
     The student need not memorize the following list. It is included here only
for illustration of the grammatical points discussed in this unit.

Root

dbr   דבר   /dabér/ "speak"   /davár/ "thing"

mc'   מצא   /moc'ím/ "find"   /nimca'ím/ "are found"

šm'   שמע   /šim'í/ "hear" (f.s.imv.)   /šamáti/ "I heard"
              /nišmá/ "is heard"

mšx   משך   /hamšéx/ "continue"   /tamšíx/ "you will continue"

r'h   ראה   /lir'ót/ "to see"   /roé/ "sees"   /raíti/ "I saw"

'sh   עשה   /laasót/ "to do"   /osé/ "does"   /asíti/ "I did"

'kl   אכל   /leexól/ "to eat"   /axálti/ "I ate"   /óxel/ "food"

sgr   סגר   /sgór/ "close"   /esgór/ "I will close"

ptx   פתח   /ptáx/ "open"   /eftáx/ "I will open"

gzm   /tagzím/   "you will exaggerate"

gdl   /gadól/   "big"

sdr   /yesudár/   "it will be arranged"   /séder/   "order"

zhr   /hizahér/   "be careful"

kns   /lehikanés/   "to enter"

[Note: In this text abstracted root consonants are indicated by underlining. Transcriptions of spoken forms are indicated by slash lines. Thus, for example, the statement "b occurs as /v/" would mean that a radical b, which alternates between /b/ and /v/, occurs as /v/ in the particular form being discussed.
      Root šbr --   3 m.s. past /šavar/ "he broke"   שבר]

RAPID RESPONSE DRILL

איזה היה בית הקפה?

מה הזמינו לשתות?

איזה קפה רצתה עטרה?

איזה עוגת יש בבית הקפה?

ואיזו עוגה נחמדה עטרה?

באיזו עוגה נזכר דוד?

מדוע דוד אינו יכול עדיין לשתות את הקפה?

REVIEW CONVERSATIONS

A: bó nigáš lištót kós kafé.

א: בוא ניגש לשתות כוס קפה.

B: éyfo bét hakafé.

ב: איפה בית הקפה?

A: šám bapiná.

א: שם בפינה.

B: esmáx meód.

ב: אשמח מאוד.

C: hatéy xám. hizaharí.

ג: התה חם. הזהרי.

D: hú ló xám. hú kvár kár.

ד: הוא לא חם. הוא כבר קר.

C: át rocá xaláv latéy?

ג: את רוצה חלב לזה?

D: ló. aní rocá limón vesukár.

ד: לא. אני רוצה לימון וסוכר.

E: melcarít. tní li kós máim karím, bevakašá.

ה: מלצרית, תני לי כוס מים קרים, בבקשה.

F: atá rocé ód mášehu?

ו: אתה רוצה עוד משהו?

E: kén. banána splít.

ה: כן. בננה ספליט.

F: tóv adoní. beracón.

ו: טוב אדוני. ברצון.

G: matáy tavó lir'ót otánu.

ז: מתי תבוא לראות אותנו?

H: avó haérev, ím atém rocím.

ח: אבוא הערב אם אתם רוצים.

G: tov. bó im hamišpaxá.

ז: טוב. בוא עם המשפחה.

H: rayón tóv. lehitraót haérev.

ח: רעיון טוב. להתראות הערב.

I: sapér li. heyxán raíta et xána.

ט: ספר לי, היכן ראית את חנה?

J: raíti otá birxóv álenbi.

י: ראיתי אותה ברחוב אלנבי.

I: má hí osá betél avív.

ט: מה היא עושה בתל אביב?

J: hí báa lekán kól šavúa.

י: היא באה לכאן כל שבוע.

I: im kén, caríx lehazmín otá
learuxát érev.

ט: אם כן, צריך להזמין אותה
לארוחת ערב.

K: haím mošé yavó héna hayóm?

כ: האם משה יבוא הנה היום?

L: aní xošév šeyavó bexaméš.

ל: אני חושב שיבוא בחמש.

K: tóv. nexaké ló kán ád šeyagía.

כ: טוב. נחכה לו כאן עד שיגיע.

16.1 <u>Conversation in the Coffee House</u> /sixá bebét hakafé/ . שיחה בבית הקפה

DAVID

I met	pagášti	פגשתי
Moshe this morning.	et mošé habóker.	את משה הבוקר.
I met	pagášti	פגשתי

ATARA

Really?	beemét?	באמת?
What did he	má hú	מה הוא
say to you?	sipér lexá.	סיפר לך?
he told	sipér (3 m.s.past)	סיפר

DAVID

He told me	hú sipér li	הוא סיפר לי
that he got	šehú kibél	שהוא קיבל
a letter	mixtáv	מכתב
from Mr. Williams.	mimár Williams.	ממר ווילימאס.
he received	kibél (3.m.s.past)	קיבל
letter	mixtáv (m)	מכתב

ATARA

From where	meáin	מאין
did he send	hú šaláx	הוא שלח
the letter?	et hamixtáv,	את המכתב?
From the U.S.?	meamérika?	מאמריקה?
he sent	šaláx (3 m.s.past)	שלח

DAVID

| No. From Tel Aviv. | ló. mitél avív. | לא. מתל אביב. |

ATARA

| From Tel Aviv? | mitél avív? | מתל אביב? |
| What is he doing there? | má hú osé šám. | מה הוא עושה שם? |

DAVID

He was appointed	hú nitmaná	הוא נתמנה
Counsellor of	leyoéc	ליועץ
the American Embassy.	hašagrirút haamerikáit.	השגרירות האמריקאית.
he was appointed	nitmaná (3 m.s.past)	נתמנה

ATARA

When	matáy	מתי
did he arrive?	hú higía.	הוא הגיע?
he arrived	higía (3 m.s.past)	הגיע

DAVID

| Last week. | bešavúa šeavár. | בשבוע שעבר. |
| he passed | avár (3 m.s.past) | עבר |

Moshe went	mošé nasá	משה נסע
to Tel Aviv	letél avív	לתל אביב,
and saw him.	veraá otó.	וראה אותו.
he travelled	nasá (3 m.s.past)	נסע
he saw	raá (3 m.s.past)	ראה

ATARA

How does he look?	éyx hú nir'é.	איך הוא נראה?
is seen, appears	nir'é (m.s.pres.)	נראה

DAVID

Moshe said that	mošé amár šé -	משה אמר ש-
he looks good.	hú nir'é tóv.	הוא נראה טוב.
he said	amár (3 m.s.past)	אמר

ATARA

Does he still	hú ód	הוא עוד
speak Hebrew?	medabér ivrít?	מדבר עברית?

DAVID

Yes. He spoke	kén. hú dibér	כן. הוא דיבר
Hebrew with Moshe.	ivrít im mošé.	עברית עם משה.
he spoke	dibér (3 m.s.past)	דיבר

16.2 ADDITIONAL VOCABULARY

She received a letter.	hí kiblá mixtáv.	היא קבלה מכתב.
They (m) received a letter.	hém kiblú mixtáv.	הם קבלו מכתב.
They (f) received a letter.	hén kiblú mixtáv.	הן קבלו מכתב.
She sent a letter.	hí šalxá mixtáv.	היא שלחה מכתב.
They sent a letter.	hém šalxú mixtáv.	הם שלחו מכתב.
What did she say?	má hí amrá.	מה היא אמרה?
What did they say?	má hén amrú.	מה הן אמרו?
She went to Haifa.	hí nas'á lexáyfa.	היא נסעה לחיפה.
They went to Haifa.	hém nas'ú lexáyfa.	הם נסעו לחיפה.
She arrived yesterday.	hí higía etmól.	היא הגיעה אתמול.
They arrived yesterday.	hén higíu etmól.	הן הגיעו אתמול.
She saw him.	hí raatá otó.	היא ראתה אותו.
They saw him.	hém raú otó.	הם ראו אותו.
He arrived here	hú higía héna	הוא הגיע הנה
last year.	bešaná šeavrá.	בשנה שעברה.

16.3 Vocabulary Drills.

A. Response Drill - /pagášti/ "I met"

    Instructor: When did you meet Atara?
    Student: I met her this morning.

matáy pagášta et atára.   pagášti otá habóker.   ?מתי פגשת את עטרה
matáy pagaštém et atára.   pagášnu otá habóker.   ?מתי פגשתם את עטרה
matáy pagášten et atára.   pagášnu otá habóker.   ?מתי פגשתן את עטרה
matáy pagášt et atára.   pagášti otá habóker.   ?מתי פגשת את עטרה

B. Substitution Drill - /nir'é/ "appears"

    When the present tense pattern has a /ni-/ prefix the feminine singular ends
in /-t/, even with lamed hey verbs. This is the exception to the general
lámed héy present tense pattern.with /-á/ feminine mentioned in the note to
Grammar Section 8.4a.

    He looks well.

hú nir'é tóv.   .הוא נראה טוב א
    nir'ét   נראית
    nir'ím   נראים
    nir'ót   נראות

C. Substitution - Agreement Drill

    How does Moshe look?

    éyx nir'é mošé.   ?איך נראה משה

    habáit šel dóv - gvéret zahávi   הבית של דוב - גברת זהבי
    haoniót haxadašót - hamalón   האוניות החדשות - המלון
    hatapuxím - hayerakót - hašagrirút   התפוחים - הירקות - השגרירות
    haugót - mišpáxat kármi - mošé   העוגות - משפחת כרמי - משה

D. Individual Response Drill

    Instructor: How does the new hotel look?
    Student: It's very beautiful.

    éyx nir'é hamalón haxadáš.   .איך נראה המלון החדש
    hú yafé meód.   .הוא יפה מאוד

    éyx nir'ét ištó šel davíd.   .איך נראית אשתו של דוד
    éyx nir'ím harexovót.   .איך נראים הרחובות
    éyx nir'é habáit šel xána.   .איך נראה הבית של חנה
    éyx nir'ót haagvaniót.   .איך נראות העגבניות
    éyx nir'ét sfát hayám.   .איך נראית שפת הים
    éyx nir'é bét hakafé.   .איך נראה בית הקפה

155

GRAMMAR NOTES

16.4 Third Person Past Tense Verb Forms

Examine the following verb forms:

hú	kibél	"he received"
hí	kiblá	"she received"
hém	kiblú	"they (m) received"
hén	kiblú	"they (f) received"

hú	šaláx	"he sent"
hí	šalxá	"she sent"
hém	šalxú	"they (m) sent"
hén	šalxú	"they (f) sent"

hú	amár	"he said"
hí	amrá	"she said"
hém	amrú	"they (m) said"
hén	amrú	"they (f) said"

Note, first of all, that the third person plural forms are the same for both genders. This is true of all past tense verbs, regardless of conjugation.

Note further that the feminine singular has the suffix /-á/, and the plural has suffix /-ú/. The preceding vowel is dropped as with the /-í/ and /-ú/ suffixes in the future.

In addition to these characteristics there are variations depending on the type of root. Some of these variations will be illustrated in the following drills. After the third person forms are drilled the corresponding first and second person forms will be described and drilled.

In the following drills the instructor gives a sentence with a 3 m.s. past tense verb. The students repeat the sentence. The instructor then gives the substitution cues, and the students give the sentence with the necessary changes.

Some of the verbs have not occurred in the third person past tense previously, but the student should have no trouble recognizing them.

a. Ordinary Roots

These are roots whose final two radicals do not require any additional variations. The consonants which may require variations in the third person pattern are /'/, /h/, and /x/. The possibilities of these variations will be described as they occur.

A. Substitution - Agreement Drill - /kibél/ "received"

He received a letter from Mr. Cohen.

hú kibél mixtáv mimár kóhen.   הוא קיבל מכתב מאת כהן.

xána - hém - mošé - hén   חנה - הם - משה - הן
már kármi - hú veištó - hí - hú   מר כרמי - הוא ואשתו - היא - הוא

156

B. Substitution - Agreement Drill - /sipér/ "told"

He told Miriam the news.

hú sipér lemiryám et haxadašót.   .הוא ספר למרים את החדשות

sára - davíd - hén - gvéret kóhen   שרה - דוד - הן - גברת כהן
hí vebaalá - dóv - mošé vedóv - hú   היא ובעלה - דוב - משה ודוב - הוא

C. Substitution - Agreement Drill - /dibér/ "spoke"

He spoke Hebrew in the office.

hú dibér ivrít bamisrád.   .הוא דבר עברית במשרד

hén - xána - davíd - hém   הן - חנה - דוד - הם
sára veléa - gvéret Williams - hú   שרה ולאה - גברת ויליאמס - הוא

D. Substitution - Agreement Drill - /šaláx/ "sent"

He sent a package to America.

hú šaláx xavilá leamérika.   .הוא שלח חבילה לאמריקה

mošé veištó - miryám - hém   משה ואשתו - מרים - הם
dóv - hén - atára - hú   דוב - הן - עטרה - הוא

E. Substitution - Agreement Drill - /saláx/ "forgave"

He forgave Miriam for the letter.

hú saláx lemiryám al hamixtáv.   .הוא סלח למרים על המכתב

xána - kulám - mošé - hí   חנה - כולם - משה - היא
már káspi - hén - hú   מר כספי - הן - הוא

F. Substitution - Agreement Drill - /amár/ "said"

He said it was cold yesterday.

hú amár šehayá kár etmól.   .הוא אמר שהיה קר אתמול

hém - sára - davíd - hén   הם - שרה - דוד - הן
gvéret kármi - hí - hú   גברת כרמי - היא - הוא

G. Substitution - Agreement Drill - /avár/ "passed"

He passed by the office this morning.

hú avár al yád hamisrád habóker.   .הוא עבר על יד המשרד הבוקר

hém - avígdor - atára - hén   הם - אביגדור - עטרה - הן
mošé - hí - dóv veištó - hú   משה - היא - דוב ואשתו - הוא

H. Substitution - Agreement Drill - /xašáv/   "thought"

He thought that today was Friday.

<u>hú xašáv šehayóm yóm šiší.</u>   .<u>הוא חשׁ שׁהיום יום שׁשׁי</u>

   hí - hém -gvéret kóhen   היא - הם - גברת כהן
   hén - yoséf - sára - hú   הן - יוסף - שרה - הוא

I. Substitution - Agreement Drill - /patáx/   "opened"

He opened the door.

<u>hú patáx et hadélet.</u>   .<u>הוא פתח את הדלת</u>

   hí - mošé vedóv - hén   היא - משה ורב - הן
   sára - már kóhen - hém - hú   שרה - מר כהן - הם - הוא

J. Substitution - Agreement Drill - /sagár/   "opened"

He closed the door.

<u>hú sagár et hadélet.</u>   .<u>הוא סגר את הדלת</u>

   hén - davíd veatára - hí   הן - דוד ועטרה - היא
   már kármi - hém - sára - hú   מר כרמי - הם - שרה - הוא

K. Substitution - Agreement Drill - /axál/   "ate"

He ate watermelon.

<u>hú axál avatíax.</u>   .<u>הוא אכל אבטיח</u>

   hém - hí - sára vexána   הם - היא - שרה וחנה
   avígdor - gvéret káspi - hú   אביגדור - גברת כספי - הוא

L. Substitution - Agreement Drill   /natán/   "gave"

He gave me all the food.

<u>hú natán li et kól haóxel.</u>   .<u>הוא נתן לי את כל האוכל</u>

   ištó šel haxenvaní - hamelcár   אשתו של החנוני - המלצר
   hém - mošé - ištexá - hú   הם - משה - אשתך - הוא

M. Substitution - Agreement Drill   /pagáš/   "met"

He met her in America.

<u>hú pagáš otá beamérika.</u>   .<u>הוא פגשׁ אותה באמריקה</u>

   atára - hén - már zahávi   עטרה - הן - מר זהבי
   gvéret zahávi - hém - hú   גברת זהבי - הם - הוא

N. Substitution - Agreement Drill /hitrašém/ "was impressed"

He was impressed by the new building.

<u>hú hitrašém mehabinyán haxadáš.</u>   .הוא התרשם מהבנין החדש

gvéret Williams - hém - atára   גברת ווילאמס - הם - עטרה
baalá - hén - hí - hú   בעלה - הן - היא - הוא

O. Substitution - Agreement Drill - /lamád/ "studied"

He studied in this school.

<u>hú lamád bebét haséfer hazé.</u>   .הוא למד בבית הספר הזה

xána vebaalá - baaléx - léa   חנה ובעלה - בעלך - לאה
hém - davíd - hí - hú   הם - דוד - היא - הוא

   b. <u>Verbs with Third Radical <u>'</u> or <u>x</u></u>

   There are two sub-classes of verbs whose third radical is <u>'</u> or <u>x</u>. The <u>'</u> and <u>x</u> of one sub-class are spelled in Hebrew with א and כ , respectively, and the <u>'</u> and <u>x</u> of the other sub-class are spelled with ע and ח .

   The first sub-class has the same general pattern as ordinary verbs. Examples are: /macá/ "he found" מצא /mocé/ "finds" מוצא , /himšíx/ "he continued" המשיך

   In verbs of the latter sub-class the vowel /a/ must immediately precede the third radical when it is final in the word. This is true even in the case of <u>'</u> which is spelled but not pronounced, as in /yodéa/ "knows"יורע.
   If the vowel /a/ precedes it anyway, then there is no problem. Examples are: /yadá/ "he knew" ירע ,/patáx/ "he opened" פתח ,/šaláx/ "he sent" שלח
   When the conjugation pattern calls for another vowel, then an unstressed /a/ is inserted. /saméax/ "happy" שמח but /nismáx/ "we will be happy" נשמח /šoméa/ "hears" שומע but /šmá/ "hear" (imv.) שמע
(pi'el) /šiléax/ "he sent away" שילח but /šaláx/ "he sent" שלח.

P. Substitution - Agreement Drill - /nasá/ "traveled"

He went to see Haifa.

<u>hú nasá lir'ót et xáyfa.</u>   .הוא נסע לראות את חיפה

hí - hém - mošé - sára   היא - הם - משה - שרה
dóv vemiryám - hén - hú   דוב ומרים - הן - הוא

Q. Substitution - Agreement Drill - /yadá/ "knew"

He didn't know that Miriam is in Tel Aviv.

<u>hú ló yadá šemiryám betél avív.</u>   .הוא לא ידע שמרים בתל אביב

gvéret kóhen - mošé - iští   גברת כהן - משה - אשתי
hém - sára - hén - hú   הם - שרה - הן - הוא

R.   Substitution - Agreement Drill - /macá/   "found"

He didn't find the bottle.

<u>hú ló macá et habakbúk.</u>   .הוא לא מצא את הבקבוק

   gvéret kóhen - mošé - iští - hén   גברת כהן - משה - אשתי - הן
   hém - yaakóv - hí - hú   הם - יעקב - היא - הוא

S.   Substitution - Agreement Drill - /šamá/   "heard"

He didn't hear the news this evening.

<u>hú ló šamá et haxadašót haérev.</u>   .הוא לא שמע את החדשות הערב

   ištó - dóv - hém - yaakóv   אשתו - דוב - הם - יעקב
   hén - gvéret óren - hú   הן - גברת אורן - הוא

   c.   <u>lamed hey Verbs</u>

Examine the pattern of the following forms:

/hayá/	"he was"	היה
/haytá/	"she was"	היתה
/hayú/	"they were"	היו

The pattern of the third person endings is:
     3 m.s.   /-á/
     3 f.s.   /-tá/
     3 pl.   /-ú/

     These endings follow the second radical regardless of the conjugation of the verb. The third radical is listed as <u>h</u>, but this is only a spelling convention.
     The 3 m.s. ending may be confusing at first since it resembles the 3 f.s. of ordinary verbs in pronunciation and spelling. It is also similar in pronunciation to verbs with third radical <u>'</u>.

T.   Substitution - Agreement Drill /hayá/   "was"

He was in Jerusalem yesterday.

<u>hú hayá beyerušaláim etmól.</u>   .הוא היה בירושלים אתמול

   ištó šel davíd - mošé vedóv - hén   אשתו של דוד - משה ודוב - הן
   yaakóv - hí - hém - léa - hú   יעקב - היא - הם - לאה - הוא

U.   Substitution - Agreement Drill - /asá/   "did"

What did he do in Jerusalém?

<u>má hú asá beyerušaláim.</u>   ?מה הוא עשה בירושלים

   hí - hém - ištexá - hén   היא - הם - אשתך - הן
   gvéret óren - baaléx - hú   גברת אורן - בעלך - הוא

V.   Substitution - Agreement Drill - /paná/   "turned"

He turned left at the intersection.

<u>hú paná smóla bahictalvút.</u>   .הוא פנה שמאלה בהצטלבוח

    haišá - hanaším - mošé veraxél   האשה - הנשים - משה ורחל
    hí - avígdor - hém - hú   היא - אביגדור - הם - הוא

W.   Substitution - Agreement Drill - /kivá/   "hoped"

He hoped for a good result.

<u>hú kivá letocaá tová.</u>   .הוא קיווה לחוצאה טובה

    gvéret zahávi - yoséf - hém   גברת זהבי - יוסף - הם
    ištó šel dóv - miryám veléa - hú   אשתו של דוב - מרים ולאה - הוא

X.   Substitution - Agreement Drill - /racá/   "wanted"

He didn't want to eat so early.

<u>hú ló racá leexól kol káx mukdám.</u>   .הוא לא רצה ליאכול כל כך מוקדם

    hém - sára - davíd veatára   הם - שרה - דוד ועטרה
    avígdor - hanaším - hí - hú   אביגדור - הנשים - היא - הוא

     d.   <u>Verbs with Second Radical ' or h</u>

Whenever the conjugation pattern or other verb pattern would result in a second radical /'/ or /h/ occurring immediately before a consonant, the vowel /a/ is inserted between them. Other examples of this have been drilled previously, such as /memahér ~memaharím/ and /hizahér ~hizaharí/.

The root of the verb "to see" is <u>r'h</u>, a <u>lamed hey</u> verb. Accordingly the third person past tense would be:
         3 m.s.   /ra'á/   "he saw"
         3 f.s.   */ra'tá/   "she saw"
         3 pl.   /ra'ú/   "they saw"

In the 3 f.s. the second radical /'/ occurs before a consonant - the suffix /tá/. The form is then /ra'atá/.
In ordinary speech the /'/ is replaced by a smooth transition, and the forms are:
         3 m.s.   /raá/   "he saw"
         3 f.s.   /raatá/   "she saw"
         3 pl.   /raú/   "the saw"

Y.   Substitution - Agreement Drill - /raá/   "saw"

He saw the new house.

<u>hú raá et habáit haxadáš.</u>   .הוא ראה את הבית החדש

    iští - hanaším šelánu - davíd   אשתי - הנשים שלנו - דוד
    hém - gvéret kóhen - hú   הם - גברת כהן - הוא

e.   <u>Verbs with Unstressed Third Person Suffixes</u>

The 3 f.s. and the 3 pl. endings /-a, -u/ are unstressed in the following cases:

1)   When the 3 m.s. is one syllable and the vowel is /á/.
/rác/   "he ran"
/ráca/   "she ran"
/rácu/   "they ran"

2)   When the final vowel of the conjugation pattern is /í/.
/himšíx/   "he continued"
/himšíxa/   "she continued"
/himšíxu/   "they continued"

This latter conjugation is traditionally called the   <u>hif'íl</u>

Z.   Substitution - Agreement Drill - /rác/   "ran"

He ran after the bus.

<u>hú rác axaréy haótobus.</u>   .הוא רץ אחרי האוטובוס

hí - hém - mošé - raxél   היא - הם - משה - רחל
yoséf veištó - hén - hú   יוסף ואשתו - הן - הוא

AA.   Substitution - Agreement Drill - /bá/   "came"

He came to see the house.

<u>hú bá lir'ót et habáit.</u>   .הוא בא לראות את הבית

gvéret zahávi - yicxák - hí   גברת זהבי - יצחק - היא
hém - léa - hén - hú   הם - לאה - הן - הוא

BB.   Substitution - Agreement Drill - /himšíx/   "continued"

He continued seeing her every day.

<u>hú himšíx lir'ót otá kól yóm.</u>   .הוא המשיך לראות אותה כל יום

már kármi - sára - dóv - hén   מר כרמי - שרה - דוב - הן
iští - hém - gvéret óren - hú   אשתי - הם - גברת אורן - הוא

CC.   Substitution - Agreement Drill - /hitxíl/   "began"

He began the diet this morning.

<u>hú hitxíl badiéta habóker.</u>   .הוא התחיל בדיאטה הבוקר

gvéret kóhen - mošé - iští   גברת כהן - משה - אשתי
sára veyoséf - hí - hén - hú   שרה ויוסף - היא - הן - הוא

DD.   Substitution - Agreement Drill - /hizmín/ "invited"

He invited them for dinner.

<u>hú hizmín otám learuxát érev.</u>   .הוא הזמין אותם לארוחת ערב

hí - dóv veištó - xána - hén   הן - חנה - דוב ואשתו - היא
yaakóv - yaakóv vemiryám - hú   הוא - יעקב ומרים - יעקב

The root of the verb /higía/ "arrived" is listed as <u>nq'</u>. The vowel /a/
precedes the third radical <u>'</u> whenever it is final in the word. See Section
16.4b above. The third person past tense forms are:

       3 m.s. /higía/ for */higí'/   הגיע
       3 f.s. /higía/ for /higí'a/   הגיעה
       3 pl.   /higíu/ for /higí'u/   הגיעו

By coincidence, therefore, the 3 m.s. and 3 f.s. are identical in
ordinary speech.

EE.   Substitution - Agreement Drill

He arrived in Israel last week.

<u>hú higía leisraél bešavúa šeavár.</u>   .הוא הגיע לישׂדאל בשׂבוע שׂעבר

hí - hém - iští - hanaším   היא - הם - אשתי - הנשים
davíd - hamišpaxá šeló - hú   דוד - המשפחה שלו - הוא

RAPID RESPONSE DRILL

The following questions are based on the conversation of this unit.

1. matáy pagáš davíd et mošé.   ?מתי פגשׂ דוד את משׂה .1

2. má sipér mošé ledavíd.   ?מה סׂפר משׂה לדוד .2

3. mimí kibél mošé mixtáv.   ?מׂמי קבׂל משׂה מכׂתׂב .3

4. meáin šaláx már Williams et hamixtáv.   ?מאין שׂלח מר ווׂילׂיאמס את המכׂתׂב .4

5. má osé már Williams betél avív.   ?מה עוׂה מר ווׂילׂיאמס בׂתׂל אבׂיב .5

6. matáy higía már Williams leisraél.   ?מׂתי הגׂיע מר ווׂילׂיאמס לׂישׂדאל .6

7. leán nasá mošé.   ?לׂאׂן נׂסׂע משׂה .7

8. heyxán raá mošé et már Williams.   ?היכן ראה משׂה את מר ווׂילׂיאמסׂ .8

9. éyx nir'é már Williams.   ?איך נראה מר ווׂילׂיאמסׂ .9

10. beéyze safá hém dibrú.   ?בׂאׂיזה שׂפׂה הם דברוׂ .10

REVIEW CONVERSATIONS

A.   pagášti et yaakóv.   .פגשתי את יעקב .א

B.   éyfo pagášta otó.   ?איפה פגשת אותו .ב

A.   pagášti otó barexóv.   .פגשתי אותו ברחוב .א

B.   má hú sipér lexá.   ?מה הוא סיפר לך .ב

A.   hú sipér li šehú sagár et hamisrád šeló.

.הוא ספר לי שהוא סגר את המשרד שלו .א

C.   šamáti šemiryám gára betél avív.   .שמעתי שמרים גרה בתל אביב .ג

D.   mimí šamát.   ?ממי שמעת .ד

C.   mimošé.   hú šamá et zót midóv.   .ממשה. הוא שמע את זאת מדוב .ג

D.   hú natán láx et haktóvet šelá?   ?הוא נתן לך את הכתובת שלה .ד

C.   ló.   áx hú yitén li et haktóvet maxár.   .לא. אך הוא יתן לי את הכתובת מחר .ג

E.   axálti glidá bebrúklin bár.   .אכלתי גלידה בברוקלין בר .ה

F.   éyx haglidá šám.   ?איך הגלידה שם .ו

E.   tChvá veteimá.   .טובה וטעימה .ה

F.   gám iští axlá šám veamrá šehaglidá tová.

.גם אשתי אכלה שם ואמרה שהגלידה טובה .ו

G.   dóv raá et menaxém habóker.   .דוב ראה את מנחם הבוקר .ז

H.   eyfó hú raá otó.   ?איפה הוא ראה אותו .ח

G.   kšehú veištó tiyelú birxóv álenbi   כשהוא ואשתו טיילו ברחוב אלנבי .ז
     hém pagšú otó al yád hašagrirút.   .הם פגשו אותו על יד השגרירות

I.   avíva hizmína otánu learuxát   אביבה הזמינה אותנו לארוחת .ט
     érev leyóm šiší.   .ערב ליום ששי

J.   beemét?   hí amrá šehí tazmín   נאמת? היא אמרה שהיא תזמין .י
     gám et yaakóv.   .גם את יעקב

I.   nismáx meód lir'ót otó.   .נשמח מאוד לראות אותו .ט
     matáy hú higía lexáyfa.   ?מתי הוא הגיע לחיפה

J.   hú ód ló higía.   hú yagía maxár.   .הוא עוד לא הגיע. הוא יגיע מחר .י

K. xána vebaalá avrú al yád
    habáit šelánu habóker.

כ. חנה ובעלה עברו על יד
    הבית שלנו הבוקר.

L. beemét? má hém amrú lexá.

ל. באמת? מה הם אמרו לך?

K. hém siprú li šedibrú im sára.

כ. הם ספרו לי שדברו עם שרה.

L. éyfo nimcét sára?

ל. איפה נמצאת שרה?

K. bexáyfa. hém natnú li et
    mispár hatélefon šelá.

כ. בחיפה. הם נתנו לי את
    מספר הטלפון שלה.

M. atára hitrašmá meód mehabáit
    haxadáš šel yoséf.

מ. עטרה התרשמה מאוד מהבית
    החדש של יוסף.

N. gám aní hitrašámti.
    habáit gadól vexadíš.

נ. גם אני התרשמתי.
    הבית גדול וחדיש.

M. matáy raít et habáit.

מ. מתי ראית את הבית?

N. raíti et habáit šilšóm.

נ. ראיתי את הבית שלשום.

M. gám atára raatá et habáit šilšóm.

מ. גם עטרה ראתה את הבית שלשום.

O. lamádnu ivrít bebét haséfer lesafót.

ס. למדנו עברית בבית הספר לשפות.

P. gám dálya lamdá šám

ע. גם דליה למדה שם.

O. matáy hí lamdá šám.

ס. מתי היא למדה שם?

P. aní xošévet šelifnéy šaná.

ע. אני חושבת שלפני שנה.

Q. haínu hašavúa benatánya.

פ. היינו השבוע בנתניה.

R. beéyze yóm haítem šám.

צ. באיזה יום הייתם שם?

Q. aní haíti beyóm šení veyéter
    hamišpaxá haytá beyóm šliší.

פ. אני הייתי ביום שני ויתר
    המשפחה היתה ביום שלישי.

S. davíd nasá leamérika.

ק. דוד נסע לאמריקה.

T. matáy.

ר. מתי?

S. lifnéy šavúa.

ק. לפני שבוע.

T. haím ištó gám ken nas'á?

ר. האם אשתו גם כן נסעה?

S. kén. hém nas'ú yáxad.

ק. כן. הם נסעו יחד.

אני רוצה לשלוח את המכתב הזה
לאמריקה...

17.1 At the Post Office

MR. WILLIAMS

I want	aní rocé	אני רוצה
to send	lišlóax et	לשלוח את
this letter	hamixtáv hazé	המכתב הזה
to the United States.	leamérika.	לאמריקה.
to send	lišlóax	לשלוח
letter	mixtáv (m)	מכתב

CLERK

By regular mail	bedóar ragíl	בדואר רגיל
or by air mail?	o bedóar avír.	או בדואר אוויר?
usual, habitual	ragíl (m.s.)	רגיל
air	avír (m)	אוויר

MR. WILLIAMS

By air mail.	bedóar avír.	בדואר אוויר.

CLERK

It will cost you	zé yaalé lexá	זה יעלה לך
thirty-five	šloším vexaméš	שלושים וחמש
agorot.	agorót.	אגורות.
agora (IL 0.01)	agorá (f)	אגורה

MR. WILLIAMS

How long	káma zmán	כמה זמן
will it take?	zé yikáx.	זה יקח?
time (duration)	zmán (m)	זמן
it will take	yikáx (3 m.s. fut.)	יקח
he took	lakáx	לקח

CLERK

I don't know.	aní ló yodéa.	אני לא יודע.
Maybe a week.	uláy šavúa.	אולי שבוע.
maybe, perhaps	uláy	אולי

MR. WILLIAMS

A week?	šavúa?	שבוע?
That's a long time.	zé harbé zmán.	זה הרבה זמן.
much, many	harbé	הרבה

CLERK

If it's	beím ze	באם זה
so urgent,	kol káx daxúf,	כל כך דחוף,
send a telegram.	šláx mivrák.	שלח מברק.
if	beím	באם
urgent	daxúf (m.s.)	דחוף
send	šláx (m.s.imv.)	שלח
telegram	mivrák (m)	מברק

MR. WILLIAMS

That's a good idea.	ze rayón tóv.	זה רעיון טוב.
Where is	heyxán	היכן
the telegraph office?	hamivraká.	המברקה?
idea	rayón (m)	רעיון
telegraph office	mivraká (f)	מברקה

CLERK

Here.	kán.	.כאן
On the second floor.	bakomá hašniá.	.בקומה השניה
story	komá (f)	קומה

MR. WILLIAMS

Thank you very much.	todá rabá.	.תודה רבה

17.2 ADDITIONAL VOCABULARY

Give me five postal cards.	tén li xaméš gluyót.	תן לי חמש .גלויות
postal card	gluyá (f)	גלויה
Give me five envelopes.	tén li xaméš maatafót.	תן לי חמש .מעטפות
envelope	maatafá (f)	מעטפה
Give me five air letters.	tén li xaméš igrót avír.	תן לי חמש .אגרות אויר
letter	igéret (f)	אגרת
Give me five ten-agora stamps.	tén li xamišá bulím šel éser agorót.	תן לי חמישה בולים .של עשר אגורות
stamp	búl (m)	בול
Send the letter special delivery.	šlax et hamixtáv eksprés.	שלח את המכתב .אקספרס
Send the letter by registered mail.	šlax et hamixtáv bedóar rašúm.	שלח את המכתב .בדואר רשום
recorded, listed	rašúm (m.s.)	רשום

17.3 Vocabulary Drills

A. Substitution-Agreement Drill - /ragíl/ "habitual"

He is used to eating on time.

hú ragíl leexól bazmán.	.הוא רגיל לאכול בזמן
xána - mošé kulám	— חנה – משה – כולם
sára veatára - aní - hú	שרה ועטרה – אני – הוא

B. Substitution Drill   /e - ~ti -/

I'll take the package.

ekáx et haxavilá.	.אקח את החבילה
atá tikáx	אתה תקח
át tikxí	את תקחי
hú yikáx	הוא יקח
hí tikáx	היא תקח
ánu nikáx	אנו נקח
atém tikxú	אתם תקחו
atén tikáxna	אתן תקחנה
hém yikxú	הם יקחו
hén tikáxna	הן תקחנה

C. Substitution-Agreement Drill

We'll take Miriam as far as Haifa.

nikáx et miryám ád xáyfa.   .ניקח את מרים עד חיפה

már óren - aní - hém - atén   מר אורן – אני – הם – אתן
raxél - hén - atém - át   רחל – הן – אתם – את
gvéret kóhen - atá - ánu   גברת כהן – אתה – אנו

D. Substitution Drill /šláx/ "send"

Send him a post card.

šláx ló gluyá.   .שלח לו גלויה

šilxí   שלחי
šilxú   שלחו
šláxna   שלחנה

GRAMMAR NOTES

17.4 Past Tense of pi'el

The complete past tense pattern of ordinary <u>pi'el</u> verbs with three-consonant roots is as follows: (dashes indicate root consonants).

		<u>spr</u>			<u>spr</u>
1 s.	/-i-á-ti/	sipárti	1 pl.	/-i-á-nu /	sipárnu
2 m.s.	/-i-á-ta/	sipárta	2 m.pl.	/-i-á-tem/	sipartém
2 f.s.	/-i-á-t /	sipárt	2 f.pl.	/-i-á-ten/	sipartén
3 m.s.	/-i-é- /	sipér	3 pl.	/-i--ú /	siprú
3 f.s.	/-i-- á /	siprá			

Note that the 3 m.s. has the vowels /-i-é-/ and the first and second person forms have the vowels /-i-á-/.

A. Substitution-Agreement Drill /sipér/ "told"

He told me about the dinner.

<u>hú sipér li ál aruxát haérev.</u>   הוא סיפר לי על ארוחת הערב.

xána - atém - mošé vedóv   חנה - אתם - משה ודוב
át - atá - sára - hú   את - אתה - שרה - הוא

B. Substitution-Agreement Drill - /kibél/ "received"

I received a telegram this morning.

<u>kibálti mivrák habóker.</u>   קבלתי מברק הבוקר.

hém - atém - davíd   הם - אתם - דוד
ánu - gvéret kármi - aní   אנו - גברת כרמי - אני

C. Substitution-Agreement Drill /mihér/ "hurried"

She hurried to the telegraph office.

<u>hí mihará lamivraká.</u>   היא מיהרה למברקה.

aní - atá - iští veʒgvéret káspi   אני - אתה - אשתי וגברת כספי
ánu - atém - yehuda - hí   אנו - אתם - יהורה - היא

D. Substitution-Agreement Drill /tiyél/ "strolled"

We took a walk on Allenby Road.

<u>tiyálnu berexóv álenbi.</u>   טיילנו ברחוב אלנבי.

atén - avígdor veatára - aní   אתן - אביגדור ועטרה - אני
át vedóv - atá - ánu   את ודוב - אתה - אנו

17.5 Past Tense of kal (pa'al)

The complete past tense pattern of ordinary <u>kal</u> verbs with three-consonant roots is as follows:

		<u>šlx</u>			<u>šlx</u>
1 s.	/-a-á-ti/	šaláxti	1 pl.	/-a-á-nu /	šaláxnu
2 m.s.	/-a-á-ta/	šaláxta	2 m. pl.	/-a-á-tem/	šaláxtem
2 f.s.	/-a-á-t /	šaláxt	2 f. pl.	/-a-á-ten/	šaláxten
3 m.s.	/-a-á- /	šaláx	3 pl.	/-a--ú /	šalxú
3 f.s.	/-a--á /	šalxá			

E. Substitution-Agreement Drill /šaláx/ "sent"

When did they sent the package?

<u>matáy hém šalxú et haxavilá.</u>   ?מתי הם שלחו את החבילה

   atém - haxenvaní - át - xána   אתם - החנווני - את - חנה
   heń - atá - már káspi - hém   הן - אתה - מר כספי - הם

F. Substitution-Agreement Drill /mazág/ "poured"

I poured the wine into the glasses.

<u>mazágti et hayáin lakosót.</u>   .מזגתי את היין לכוסות

   iští - át - atá - mošé   אשתי - את - אתה - משה
   ánu - baaléx - hén - aní   אנו - בעלך - הן - אני

G. Substitution-Agreement Drill /macá/ "found"

She found the package on the third floor.

<u>hí mac'á et haxavilá bakomá hašlišít.</u>   .היא מצאה את החבילה בקומה השלישית

   aní - hém - atá - avígdor   אני - הם - אתה - אביגדור
   át - ištó - hú - hí   את - אשתו - הוא - היא

Verbs such as /rác/ "ran" are traditionally listed as pa'al conjugations.
They resemble the ordinary pa'al verbs in the past tense in that the same vowel
/a/ occurs in all forms:

1 s.	/rácti/	"I ran"	1 pl.	/rácnu/	"we ran"
2 m.s.	/rácta/	"you ran"	2 m. pl.	/ráctem/	"you ran"
2 f.s.	/ráct/	"you ran"	2 f. pl.	/rácten/	"you ran"
3 m.s.	/rác/	"he ran"	3 pl.	/rácu/	"they ran"
3 f.s.	/ráca/	"she ran"			

Note that the stress remains on the infixed /á/ in the 3 f.s. and the 3 pl.:

/ráca/ "she ran"   /rácu/ "they ran"

Verbs such as /rác/ have only two consonants in the root, but are listed in
dictionaries with yav (ו) or yud (י) as the second root consonant. Thus, /rác/
רץ will be listed alphabetically under רוץ

The verb /bá/ "he came" is listed under בוא . Its pattern is similar to /rác/
except that it has only one consonant. All forms, though, are spelled with א ,

H.   Substitution-Agreement Drill /rác/ "ran"

Dov ran to the office this morning.

<u>dóv rác habóker lamisrád .</u>   .דוב רץ הבוקר למשרד

aní – atá – már káspı – át   אני - אתה - מר כספי - את
ánu – raxél – raxél vesára – dóv   אנו - רחל - רחל ושרה - דוב

I.   Substitution-Agreement Drill /ba/ "came"

David came to the office yesterday.

<u>davíd bá etmól lamisrád.</u>   .דוד בא אתמול למשרד

atá – át –hanaším – aní   אתה - את - הנשים - אני
hem – ánu – atém – hí – davíd   הם - אנו - אתם - היא - דוד

17.6 Past Tense of hitpa'el

The hitpa'el is characterized by a prefix of the pattern /Cit-/. The first
consonant of the prefix is usually /h/ in the past tense.

The hitpa'el resembles the pi'el in that the second stem vowel is /e/ in the
3 m.s. and /a/ in the first and second person in verbs with three root consonants.

/hitrašámti/   " I was impressed"
/hitrašém/   " he was impressed"

The first stem vowel is either /a/ or /o/.

/hitrašém/   " he was impressed"
/hitkonén/   " he planned"

The complete past tense pattern of the <u>hitpa'el</u> is as follows:

1 s.	/hit-a-á-ti/	hitrašámti		1 pl.	/hit-a-á-nu/	hitrašámnu
2 m.s.	/hit-a-á-ta/	hitrašámta		2 m.pl.	/hit-a-á-tem/	hitrašámtem
2 f.s.	/hit-a-á-t /	hitrašámt		2 f.pl.	/hit-a-á-ten/	hitrašámten
3 m.s.	/hit-a-é- /	hitrašém		3 pl.	/hit-a--ú/	hitrašmú
3 f.s.	/hit-a--á /	hitrašmá				

J. Substitution-Agreement Drill /hitrašém/ "was impressed"

We were impressed by the new stamps.

hitrašámnu mehabulím haxadaším.   .התרשמנו מהבולים החדשים

haamerikáim - atém - aní - iští   האמריקאים - אתם - אני - אשתי
át - baalá - atá - gvéret kóhen   את - בעלה - אתה - גברת כהן

K.   Substitution-Agreement Drill /hitkonén/ "got ready"

He got ready to move to a new house.

hú hitkonén laavór lebáit xadáš.   .הוא התכונן לעבור לבית חדש

áta - ánu - mišpáxat zahávi   אתה - אנו - משפחת זהבי
hayoéc haxadáš - aní - hém - át   היועץ החדש - אני - הם - את

17.7 Past Tense of hif'il.

The hif'il conjugation is characterized in the past tense by the prefix /hi-/, /he-/, or /ho-/.

Verbs whose first root consonant is <u>x</u> (spelled with ח , but not <u>x</u> when spelled with כ) or <u>'</u> will have the prefix /he-/.

/hexlít/ "he decided" - root xlt חלט
/he'evír/ "he brought over" - root 'vr עבר

The prefix /he-/ also occurs with some verbs whose first root consonant is <u>r</u>.

Verbs with only two root consonants also have the prefix /he-/. These verbs are listed in the dictionary with <u>vav</u> (ו) or <u>yud</u> (י) as the second root consonant.

/heríc/ "he caused to run" - root <u>r-c</u>   רוץ
/hekím/ "he set up" - root <u>k-m</u>   קום

Roots listed with <u>yud</u> (י) as the first consonant will have the prefix /ho-/, with a <u>vav</u> replacing the <u>yud</u> of the root.

/hodía/ "he informed" - root <u>yd'</u>   ידע
/hošív/ "he seated"   - root <u>yšv</u>   ישב

The root hlx "go" also has the prefix /ho-/ in the hif'il, with the <u>vav</u> replacing the <u>h</u> of the root.

/holíx/ "he led"   - root hlx   הלך

All other verbs have the prefix /hi-/.

/himšíx/ "he continued"	- root mšx	משך
/hizmín/ "he invited"	- root zmn	זמן
/higzím/ "he exaggerated"	- root gzm	גזם

If the first of the three consonants is <u>n</u>, then the <u>n</u> will be dropped in the hif'il conjugation.

/hikír/ "he recognized"	- root nkr	נכר
/higía/ "he arrived"	- root ng'	נגע

The full pattern of the past tense is as follows: (The prefix /hi-/ is used as an example).

		mšx			mšx
1 s.	/hi--á-ti/	himšáxti	1 pl.	/hi-á-nu/	himšáxnu
2 m.s.	/hi--á-ta/	himšáxta	2 m.pl.	/hi--á-tem/	himšáxtem
2 f.s.	/hi--á-t/	himšáxt	2 f.pl.	/hi--á-ten/	himšáxten
3 m.s.	/hi--í- /	himšíx	3 pl.	/hi--í-u/	himšíxu
3 f.s.	/hi--í-a/	himšíxa			

Note that the stress remains on the infixed vowel in the third person forms:

/himšíxa/ "she continued"
/himšíxu/ "they continued"

L. Substitution-Agreement Drill /himšíx/"continued".

He continued studying in Israel.

<u>hú himšíx lilmód baárec.</u>   <u>הוא המשיך ללמוד בארץ.</u>

gvéret Smith - yónatan - hém	גברת סמית – יונתן – הם
aní - át - ánu - kulám - atém	אני – את – אנו – כולם – אתם
iští veaní - atá - hú	אשתי ואני – אתה – הוא

M. Substitution-Agreement Drill /hitxíl/ "began"

Yosef started eating an hour ago.

<u>yoséf hitxíl leexól lifnéy šaá.</u>   <u>יוסף החחיל לאכול לפני שעה.</u>

raxél - mošé - aní - atá	רחל – משה – אני – אתה
ánu - atém - hém - xána	אנו – אתם – הם – חנה
hén - atén - át - yoséf	הן – אתן – את – יוסף

N. Substitution-Agreement Drill /hizmín/ "invited"

Mr. Zahavi invited them for dinner.

<u>már zahávi hizmín otám learuxát érev.</u>   <u>מר זהבי הזמין אותם לארוחת ערב.</u>

hén - ánu - ištó - aní	הן – אנו – אשתו – אני
yaakóv - atém - át - hí	יעקב – אתם – את – היא
atén - atá - hém - már zahávi	אתן – אתה – הם – מר זהבי

O. Substitution-Agreement Drill /hikír/ "recognized, knew"

He was introduced to her in the Brooklyn Bar.

<u>hú hikír otá bebrúklin bár.</u>　　　　　　　　　.הוא הכיר אותה בברוקלין בר

xána - át - atá - ánu　　　　　　　　　חנה – את – אתה – אנו
dóv - aní - hén - hú　　　　　　　　　רוב – אני – הן – הוא

P. Substitution-Agreement Drill /higía/ "arrived"

The counsellor arrived in Tel Aviv this morning.

<u>hayoéc higía letél avív habóker.</u>　　　　　　.היועץ הגיע לתל אביב הבוקר

ánu - atém - sára veyoséf　　　　　　　אנו – אתם – שרה ויוסף
hí - atá - hém - át - hayoéc　　　　היא – אתה – הם – את – היועץ

Q. Substitution-Agreement Drill /higzím/ "exaggerated"

He exaggerated his story.

<u>hú higzím basipúr šeló.</u>　　　　　　　　　.הוא הגזים בסיפור שלו

hém - atá - aní - át,　　　　　　　　　הם – אתה – אני – את
menaxém - atára - atém - hú　　　　מנחם – עטרה – אתם – הוא

R. Substitution-Agreement Drill /hexlít/ "decided"

(Note: In the first and second person forms an /e/ is inserted before the
suffix - /hexláteti/.)

He decided not to go by ship.

<u>hú hexlít ló linsóa beoniá.</u>　　　　　　.הוא החליט לא לנסוע באוניה

atém - aní - haxenvaní - hí　　　　אתם – אני – החנווני – היא
atá - hém - ánu - át - hú　　　　　אתה – הם – אנו – את – הוא

S. Substitution-Agreement Drill /heríc/ "caused to run"

He had us running the whole morning.

<u>hú heríc otánu kol habóker.</u>　　　　　　.הוא הריץ אותנו כל הבוקר

hí - atém - át - yónatan　　　　　　היא – אתם – את – יונתן
atá - hém - atára - hú　　　　　　　אתה – הם – עטרה – הוא

T. Substitution-Agreement Drill /hodía/ "informed"

He told Yonatan that he didn't get the telegram.

<u>hú hodía leyónatan šeló kibél et hamivrák.</u>　.הוא הודיע ליונתן שלא קבל את המברק

aní - atára - atém - át　　　　　　אני – עטרה – אתם – את
sára veaní - hém - atá - hú　　　שרה ואני – הם – אתה – הוא

175

17.8 Past Tense of lamed hey verbs

Regardless of the conjugation (binyan) these verbs have the following similarities:

a) The vowel before the 1st and 2nd person suffixes is /-í-/ or /-é-/. In the kal and pi'el the vowel is /-í /. In the other binyanim it is /-é /.

b) The 3rd person forms are as described in Grammar Section 16.4c.

    3 m.s. -á
    3 f.s. -tá
    3 pl.   ú

A complete past tense is as follows:
(The verb illustrated is /xiká/ חכה "waited")

1 s.	/-V-íti/	xikíti	חכיתי	1 pl.	/-V ínu/	xikínu	חכינו
2 m.s.	/-V-íta/	xikíta	חכית	2 m.pl.	/-V-ítem/	xikítem	חכיתם
2 f.s.	/-V-ít/	xikít	חכית	2 f.pl.	/-V-íten/	xikíten	חכיתן
3 m.s.	/-V-á/	xiká	חכה	3 pl.	/-V-ú/	xikú	חכו
3 f.s.	/-V-tá /	xiktá	חכתה				

U. Substitution-Agreement Drill /kivá/ "hoped"

I hoped to go to Haifa.

kivíti linsóa lexáyfa.   .קוויתי לנסוע לחיפה

yónatan - raxél - hén - át   יונתן - רחל - הן - את
ánu   atá - atén - aní   אנו - אתה - אתן - אני

V. Substitution-Agreement Drill /xiká/ "waited"

I waited and waited for Friday to come.

xikíti vexikíti leyóm šiší ševavó.   .חכיתי וחכיתי ליום ששי שיבוא

ánu - atá - hém - hí   אנו - אתה - הם - היא
mošé - át - atén - sára   משה - את - אתן - שרה
atém - dóv vexána - aní   אתם - דוב וחנה - אני

W. Substitution-Agreement Drill /racá/ "wanted"

I wanted to go to the tourist office.

racíti laléxet lemisrád hatayarút.   .רציתי ללכת למשרד התיירות

atén - át - iští veaní - mí   אתן - את - אשתי ואני - מי
atá - avígdor - atára - hém   אתה - אביגדור - עטרה - הם
már Williams - atém - aní   מר ווילימס - אתם - אני

X. Substitution-Agreement Drill /asá/ "made, did"

I did well to get here early.

tóv asíti šehigáti mukdám .   .טוב עשיתי שהגעתי מוקדם

át - davíd - atá - léa   את - דוד - אתה - לאה
ánu - hém - atén - aní   אנו - הם - אתן - אני

Y. Substitution-Agreement Drill /kaná/ "bought"   קנה

He bought a new house.

<u>hú kaná báit xadáš.</u>   <u>.הוא קנה בית חדש</u>

   ánu - xána vebaalá - aní   אנו – חנה וכעלה – אני
   gvéret kóhen - atém - hí   גברת כהן – אתם – היא
   atá - yoséf - hém - hú   אתה – יוסף – הם – הוא

Z. Substitution-Agreement Drill / raá/ "saw"   ראה

He saw her this morning.

<u>hú raá otá habóker.</u>   <u>.הוא ראה אותה הבוקר</u>

   aní - át - hí - ánu   אני – את – היא – אנו
   atén - hén - yónatan   אתן – הן – יונתן
   atá - ištó - hú   אתה – אשתו – הוא

AA. Substitution-Agreement Drill /paná/ "turned"   פנה

He addressed him in English.

<u>hú paná eláv beanglít.</u>   <u>.הוא פנה אליו באנגלית</u>

   át - hayoéc haxadáš - atá   את – היועץ החרש – אתה
   aní -gvéret káspi - hém - hú   אני – גברת כספי – הם – הוא

BB. Substitution-Agreement Drill /šatá/ "drank"   שתה

I didn't drink the water.

<u>ló šatíti et hamáim.</u>   <u>.לא שתיתי את המים</u>

   ánu - atém - hém - dóv   אנו – אתם – הם – רב
   avíva - hén - sára - atá   אביבה – הן – שרה – אתה
   haamerikáim - át - aní   האמריקאים – את – אני

CC. Substitution-Agreement Drill /alá/ "went up"   עלה

We went up to the third floor.

<u>alínu lakomá hašlišít.</u>   <u>.עלינו לקומה השלישית</u>

   aní - kulám - atém - át   אני – כולם – אתם – את
   már alón - ištexá   hém   מר אלון – אשתך – הם
   atá - atén - hú - ánu   אתה – אתן – הוא – אנו

DD. Substitution-Agreement Drill /nitmaná/ "was appointed"   נתמנה

We were appointed as advisers in the foreign office.

<u>nitmanénu keyoacím bemisrád haxúc.</u>   <u>.נתמנינו כיועצים כמשרד החרץ</u>

   atém - hém - már kóhen - aní   אתם – הם – מר כהן – אני
   hén - hí   át - ánu   הן – היא – את – אנו

EE. Substitution-Agreement Drill /hayá/ "was"

The verb /hayá/ poses problems other than the <u>lamed hey</u> pattern. In ordinary speech the /h/ is often dropped, and the /y/ is often a very slight glide between the surrounding vowels. A spelling consistent with other <u>lamed hey</u> verbs would be as in the left-hand column.

Transcriptions of frequently heard pronunciations are in the middle and right hand columns.

1 s.	hayíti	/haíti/	or	/aíti/
2 m.s.	hayíta	/haíta/	or	/aíta/
2 f.s.	hayít	/haít/	or	/aít/
3 m.s.	hayá			/ayá/
3 f.s.	haytá			/aytá/
1 pl.	hayínu	/haínu/	or	/aínu/
2 m.pl.	hayítem	/haítem/	or	/aítem/
2 f.pl.	hayíten	/haíten/	or	/aíten/
3 pl.	hayú			/ayú/

In previous units the transcriptions in the middle column have been used since they represent the most generally acceptable pronunciation.

I was in Haifa a week ago.

haíti bexáyfa lifnéy šavúa.　　　　　　　　　.הייתי בחיפה לפני שבוע

hém - baalá - mošé - ánu			אנו – משה – בעלה – הם
atén - xána - atá - át			את – אתה – חנה – אתן
hí - hén - dóv - aní			אני – דוב – הן – היא

FF. Substitution-Agreement Drill /nir'á/ "seemed, was seen"

This <u>binyan, nif'al</u>, will be discussed in detail in Unit 19. However, the forms of /nir'á/ may be drilled here as an example of a <u>lamed hey</u> verb. The prefix /ni-/ is the same in all forms.

You looked well yesterday.

nir'ét tóv etmól.　　　　　　　　　.נראית טוב אתמול

atá - sára - hú - aní			אני – הוא – שרה – אתה
ánu - xána vemošé - hí			היא – חנה ומשה – אנו
davíd - atém - hém - át			את – הם – אתם – דוד

RAPID RESPONSE DRILL

1. má rocé már Williams lišlóax.	?1. מה רוצה מר וויליאמס לשלוח
2. leán hú rocé lišlóax et hamixtáv.	?2. לאן הוא רוצה לשלוח את המכתב
3. haím hú yišláx et hamixtáv bedóar avír o bedóar ragíl.	3. האם הוא ישלח את המכתב בדואר ?אוויר או בדואר רגיל
4. káma yaalé lo lišlóax et hamixtáv.	?4. כמה יעלה לו לשלוח את המכתב
5. káma zmán yikáx lamixtáv lehagía leamérika.	5. כמה זמן יקח למכתב להגיע ?לאמריקה
6. haím hamixtáv daxúf?	?6. הם המכתב רחוף
7. haím mar Williams yišláx mivrák?	?7. האם מר וויליאמס ישלח מברק
8. heyxán nimcét hamivraká.	?8. היכן נמצאת המברקה

REVIEW CONVERSATIONS

A: aní rocé lišlóax et haxavilá   א : אני רוצה לשלוח את החבילה
hazót letél avív.   הזאת לתל אביב.

B: éyx atá rocé lišlóax otá.   ב : איך אתה רוצה לשלוח אותה,
ragíl o exprés.   רגיל או אקספרס?

A: káma zmán yikáx bedóar ragíl,   א : כמה זמן יקח בדואר רגיל,
vekáma beeksprés.   וכמה באקספרס'?

B: ragíl yikáx xamišá yamím,   ב : רגיל יקח חמישה ימים,
beeksprés yomáim.   באקספרס יומים.

A: im káx, šláx et haxavilá ragíl.   א : אם כך, שלח את החבילה רגיל.
zé ló kol káx daxúf.   זה לא כל כך דחוף.

C: tén li bevakašá, xaméš igrót avír.   ג : תן לי בבקשה, חמש אגרות אויר.

D: kén. bevakašá.   ד : כן. בבקשה.

C: káma zé olé.   ג : כמה זה עולה?

D: šlosím vexaméš agorót kol axát.   ד : שלושים וחמש אגורות כל אחת.
yáxad líra vesív'ím vexaméš agorót.   יחד לירה ושבעים וחמש אגורות.

E: kibálnu habóker gluyá mimišpáxat zahávi.   ה : קבלנו הבוקר גלויה ממשפחת זהבי.

F: má hém kotvím.   ו : מה הם כותבים?

E: hém kotvím šeyavóu lir'ót otánu bekaróv.   ה : הם כותבים שיבואו לראות אותנו בקרוב.

F: tóv méod. hém katvú matáy šehém yavóu?   ו : טוב מאוד. הם כתבו מתי שהם יבואו?

E: ló. ax hém yišlexú mivrák lifnéy šeyagíu.   ה : לא. אך הם ישלחו מברק לפני שיגיעו.

G: aní caríx bulím. éyfo aní yaxól   ז : אני צריך בולים. איפה אני יכול
liknót otám.   לקנות אותם'?

H: bulím efšar liknót badóar.   ח : בולים אפשר לקנות בדואר.

G: éyfo hadóar?   ז : איפה הדואר?

H: hadóar nimcá birxóv álenbi,   ח : הדואר נמצא ברחוב אלנבי,
lo raxók mikán.   לא רחוק מכאן.

G: ad éyze šaá hadóar patúax.   ז : עד איזה שעה הדואר פתוח?

H: ad xaméš.   ח : עד חמש.

NOTE ON TRANSCRIPTION

In the remainder of the book the stress mark ⁻ is
used only when a syllable other than the last ⁻in a
a word is stressed.

היית רוצה להגיע חצי שעה לפני הזמן...

18.1 Telling Time

DOV

What time is it?	ma hašaa.	מה השעה?
hour	šaa (f)	שעה

AVIVA

It's	hašaa	השעה
a quarter to seven.	réva lešéva.	רבע לשבע.
quarter	réva (m)	רבע

DOV

When are (your) parents	matay omdim	מתי עומרים
supposed to arrive?	hahorim lehagía.	ההורים להגיע?
he stood	amad	עמד
parents	horim (m.pl)	הורים

AVIVA

I don't know	ani lo yodáat	אני לא יודעת
exactly.	bediyuk.	בדיוק.
It seems to me	nidme li	נדמה לי
at eight thirty.	šebešmóne vaxéci.	שבשמונה וחצי.
seems	nidme (m.s. pres.)	נדמה

DOV

Please check	bidki bevakaša,	בירקי בבקשה
when	matay	מתי
the plane will arrive.	šehamatos yagía.	שהמטוס יגיע.
I'd like	hayíti roce	הייתי רוצה
to get (there)	lehagía	להגיע
a half hour	xaci šaa	חצי שעה
ahead of time.	lifney hazman.	לפני הזמן.
he examined	badak	בדק
airplane	matos (m)	מטוס

AVIVA

All right.	beracon.	ברצון.
I want	gam ani roca	גם אני רוצה
to go with you, too.	linsóa itxa.	לנסוע אתך.
to travel	linsóa	לנסוע
he traveled	nasa	נסע
with me	iti	אתי

DOV

Good, I'll take you.	tov, ekax otax.	טוב. אקח אותך.
We'll have to	nictarex	נצטרך
wait	lexakot	לחכות
until they clear	ad šehem yaavru	עד שהם יעברו
customs.	et haméxes.	את המכס.
he needed, had to	hictarex	הצטרך
customs	méxes (m)	מכס

181

AVIVA

We have	yeš lánu	יש לנו
enough time.	maspik zman.	מספיק זמן.
enough	maspik	מספיק
he made it in time	hispik	הספיק

DOV

I hope so.	ani mekave kax.	אני מקווה כך.
Call up right away.	hitkašri miyad.	התקשרי מיד.
he got in touch	hitkašer	התקשר
immediately	miyad	מיד

18.2 ADDITIONAL VOCABULARY

The following are several of the expressions for telling time. The feminine numbers are used with /dakot/ "minutes", and the masculine numbers with /regaim/ "minutes".

/hašaa/ may be omitted in the reply.

What time do you have?	ma hašaa eclexa?	מה השעה אצלך?
The time is ten minutes before seven.	hašaa éser dakot lifney šéva.	השעה עשר דקות לפני שבע.
minute	daka (f)	דקה
The time is ten to seven.	hašaa asara lešéva.	השעה עשרה לשבע.
The time is ten to seven.	šéva paxot asara.	השעה שבע פחות עשרה.
less	paxot	פחות
The time is ten minutes after seven.	hašaa éser dakot axarey šéva.	השעה עשר דקות אחרי שבע.
The time is 7:10.	hašaa šéva veasara.	השעה שבע ועשרה.
The time is 7:15.	hašaa šéva varéva.	השעה שבע ורבע.
I'll meet her at 9:00 A.M.	efgoš ota betéša babóker.	אפגוש אותה בתשע בבוקר.
I'll meet her at 3:00 P.M.	efgoš ota bešalóš axarey hacohoráim.	אפגוש אותה בשלוש אחרי הצהריים.
I'll meet her at 8:00 P.M.	efgoš ota bešmóne baérev.	אפגוש אותה בשמונה בערב.
I'll arrive at midnight.	agía bexacot.	אגיע בחצות.
midnight	xacot	חצות
It'll take us 24 hours to get there.	yikax lánu yemama lehagía.	יקח לנו יממה להגיע.
24 hour period	yemama (f)	יממה
Wait a minute.	xake réga.	חכה רגע.
minute, moment	réga	רגע

My watch	hašáon šeli	השעון שלי
is slow.	mefager.	מפגר.
retarded	mefager (m.s. pres) מפגר	

| My watch is fast. | hašáon šeli memaher. | השעון שלי ממהר. |

The big hand	hamaxog hagadol	המחוג הגדול
is on the five,	al xameš,	על חמש,
and the little hand	vehamaxog hakatan	והמחוג הקטן
is on the three.	al šaloš.	על שלוש.
dial hand	maxog	מחוג
(plural)	mexugim	מחוגים

18.3 Vocabulary Drills

A. Substitution-Agreement Drill /omed/ "stand" (pres.)

He is standing next to the movie.

<u>hu omed al yad hakolnóa.</u>   <u>הוא עומד על יד הקולנוע.</u>

at - hem - sára vebaala - hi   את – הם – שרה ובעלה – היא
ani - hanašim - ata - hu   אני – הנשים – אתה – הוא

B. Substitution-Agreement Drill /amad/ "stood" (past)

He stood on the corner all morning.

<u>hu amad bapina kol habóker.</u>   <u>הוא עמד בפינה כל הבוקר.</u>

hem - ani - atem - at   הם – אני – אתם – את
hi - moše - ánu - hu   היא – משה – אנו – הוא

C. Substitution Drill /bdok/ "examine" (imv.)

Check all the doors.

bdok et kol hadlatot.   בדוק את כל הדלתות.
bidki   בדקי
bidku   בדקו
bdókna   בדוקנה

D. Transformation Drill - Negative to Affirmative
(The first column may be done as a substitution drill first.)

Don't examine the packages.

al tivdok et haxavilot. bdok et haxavilot.   אל תבדוק את החבילות.
al tivdeki et haxavilot. bidki et haxavilot.   אל תבדקי את החבילות.
al tivdeku et haxavilot. bidku et haxavilot.   אל תבדקו את החבילות.
al tivdókna et haxavilot.bdókna et haxavilot.   אל תבדוקנה את החבילות.

E. Transformation Drill - Affirmative to Negative

Do Drill D in reverse.

F. Substitution Drill /e - ~ti -/

I'll check his phone number.

evdok et mispar hatélefon šelo.		אבדוק את מספר הטלפון שלו.
ata	tivdok	אתה תבדוק
at	tivdeki	את תבדקי
dov	yivdok	דוב יבדוק
hi	tivdok	היא תבדוק
	nivdok	נבדוק
	tivdeku	תבדקו
	tivdókna	תבדוקנה
hem	yivdeku	הם יבדקו
hen	tivdókna	הן תבדוקנה

G. Substitution-Agreement Drill

David will check the mail.

<u>david yivdok et hadóar.</u>   <u>דוד יבדוק את הדואר.</u>

ani - xána - hem - ata	אני - חנה - הם - אתה
ánu - at - atem - mi	אנו - את - אתם - מי
aten - hen - hi - david	אתן - הן - היא - דוד

H. Substitution-Agreement Drill /badak/ "examined"

He checked the address in the phone book.

<u>hu badak et haktóvet beséfer hatelefónim.</u>   <u>הוא בדק את הכתובת בספר הטלפונים.</u>

hi - ata - ánu - ani	היא - אתה - אנו - אני
hem - yosef - at - hu	הם - יוסף - את - הוא

I. Substitution Drill /e - ~ti -/

I'll have to get to Lydda by five o'clock.

ectarex lehagiá lelud ad xameš.		אצטרך להגיע ללוד עד חמש.
	tictarex	תצטרך
at	tictarxi	את תצטרכי
hu	yictarex	הוא יצטרך
hi	tictarex	היא תצטרך
	nictarex	נצטרך
atem	tictarxu	אתם תצטרכו
aten	tictaréxna	אתן תצטרכנה
hem	yictarxu	הם יצטרכו
hen	tictaréxna	הן תצטרכנה

J. Substitution-Agreement Drill

He'll have to send the letter special delivery.

<u>hu yictarex lišlóax et hamixtav ekspres.</u>   <u>הוא יצטרך לשלוח את המכתב אקספרס.</u>

ánu - aten - raxel - hem	אנו - אתן - רחל - הם
at - ata - ani - hen - hi	את - אתה - אני - הן - היא
atem - mar káspi - hi - hu	אתם - מר כספי - היא - הוא

K. Substitution-Agreement Drill /hispik/ "he had the time to"

Dov didn't have time to eat breakfast.

<u>dov lo hispik leexol aruxat bóker.</u>   .דוב לא הספיק לאכול ארוחת בוקר

```
ani - ata - išto - baala                              אני - אתה - אשתו - בעלה
hem - ánu - at - dov                                  הם - אנו - את - דוב
```

L. Substitution Drill

I won't get a chance to see the whole city.

```
        lo aspik lir'ot et kol hair.          לא אספיק לראות את כל העיר.
        lo taspík                                          לא תספיק
        lo taspíki                                         לא תספיקי
   hu   lo yaspik                                     הוא לא יספיק
   hi   lo taspik                                     היא לא תספיק
        lo naspik                                          לא נספיק
        lo taspíku                                         לא תספיקו
 aten   lo taspékna                                  אתן לא תספקנה
  hem   lo yaspíku                                   הם  לא יספיקו
  hen   lo taspékna                                  הן  לא תספקנה
```

M. Expansion Drill

Instructor: I didn't get a chance to see him.
Student : I didn't get a chance to see him,
           I'll have to come tomorrow.

```
lo hispákti lir'ot oto.                                     לא הספקתי לראות אותו.
          ectarex lavo maxar.          אצטרך לבוא מחר.
lo hisoáknu lir'ot oto.                                     לא הספקנו לראות אותו.
          nictarex lavo maxar.          נצטרך לבוא מחר.
xána lo hispíka lir'ot oto.                         חנה לא הספיקה לראות אותו.
          hi tictarex lavo maxar.          היא תצטרך לבוא מחר.
ata lo hispákta lir'ot oto.                         אתה לא הספקת לראות אותו.
          tictarex lavo maxar.          תצטרך לבוא מחר.
hem lo hispíku lir'ot oto.                          הם לא הספיקו לראות אותו.
          yictarxu lavo maxar.          יצטרכו לבוא מחר.
lo hispákta lir'ot oto.                                     לא הספקת לראות אותו.
          tictarex lavo maxar.          תצטרך לבוא מחר.
aten lo hispákten lir'ot oto.                       אתן לא הספקתן לראות אותו.
          tictaréxna lavo maxar.          תצטרכנה לבוא מחר.
hen lo hispíku lir'ot oto.                          הן לא הספיקו לראות אותו.
          tictaréxna lavo maxar.          תצטרכנה לבוא מחר.
at lo hispakt lir'ot oto.                           את לא הספקת לראות אותו.
          tictarxi lavo maxar.          תצטרכי לבוא מחר.
```

N. Substitution Drill

Call right away; it's urgent.

hitkašer miyad. ze daxuf.	התקשר מיר. זה דחוף.
hitkašri	התקשרי
hitkašru	התקשרו
hitkašérna	התקשרנה

O. Substitution Drill   /e- ~ ti - /

I'll get in touch with Mr. Caspi.

ani etkašer im mar káspi.	אני אתקשר עם מר כספי.
ata titkašer	אתה תתקשר
at titkašri	את תתקשרי
hu yitkašer	הוא יתקשר
hi titkašer	היא תתקשר
ánu nitkašer	אנו נתקשר
atem titkašru	אתם תתקשרו
aten titkašérna	אתן תתקשרנה
hem yitkašru	הם יתקשרו
hen titkašérna	הן תתקשרנה

P. Substitution-Agreement Drill

I'll call them this week.

<u>etkašer itam hašavúa.</u>	<u>אתקשר אתם השבוע.</u>
moše veišto - dov - sára	משה ואשתו - דוב - שרה
ata - aten - ánu - hi	אתה - אתן - אנו - היא
at - hen - atem - ani	את - הן - אתם - אני

R. Substitution-Agreement Drill /hitkašer/ "he contacted"

He got in touch with Mrs. Cohen this morning.

<u>hu hitkašer im gvéret kóhen habóker.</u>	<u>הוא התקשר עם גברת כהן הבוקר.</u>
ani - at - hem - sára	אני - את - הם - שרה
ata - atem - išto - hi	אתה - אתם - אשתו - היא
ánu - yosef - hen - hu	אנו - יוסף - הן - הוא

S. Expansion Drill   /iti /   "with me"

Instructor: I'll go to school.
Student: I'll go to school, and Moshe
            will go with me.

ani elex lebet haséfer, vemoše yelex iti.			אני אלך לבית הספר ומשה ילך אתי.
ata telex	itxa.	אתך.	אתה תלך
dov yelex	ito.	אתו.	דוב ילך
xána telex	ita.	אתה.	חנה תלך
ánu nelex	itánu.	אתנו.	אנו נלך
hem yelxu	itam.	אתם.	הם ילכו
atem telxu	itxem.	אתכם.	אתם תלכו
at telxi	itax.	אתך.	את תלכי
aten teléxna	itxen.	אתכן.	אתן תלכנה
hen teléxna	itan.	אתן.	הן תלכנה

The unsuffixed form of this preposition is /et/, identical to the preposition /et/ indicating a direct object. The unsuffixed form /et/ is used with the meaning "with" only in special literary styles. In ordinary Hebrew the preposition /im/ is used, and /et/ is used for the direct object. With the pronominal suffixes all three are in common use: /oti/ "me", /iti/, /imi/ "with me".

T. Substitution Drill   /iti ~ imi/

The student repeats the sentence, substituting the preposition /im-/. The drill may then be done in reverse.

Yonatan will go with me this evening.

yónatan yelex iti haérev.	יונתן ילך אתי הערב.
yónatan yelex imi haérev.	יונתן ילך עמי הערב.
axálti ito aruxat cohoráim.	אכלתי אתו ארוחת צהריים.
(imo)	(עמו)
mi hitkašer itxa habóker.	מי התקשר אתך הבוקר?
(imxa)	(עמך)
šaláxnu et haxavila itam.	שלחנו את החבילה אתם.
(imam)	(עמם)
hu roce linsóa itánu lexáyfa.	הוא רוצה לנסוע אתנו לחיפה.
(imánu)	(עמנו)
išti telex ita lakolnóa.	אשתי תלך אתה לקולנוע.
(ima)	(עמה)
tikxu et moše itxem.	תקחו את משה אתכם.
(imaxem)	(עמכם)
hen lo tikáxna et hasfarim itan.	הן לא תקחנה את הספרים אתן.
(iman)	(עמן)
haim hem lamdu itax bebet haséfer?	האם הם למדו אתך בבית הספר?
(imax)	(עמך)
haim hen garot itxen bebáit exad?	האם הן גרות אתכן בבית אחד?
(imaxen)	(עמכן)

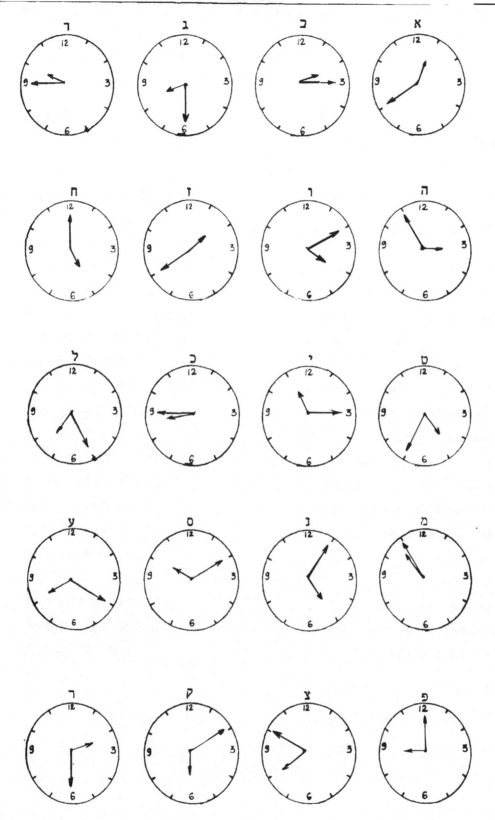

Drills_____

A. The students cover this page, and the instructor asks at random for the
time on the clocks.

What time is it on clock_____.

ma hašaa al šaon ____.   •_____ מה השעה על שעון

א	hašaa esrim dakot lifney axat.	השעה עשרים דקות לפני אחת. א
ב	hašaa štáim varéva.	השעה שתיים ורבע. כ
ג	hašaa šmóne vaxéci.	השעה שמונה וחצי. ג
ד	hašaa réva leéser.	השעה רבע לעשר. ד
ה	hašaa xaméš dakot lifnéy šaloš.	השעה חמש דקות לפני שלוש. ה
ו	hašaa éser dakot axarey árba.	השעה עשר דקות אחרי ארבע. ו
ז	hašaa esrim dakot lifney štáim.	השעה עשרים דקות לפני שתיים. ז
ח	hašaa xameš (bediyuk).	השעה חמש (בדיוק). ח
ט	hašaa esrim vexameš dakot lifney xaméš.	השעה עשרים וחמש דקות לפני חמש. ט
י	hašaa axát'esre varéva.	השעה אחת עשרה ורבע. י
כ	hašaa réva letéša.	השעה רבע לתשע. כ
ל	hašaa esrim vexameš dakot axarey šéva.	השעה עשרים וחמש דקות אחרי שבע. ל
מ	hašaa xameš dakot leaxát'esre.	השעה חמש דקות לאחת עשרה. מ
נ	hašaa xameš vexamiša.	השעה חמש וחמישה. נ
ס	hašaa éser veasara.	השעה עשר ועשרה. ס
ע	hašaa šmóne veesrim.	השעה שמונה ועשרים. ע
פ	hašaa téša.	השעה תשע. פ
צ	hašaa asara lešmóne.	השעה עשרה .לשמונה. צ
ק	hašaa éser dakot axarey šeš.	השעה עשר דקות אחרי שש. ק
ר	hašaa štáim vaxéci.	השעה שתיים וחצי. ר

GRAMMAR NOTES

18.5 The Expected Future

Note the following sentence from the Basic Conversation of this unit:

matay omdim hahorim lehagia. "when are your parents supposed to arrive?"

The construction /omdim lehagía/ (literally "stand to arrive") may also be translated "expect to arrive". It is a paraphrase of the future with the added meaning of expectation. The first verb, "stand" may occur in the past tense /amad/ in this construction. It then may be translated "was supposed to have", and usually implies that the second verb did not occur. hem amdu liknot báit. (velo kanu). "They were supposed to have bought a house.(but didn't)" With the present tense it may mean "about to".
/hu omed lehagía./   "He is about to arrive."

A. Substitution-Agreement Drill

He's supposed to go to America.

<u>hu omed linsóa leamérika.</u>   הוא עומד לנסוע לאמריקה.

gvéret zahávi - ánu - hen   גברת זהבי - אנו - הן
ani - dov - xána - hu   אני - דוב - חנה - הוא

B. Transformation Drill

Instructor: She'll receive a letter today.
Student: She's supposed to received a letter today.

hi tekabel mixtav hayom.   היא תקבל מכתב היום.
    hi omédet lekabel mixtav hayom.   היא עומרת לקבל מכתב היום.
moše veišto yiknu báit.   משה ואשתו יקנו בית.
    moše veišto omdim liknot báit.   משה ואשתו עומדים לקנות בית.
hamišpaxa tagía beod xódeš.   המשפחה תגיע בעור חורש.
    hamišpaxa omédet lehagia beod xódeš.   המשפחה עומרת להגיע בעור חורש.
mar Williams yišlax et haxavila.   מר ווילאמס ישלח את החבילה.
    mar Williams omed lišlóax et haxavila. מר ווליאמס עומר לשלוח את החבילה.
hanašim tagána lifney xameš.   הנשים תגענה לפני חמש.
    hanašim omdot lehagía lifney xameš.   הנשים עומרות להגיע לפני חמש.

C. Transformation Drill

Instructor: I sent him a telegram.
Student: I was supposed to have sent him
            a telegram, but I didn't.

šaláxti lo mivrak.   שלחתי לו מברק.
    amádeti lišlóax lo mivrak, velo šaláxti.   עמרתי לשלוח לו מברק ולא שלחתי.
kibálti et hagluya.   קבלתי את הגלויה.
    amádeti lekabel et hagluya, velo kibálti.   עמרתי לקבל את הגלויה ולא קבלתי.
hu kibel xavila habóker.   הוא קבל חבילה הבוקר.
    hu amad lekabel xavila habóker, velo kibel. הוא עמר לקבל חבילה הבוקר ולא קבל.
kanínu báit benatánya.   קנינו בית בנתניה.
    amádnu liknot báit benatánya, velo kanínu. עמרנו לקנות בית בנתניה ולא קנינו.
hem higíu lelud etmol.   הם הגיעו ללור אתמול.
    hem amdu lehagía lelud etmol, velo higíu. הם עמרו להגיע ללור אתמול ולא הגיעו.
sára avra lebáit xadaš.   שרה עברה לבית חרש.
    sára amda laavor lebáit xadaš, velo avra.. שרה עמרה לעבור לבית חרש ולא עברה.
david axal itánu haérev.   דוד אכל אתנו הערב.
    david amad leexol itánu haérev, velo axal.. דור עמר לאכול אתנו הערב ולא אכל.

18.6 /matay še-/

Compare the following sentences:

/matay yagía hamatos./ "when will the plane arrive?"

/bidki matay šehamatos yagía/ "check [as to] when the plane will arrive."

This is another example of an included sentence. [See Grammar Note 10.4]
in this case the included sentence is a question beginning with the interrogative
/matay/ "when". When the subject is an independent noun, as /hamatos/ in the
example above, the word order in the included sentence, may differ from that of
the original sentence.

/matay tagía hamišpaxa šelxa./ "When will your family arrive?"

or /emor li matay šetagía hamišpaxa šelxa./ "Tell me when your family will arrive."
or /emor li matay šehamišpaxa šelxa tagía./

A. Transformation Drill /matay ~ matay še - /

In the following drill the instructor will ask a question beginning with
/matáy/ "When?". The student will respond by paraphrasing the same question
with a sentence beginning with /emor li matáy še-/ "Tell me when..."

Example: Instructor: matáy tagia hamišpaxa šelxá. "When will your family arrive?"
Student: emor li matáy šetagia hamišpaxá šelxá. "Tell me when your
family will arrive".

The instructor may vary this drill by having the students respond with the
feminine form /imri/ or with a plural form /imru/ or /emórna/.

1. matay tavo.   מתי תבוא? .1
אמור לי מתי שתבוא.

2. matay nigaš lemoše.   מתי ניגש למשה? .2
אמור לי מתי שניגש למשה.

3. matay nelex lir'ot et haxanut haxadaša.   מתי נלך לראות את החנות החדשה? .3
אמור לי מתי שנלך לראות את החנות החדשה.

4. matay lamadeta ledaber ivrit.   מתי למדת לדבר עברית? .4
אמור לי מתי שלמדת לדבר עברית.

5. matay tatxil bedieta.   מתי תתחיל בדיאטה? .5
אמור לי מתי שתתחיל בדיאטה.

6. matay raita et miryam.   מתי ראית את מרים? .6
אמור לי מתי שראית את מרים.

7. matay ata roce lišloax mivrak.   מתי אתה רוצה לשלוח מברק? .7
אמור לי מתי שאתה רוצה לשלוח מברק.

RAPID RESPONSE DRILL

1. matay omdim hahorim šel avíva lehagía.   מתי עומדים ההורים של אבינה להגיע? .1
2. ma crixa avíva livdok.   מה צריכה אבינה לבדוק? .2
3. káma zman lifney šehamatos yagía   כמה זמן לפני שהמטוס יגיע .3
   roce dov lehagía lelud.   רוצה דוב להגיע ללוד?
4. lean roca avíva linsóa.   לאן רוצה אבינה לנסוע? .4
5. haim dov yikax ota ito?   האם דוב יקח אותה אתו? .5
6. lema hem yictarxu lexakot.   למה הם יצטרכו לחכות? .6
7. haim hem yagíu bazman?   האם הם יגיעו בזמן? .7
8. im mi avíva crixa lehitkašer.   עם מי אבינה צריכה להתקשר? .8

REVIEW CONVERSATIONS

A: ma hašaa.   א: מה השעה?

B: hašaa šeš bediyuk.   ב: השעה שש בדיוק.

A: toda raba.   א: תודה רבה.

C: matay hahorim šelxa omdim lehagía.   ג: מתי ההורים שלך עומדים להגיע?

D: beod yomáim.   ד: בעוד יומיים.

C: hem hitkašru itxa telefónit?   ג: הם התקשרו אתך טלפונית?

D: lo, hem šalxu mixtav.   ד: לא. הם שלחו מכתב.

E: ani roca linsóa itxa lexáyfa.   ה: אני רוצה לנסוע אתך לחיפה.

F: tov. beracon.   ו: טוב. ברצון.

E: beéyze šaa tisa.   ה: באיזה שעה תיסע.

F: bešéva varéva.   ו: בשבע ורבע.

G: matay carix moše lehagía.   ז: מתי צריך משה להגיע?

H: ani lo yodáat bediyuk.   ח: אני לא יודעת בדיוק.

G: hu lo hitkašer itax?   ז: הוא לא התקשר אתך?

H: lo, hu amar šeyišlax mivrak.   ח: לא. הוא אמר שישלח מברק.

I: ata noséa lelud habóker?   ט: אתה נוסע ללוד הבוקר?

J: ken.   י: כן.

I: beéyze šaa ata noséa.   ט: באיזה שעה אתה נוסע?

J: bešmóne.   י: בשמונה.

I: yeš lexa maspik zman.   ט: יש לך מספיק זמן.

K: ani mekave šelo nictarex   כ: אני מקוה שלא נצטרך
   lexakot harbe zman.   לחכות הרבה זמן.

L: gam ani mekava kax.   ל: גם אני מקוה כך.

K: káma zman yikax lahem   כ: כמה זמן יקח להם
   laavor et haméxes.   לעבור את המכס?

L: kexaci šaa.   ל: כחצי שעה.

K: xaci šaa? ze lo harbe zman.   כ: חצי שעה? זה לא הרבה זמן.

M: bidki matay šehamatos omed lehagía.   מ: בדקי מחי שהמטוס עומד להגיע.

N: ken. etkašer miyad.   נ: כן. אתקשר מיד.

M: ani xošev šebešaa šeš.   מ: אני חורשב שבשעה שש.

N: gam ani xošévet kax.   נ: גם אני חושבת כך.

O: matay omédet hamišpaxa šelxa lehagía.   ס: מתי עומרת המשפחה שלך להגיע.

P: hamišpaxa šeli tagía beod   xódeš yamim.   ע: המשפחה שלי תגיע בעוד חורש ימים.

O: heyxan tagúru?   ס: היכן תגורו?

P: yesudar avurénu báit berámat gan.   ע: יסורד עבורנו בית כרמת גן.

O: rámat gan hi ir yafa meod.   ס: רמח גן היא עיר יפה מאור.

Q: ma at xošévet? yikax lemoše harbe   פ: מה את חושבת? יקח למשה הרבה
   zman laavor et haméxes?   זמן לעבור את המכס?

R: ken. ki yeš lo harbe xavilot.   צ: כן. כי יש לו הרבה חבילות.

Q: O ken. naxon. ad šeyivdeku et kol   פ: אה, כן, נכון. עד שיבדקו את כל
   haxavilot yikax šaa, šaatáim.   החבילות יקח שעה - שעתים.

193

הלו, יפה שּחייט שּבע שּ א־בע אסא?
חל אכיכ קוראֿ. רברו נבקשה...

19.1 Calling Long Distance

YONATAN

Atara, do you know	atára. at yodáat	עטרה, את יורעת
the telephone number	et mispar hatélefon	את מספר הטלפון
of Uncle Reuven?	šel hadod reuven?	של הרוד ראובן?
uncle	dod (m)	דור
aunt	doda (f)	רודה

ATARA

No. Call	lo. hitkašer im	לא. התקשר עם
information.	modiin.	מודיעין.
Dial "zero".	xayeg éfes.	חייג אפס.
information(service)	modiin (m.s.)	מודיעין
he dialed	xiyeg	חייג
zero	éfes	אפס

YONATAN

Hello, information?	halo. modiin?	הלו. מודיעין?
Please give me	tni li bevakaša	חני לי בבקשה
a number in Haifa.	mispar bexáyfa.	מספר בחיפה.
The name is	hašem hu	השם הרא
Reuven Duvdevani,	reuven duvdeváni.	ראובן רובדבני,
Jaffa Street 76.	rexov yáfo šiv'im vešeš.	רחוב יפו שבעים ושש.
name	šem (m)	שם
names	šemot (m.pl.)	שמות

INFORMATION

The number is	hamispar hu	המספר הרא
27640.	štáim šéva šeš árba éfes.	שחיים שבע שש ארבע אפס.
You can dial	ata yaxol	אתה יכול
direct or	lexayeg yeširot	לחייג ישירות
through long distance,	o dérex sixot xuc	או דרך שיחות-חרץ,
number 19.	mispar tšá'esre.	מספר חשע-עשרה.
direct	yašir (m.s.)	ישיר
conversation	sixa (f)	שיחה

YONATAN

Thank you.	toda raba.	תורה רבה.
I'll make the call	azmin et hasixa	אזמין את השיחה
through number 19.	bemispar tšá'esre.	במספר חשע-עשרה.

LONG DISTANCE

Long distance. Hello.	sixot xuc. šalom.	שיחות חרץ. שלום.

YONATAN

Please give me	tni li bevakaša	חני לי בבקשה
Haifa 27640.	xáyfa štáim šéva šeš	חיפה שחיים שבע שש
	árba éfes.	ארבע אפס.

LONG DISTANCE

What is your number?	ma hamispar šelxa?	מה המספר שלך?

YONATAN

60783.	šeš éfes šéva šmóne	שש אפס שבע שמונה
	šaloš.	שלוש.

LONG DISTANCE

One moment.	xake réga.	חכה רגע.
The line is busy.	hakav tafus.	הקו תפוס.
line	kav (m)	קו
occupied	tafus (m.s.)	תפוס

Hello, Haifa 27640?	haló - xáyfa štaim ševa šeš árba éfes?	הלו, חיפה שתיים שבע שש ארבע אפס?
Tel Aviv calling.	tel aviv koret.	תל אביב קוראת.
Go ahead please.	dabru bevakaša.	דברו בבקשה.
calls, reads	kore (m.s. pres.)	קורא

19.2   ADDITIONAL VOCABULARY

A call from a phone booth costs 20 "grush".	sixa mita télefon ola esrim gruš.	שיחה מתא טלפון עולה עשרים גרוש.
booth	ta (m)	תא
(old name for agora)	gruš (m)	גרוש

Tokens are sold in every post office.	asimonim nimkarim bexol misrad dóar.	אסימונים נמכרים בכל משרד דואר.
token	asimon (m)	אסימון
is sold	nimkar (m.s.)	נמכר
he sold	maxar	מכר

In order to find out what time it is dial 15.	kedey levarer ma hašaa xayeg xaméš'esre.	כדי לברר מה השעה חייג חמש-עשרה.
in order to	kedey	כדי
he found out	birer	בירר

When the phone is out of order dial 16.	kšehatélefon mekulkal xayeg šéš'esre.	כשהטלפון מקולקל חייג שש-עשרה.
out of order	mekulkal (m.s.)	מקולקל
he damaged	kilkel	קלקל

| To call outside the country dial 18. | lehitkašer im xuc laárec xayeg šmóne'esre. | להתקשר עם חוץ לארץ חייג שמונה-עשרה. |

19.3 Vocabulary Drills

A. Substitution-Agreement Drill

This drill may be done as a substitution drill using either verb as a cue and also as an expansion drill.

Dial 15 and check the time.

xayeg xaméš'esre ubdok ma hašaa.		חייג חמש-עשרה ובדוק מה השעה.
xaygi	vebidki	חייגי חמש-עשרה ובדקי מה השעה.
xaygu	vebidku	חייגו חמש-עשרה ובדקו מה השעה.
xayegna	ubdókna	חייגנה חמש-עשרה ובדוקנה מה השעה.

(Both /u-/ and /ve-/ have been used to illustrate possible variations).

B. Substitution Drill   / a - ~ te - /

I'll dial direct to Rehovot.

	axayeg yeširot lerexóvot.	אחייג ישירות לרחובות.
	texayeg	תחייג
at	texaygi	תחייגי את
hu	yexayeg	יחייג הוא
hi	texayeg	תחייג היא
	nexayeg	נחייג
atem	texayǫu	תחייגו אתם
aten	texayégna	תחייגנה אתן
hem	yexayǫu	יחייגו הם
hen	texayégna	תחייגנה הן

C. <u>Substitution-Agreement Drill</u>   /xiyeg/ "he dialed"

He didn't dial the right number.

<u>hu lo xiyeg et hamispar hanaxon.</u>	<u>הוא לא חייג את המספר הנכון.</u>
hi - ani - at - hu	היא – אני – את – הוא
hem - ánu - ata - hi	הם – אנו – אתה – היא
atem - hen - hu	אתם – הן – הוא

D. <u>Substitution-Agreement Drill</u>   /kore/ "calls"

The root of this verb is <u>kr'</u> קרא , and it is conjugated like <u>mc'</u> מצא "find".

Miriam is calling us. Hurry.

<u>miryam koret lánu. maharu.</u>	<u>מרים קוראת לנו. מהרו.</u>
dov - hem - hi - hen	דוב – הם – היא – הן
moše veišto - hu - miryam	משה ואשתו – הוא – מרים

E. <u>Substitution-Agreement Drill</u>   /birer/ "he found out"

We found out Mrs. Zahavi's address.

<u>birárnu et haktóvet šel gvéret zahávi.</u>	<u>בררנו את הכתובת של גברת זהבי.</u>
atem - at - hu - hi	אתם – את – הוא – היא
hem - ani - moše - ata	הם – אני – משה – אתה
xana - hen - ánu	חנה – הן – אנו

F. Substitution Drill   / a - ~ te - /

I'll find out if the bus goes to Lydda.

	avarer im haótobus noséa lelud.	אברר אם האוטובוס נוסע ללוד.
	tevarer	תברר
	tevareri	תבררי
hu	yevarer	יברר הוא
hi	tevarer	תברר היא
	nevarer	נברר
atem	tevareru	תבררו אתם
aten	tevarérna	תבררנה אתן
hem	yevareru	יבררו הם
hen	tevarérna	תבררנה הן

G. Substitution-Agreement Drill

She'll find out if Miriam is going.

<u>hi tevarer im miryam nosáat.</u>   .היא תברר אם מרים נוסעת

ani - ánu - hen - hu   אני - אנו - הן - הוא
ata - at - hem - hi   אתה - את - הם - היא

H. Substitution-Agreement Drill

Moshe is checking when the plane arrives.

<u>moše</u> mevarer maţay šehamatos megía.   .משה מברר מתי שהמטוס מגיע
<u>sára</u> mevaréret   שרה מבררת
<u>ánu</u> mevarerim   אנו מבררים
<u>hen</u> mevarerot   הן מבררות

GRAMMAR NOTES

19.4 <u>Adverbs</u>

Adverbs or adverbial phrases are of several types.

(a)   The masculine singular form of the adjective is often used.
/at medabéret yafe./ "You speak beautifully."
/tov asíta./ "You did well."

This was discussed earlier in Grammar Note 10.5.

(b)   The /t/ feminine singular of some adjectives ending in / - i / is used.
This is so with the ordinal numbers.

/šenit/ "secondly"
/šlišit/ "thirdly"

Note that the feminine singular form of the adjective "second" is /šnia/.
There are some adverbs of this type which have no corresponding masculine
singular form.

/rešit/ "first" (cf. /rišon/)

(c)   The feminine plural adjective is sometimes used.

/xayeg yeširot./ "Dial directly."

(d)   Some adverbs have unique forms, though with recognizable roots.
/kódem/   "early, preceding" (cf. /mukdám/)
/heytev/ "well"   (/cf. /tov/)

(e)   The preposition /be-/ is often used with a corresponding noun.

/bekol/   "loudly"
/beemet/   "really"
/bediyuk/ "exactly"
/beracon/ "willingly"
/behexlet/ "decidely"
/bekarov/ "shortly"

(f)   Other prepositions are sometimes used.

/miyad/   "immediately"

199

19.5 <u>The nif'al Conjugation</u> - Present and Past Tenses

Compare the following forms.

/moxer/	"sells"	/nimkar/	"is sold"
/moce/	"find"	/nimca/	"is found"
/roe/	"sees"	/nir'e/	"is seen, seems"

Note that the meaning of the forms on the right is the passive or intransitive of the verbs on the left.

Most <u>nif'al</u> verbs have a counterpart in the <u>pa'al</u> with the corresponding active meaning. A few have active counterparts in the <u>pi'el</u> or <u>hif'il</u>. The correspondence of form is sometimes remote in the English translations, but the Hebrew speaker has a definite feeling for the basic meaning of the root.

1. Prefix of the <u>nif'al</u>:

The present and past tenses of the <u>nif'al</u> have a prefix to the root. The prefix is / ni - / except in the following cases:

(a) If the first consonant of the root is / x / (ח) then the prefix is /ne-/.

/nexšav/   "is considered"   נֶחְשָׁב

(b) If the first consonant of the root is / ' / (א or ע) then the form begins /ne'e-/ with the /'/ usually replaced by a smooth transition.

/ne'exal/ or /neexal/   "eaten"   נֶאֱכָל

(c) If the first consonant is /'/ represented by ע , the form may begin /na'a-/ or, with smooth transition, /naa-/.

/naase/   "done, made"   נֶעֱשֶׂה

(d) If the first consonant of the root is /h/ then the form begins /nehe-/.

/nehedar/   "wonderful"   נֶהְדָּר

(e) If the first consonant of the root is y, then the prefix and the y coalesce to /no-/, spelled נו . Compare this with the comment on /hodia/ "he informed" in Grammar Note 17.7.

/yada/ "he knew"	ידע	/yalda/ "she gave birth"	ילדה
/noda/ "known"	נודע	/nolda/ "she was born"	נולדה

2. Alternation of root consonants in the <u>nif'al</u>:

(a) If the first radical is <u>n</u> , then it is dropped in the present and past tenses.

/natan/ "he gave"
/nitan/ "was given"   for */nintan/

(b) If the first radical is <u>b</u> or <u>p</u> , then it occurs as /v/ or /f/, respectively.

/badak/	"he checked"	בדק
/nivdak/	"was checked"	נבדק

/patax/	"he opened"	פתח
/niftax/	"was opened"	נפתח

[Note the designation /ni<u>f</u>'al/ itself.]

(c) If the first radical is <u>k</u>, spelled כ , then it occurs as /x/. However, the prefix is /ni-/, not /ne-/ as with /x/ spelled ח .

/nixnas/	"he entered"	נכנס
but /nexšav/	"is considered"	נחשב

(d) If the <u>second</u> radical is <u>b</u> or <u>p</u> , then it occurs as /b/ or /p/, respectively.

/nišbar/	"was broken"	נשבר
/nišpax/	"was spilled"	נשפך

(e) If the second radical is <u>k</u>, spelled כ , then it occurs as /k/.

/nimkar/	"is sold"	נמכר

There is an exception to rules (d) and (e). If the second radical is preceded by /nee/ or /no/ then the variants /v/, /f/, and /x/ occur.

/neevad/	"lost"	נאבד
/neefe/	"baked"	נאפה
/neexal/	"eaten"	נאכל

There are other relatively minor features of the present and past tense forms of the nif'al which should be learned by the student as they are met, but which need not be discussed here. A more complete description of the consonant alternations is given in Unit 23.

19.6 The Present Tense of the nif'al

The pattern of the present tense is as follows: (The prefix is given as /ni-/ since this is the most frequent form.)

m.s.	/ni - - a - /	nimkar	נמכר
f.s.	/ni - - é - et/	nimkéret	נמכרת
m.pl.	/ni - - a - im/	nimkarim	נמכרים
f.pl.	/ni - - a - ot/	nimkarot	נמכרות

The feminine singular always ends in /-t/, even in <u>lamed hey</u> verbs.

m.s.	/nir'e / "seems"	נראה
f.s.	/nir'et/	נראית

This is the exception to the f.s. /-a/ endings mentioned in Grammar Note 8.4a and section 16.3, Drill B. It avoids confusion with the 3 m.s. past tense form /nir'a/ "he seemed".

When the third root consonant is י (ע) or <u>x</u> (ח) the feminine singular has the suffix / - at/. Cf. m.s. /šoméa/ f.s. /šomáat/ "hears"

m.s.	/nišma/ "is heared"	נשמע
f.s.	/nišmáat/	נשמעת

When the third root consonant is <u>'</u> (א) the feminine singular ends in /-et/.

m.s. /nimca/   "is located"   נמצא
f.s. /nimcet/   נמצאת

A. Substitution-Agreement Drill   /nimkar/ "is sold"   נמכר

   Tokens are sold in the post office.

   <u>asimonim nimkarim badóar.</u>   <u>אסימונים נמכרים בדואר.</u>

   bulim - gluyot - igrot avir   כולים - גלויות - אגרות אויר
   maatafa - bul - gluya - asimonim   מעטפה - כול - גלויה - אסימונים

B. Substitution-Agreement Drill   /neexal/ " is eaten"   נאכל

   Chala is eaten on the Sabbath.

   <u>xala neexélet bešabat.</u>   <u>חלה נאכלת בשבת.</u>

   dagim memulaim - ugot - basar   רגים ממולאים - עוגות - בשר
   beycim - melafefonim - xala   ביצים - מלפפונים - חלה

C. Substitution-Agreement Drill   /nišma/ "is heard"   נשמע

   He is heard well over the phone.

   <u>hu nišma tov batélefon.</u>   <u>הוא נשמע טוב בטלפון.</u>

   išti - hem - ata - aten   אשתי - הם - אתה - אתן
   yónatan - sára - atem - hu   יונתן - שרה - אתם - הוא

D. Substitution-Agreement Drill   /nexšav/ "is considered"   נחשב

   She is considered a good teacher.

   <u>hi nexšévet lemora tova.</u>   <u>היא נחשבת למורה טובה.</u>

   ata - kulam - sára veatára   אתה - כולם - שרה ועטרה
   ištexa - ánu - hu - hi   אשתך - אנו - הוא - היא

E. Substitution-Agreement Drill   /nir'e/ "seems"   נראה

   They don't look well today.

   <u>hem lo nir'im tov hayom.</u>   <u>הם לא נראים טוב היום.</u>

   at - sára vexána - ata   את - שרה וחנה - אתה
   baalex - hi - aten - hem   בעלך - היא - אתן - הם

F. Substitution-Agreement Drill   /nimca/ "is located"

The books are in my house.

<u>hasfarim nimcaim bebeyti.</u>   .הספרים נמצאים בביתי

haóxel – hašulxanot – haxala – habakbuk   הבקבוק – החלה – השולחנות – האוכל

hateenim – hakufsa – haxavilot – hasfarim   הספרים – החבילות – הקופסה – התאנים

The following drills require the student to transform a sentence with the verb in the <u>kal (pa'al)</u> conjugation into a more-or-less equivalent sentence with the verb in the <u>nif'al</u> conjugation. The drills should also be done in reverse.

The native English speaker is often stunned when the Hebrew speaker assumes, for example, that the meaning of   /histadárnu tov./   "we got along well" should be clear from /séder/ "order". The astonishment is increased when he adds, "You know /yesudar/ 'will be arranged', don't you?" The point is that the Hebrew speaker is primarily aware of the consonant sequence <u>s-d-r</u>, and the English speaker is not.

English has only a few comparable patterns (<u>sing</u> – <u>sang</u> – <u>sung</u> – <u>song</u>), but each of these is unique. (There is the pattern <u>ring-rang-rung</u>, but not <u>rong</u>.) Similarities of spelling train the English speaker to be unaware of others, such as <u>democrat</u> – <u>democracy</u>, which do not share a single vowel in pronunciation in corresponding syllables.

It cannot be emphasized too strongly that the student must learn to handle the roots, conjugations, and paradigms with great ease. Most students will learn to "encode" the forms without much trouble, but drilling should be continued until correct forms and sentences are produced rapidly and automatically.

G. Transformation Drill

Instructor: [They] sell tokens at the post office.

Student: Tokens are sold at the post office.

1. moxrim asimonim badóar.   .מוכרים אסימונים בדואר .1
   asimonim nimkarim badóar.   .אסימונים נמכרים בדואר

2. moxrim gluyot badóar.   .מוכרים גלויות בדואר .2
   gluyot nimkarot badóar.   .גלויות נמכרות בדואר

3. moxrim igrot avir badóar.   .מוכרים אגרות אויר בדואר .3
   igrot avir nimkarot badóar.   .אגרות אויר נמכרות בדואר

4. moxrim maatafa badóar.   .מוכרים מעטפה בדואר .4
   maatafa nimkéret badóar.   .מעטפה נמכרת בדואר

5. moxrim bul badóar.   .מוכרים בול בדואר .5
   bul nimkar badóar.   .בול נמכר בדואר

6. moxrim gluya badóar.   .מוכרים גלויה בדואר .6
   gluya nimkéret badóar.   .גלויה נמכרת בדואר

7. moxrim bulim badóar.   .מוכרים בולים בדואר .7
   bulim nimkarim badóar.   .בולים נמכרים בדואר

H. Transformation Drill

    Instructor: We eat <u>chala</u> on the Sabbath.
    Student: <u>chala</u> is eaten on the Sabbath.

1. ánu oxlim xala bešabat.   .אנו אוכלים חלה בשבת. 1.
    xala neexélet bešabat.   חלה נאכלת בשבת.

2. ánu oxlim basar bešabat.   .אנו אוכלים בשר בשבת. 2.
    basar neexal bešabat.   בשר נאכל בשבת.

3. ánu oxlim dagim memulaim bešabat.   .אנו אוכלים דגים ממולאים בשבת. 3.
    dagim memulaim neexalim bešabat.   דגים ממולאים נאכלים בשבת.

4. ánu oxlim ugot bešabat.   .אנו אוכלים עוגות בשבת. 4.
    ugot neexalot bešabat.   עוגות נאכלות בשבת.

5. ánu oxlim perot bešabat.   .אנו אוכלים פירות בשבת. 5.
    perot neexalim bešabat.   פירות נאכלים בשבת.

6. ánu oxlim beycim bešabat.   .אנו אוכלים ביצים בשבת. 6.
    beycim neexalot bešabat.   ביצים נאכלות בשבת.

19.7 The Past Tense of the nif'al

    The pattern of the past tense is as follows:

                     <u>šlx</u>

1. s.	/ni--á-ti/	nišláxti	"I was sent"
2. m.s.	/ni--á-ta/	nišláxta	"you were sent"
2. f.s.	/ni--á-t /	nišláxt	"you were sent"
3. m.s.	/ni--a- /	nišlax	"he was sent"
3. f.s.	/ni---a /	nišlexa	"she was sent"
1. pl.	/ni--á-nu/	nišláxnu	"we were sent"
2. m.pl.	/ni--á-tem/	nišláxtem	"you were sent"
2. f.pl.	/ni--á-ten/	nišláxten	"you were sent"
3.pl.	/ni---u/	nišlexu	"they were sent."

    There are no surprises at all in the above chart. The first and second person forms differ only in the suffixes, as described back in Grammar Note 5.4. The pattern of the third person forms is quite regular, as described in Grammar Note C.9 and 16.4. The / - e - / in 3 f.s. and 3 pl. /nišlexa , nišlexu/ is introduced to break up the three-consonant cluster which results in these forms.

    The past tense of <u>lamed hey</u> verbs has the vowel / e / before the suffix.

               /nir'éti/   "I was seen"

A. Substitution-Agreement Drill   /nišlax/ "was sent"   נשלח

    I was sent to the grocery store.

<u>nišláxti lexanut hamakólet.</u>   .נשלחתי לחנות המכולת

hem - moše - dálya - ánu   הם – משה – דליה – אנו
ata - at - atára - ani   אתה – את – עטרה – אני

B. Substitution-Agreement Drill   /nifgaš/   "met"   נפגש

We got together with Dov this morning.

<u>nifgášnu im dov habóker.</u>   .נפגשנו עם דוב הבוקר

    ani - avíva - baali - hen   אני - אביבה - בעלי - הן
    ata - atem - hem - ánu   אתה - אתם - הם - אנו

C. Substitution-Agreement Drill   /nigaš/   "approached"   נִגַּשׁ

(This verb is irregular in that in the present and past tenses it is
conjugated in the <u>nif'al</u>, but in the imperative and future it is conjugated
in the <u>pa'al</u>.   The future was drilled in Grammar Section 13.6, Drills G & H.)

I went to the main post office.

<u>nigášti ladóar hamerkazi.</u>   .נגשתי לדואר המרכזי

    hi - dov - atem - ánu   היא - דוב - אתם - אנו
    at - david veyónatan - ani   את - דוד ויונתן - אני

    The following drills should be done in reverse, also.

D. Transformation Drill /nišlax/ "was sent"   נשלח

Instructor: They sent me to the store.
Student: I was sent to the store.

    šalxu oti laxanut.   .שלחו אותי לחנות
        nišláxti laxanut.   .נשלחתי לחנות
    šalxu otxa laxanut.   .שלחו אותך לחנות
        nišláxta laxanut.   .נשלחת לחנות
    šalxu et moše laxanut.   .שלחו את משה לחנות
        moše nišlax laxanut.   .משה נשלח לחנות
    šalxu otánu laxanut.   .שלחו אותנו לחנות
        nišláxnu laxanut.   .נשלחנו לחנות
    šalxu otxem laxanut.   .שלחו אתכם לחנות
        nišláxtem laxanut.   .נשלחתם לחנות
    šalxu et léa laxanut.   .שלחו את ליה לחנות
        léa nišlexa laxanut.   .לאה נשלחה לחנות
    šalxu otax laxanut.   .שלחו אותך לחנות
        nišlaxt laxanut.   .נשלחת לחנות
    šalxu otan laxanut.   .שלחו אותן לחנות
        hen nišlexu laxanut.   .הן נשלחו לחנות
    šalxu otam laxanut.   .שלחו אותם לחנות
        hem nišlexu laxanut.   .הם נשלחו לחנות
    šalxu otxen laxanut.   .שלחו אתכן לחנות
        nišláxten laxanut.   .נשלחתן לחנות
    šalxu oti laxanut.   .שלחו אותי לחנות
        nišláxti laxanut.   .נשלחתי לחנות

E. Transformation Drill   /nifgaš/   "met"   נפגש

Instructor: I met Yael the day before yesterday.

Student: I got together with Yael the day before yesterday.

pagášti et yael šilšom.   .פגשתי את יעל שלשום
         nifgášti im yael šilšom.   .נפגשתי עם יעל שלשום
išti pagša et yael šilšom.   .אשתי פגשה את יעל שלשום
         išti nifgeša im yael šilšom.   .אשתי נפגשה עם יעל שלשום
hu pagaš et yael šilšom.   .הוא פגש את יעל שלשום
         hu nifgaš im yael šilšom.   .הוא נפגש עם יעל שלשום
pagášta et yael šilšom.   .פגשת את יעל שלשום
         nifgášta im yael šilšom.   .נפגשת עם יעל שלשום
atem pagáštem et yael šilšom.   .אתם פגשתם את יעל שלשום
         atem nifgáštem im yael šilšom.   .אתם נפגשתם עם יעל שלשום
pagášnu et yael šilšom.   .פגשנו את יעל שלשום
         nifgášnu im yael šilšom.   .נפגשנו עם יעל שלשום
pagašt et yael šilšom.   .פגשת את יעל שלשום
         nifgašt im yael šilšom.   .נפגשת עם יעל שלשום
mi pagaš et yael šilšom.   ?מי פגש את יעל שלשום
         mi nifgaš im yael šilšom.   ?מי נפגש עם יעל שלשום
hem pagšu et yael šilšom.   .הם פגשו את יעל שלשום
         hem nifgešu im yael šilšom.   .הם נפגשו עם יעל שלשום
pagášten et yael šilšom.   .פגשתן את יעל שלשום
         nifgášten im yael šilšom.   .נפגשתן עם יעל שלשום
pagášti et yael šilšom.   .פגשתי את יעל שלשום
         nifgášti im yael šilšom.   .נפגשתי עם יעל שלשום

F. Transformation Drill   /nišma/   "was heard"   נשמע

Instructor: We heard well over the phone.
Student: We were heard well over the phone.

         šamánu tov batélefon.   .שמענו טוב בטלפון
                  nišmánu tov batélefon.   .נשמענו טוב בטלפון
         šamátem tov batélefon.   .שמעתם טוב בטלפון
                  nišmátem tov batélefon.   .נשמעתם טוב בטלפון
         šamáti tov batélefon.   .שמעתי טוב בטלפון
                  nišmáti tov batélefon.   .נשמעתי טוב בטלפון
moše šama tov batélefon.   .משה שמע טוב בטלפון
         moše nišma tov batélefon.   .משה נשמע טוב בטלפון
hem šam'u tov batélefon.   .הם שמעו טוב בטלפון
         hem nišme'u tov batélefon.   .הם נשמעו טוב בטלפון
         šamat tov batélefon.   .שמעת טוב בטלפון
                  nišmat tov batélefon.   .נשמעת טוב בטלפון
ištexa šam'a tov batélefon.   .אשתך שמעה טוב בטלפון
         ištexa nišme'a tov batélefon.   .אשתך נשמעה טוב בטלפון
         šamáten tov batélefon.   .שמעתן טוב בטלפון
                  nišmáten tov batélefon.   .נשמעתן טוב בטלפון
         šamáta tov batélefon.   .שמעת טוב בטלפון
                  nišmáta tov batélefon.   .נשמעת טוב בטלפון

G. Transformation Drill   /nir'a/   "was seen"   נראה

Instructor: He saw me in the Dan Hotel.
Student: I was seen in the Dan Hotel.

hu raa oti bemalon dan.   הוא ראה אותי כמלון דן.
    nir'éti bemalon dan.   נראיתי כמלון דן.

hu raa otxá bemalon dan.   הוא ראה אותך כמלון דן.
    nir'éta bemalon dan.   נראית כמלון דן.

hu raa otánu bemalon dan.   הוא ראה אותנו כמלון דן.
    nir'énu bemalon dan.   נראינו כמלון דן.

hu raa otax bemalon dan.   הוא ראה אותך כמלון דן.
    nir'et bemalon dan.   נראית כמלון דן.

hu raa et mošе bemalon dan.   הוא ראה את משה כמלון דן.
    mošе nir'a bemalon dan.   משה נראה כמלון דן.

hu raa otan bemalon dan.   הוא ראה אותן כמלון דן.
    hen nir'u bemalon dan.   הן נראו כמלון דן.

hu raa et sára bemalon dan.   הוא ראה את שרה כמלון דן.
    sára nir'ata bemalon dan.   שרה נראתה כמלון דן.

hu raa otxem bemalon dan.   הוא ראה אתכם כמלון דן.
    nir'étem bemalon dan.   נראיתם כמלון דן.

hu raa otxen bemalon dan.   הוא ראה אתכן כמלון דן.
    nir'éten bemalon dan.   נראיתן כמלון דן.

hu raa otam bemalon dan.   הוא ראה אותם כמלון דן.
    hem nir'u bemalon dan.   הם נראו כמלון דן.

H. Transformation Drill   /nivdak/   "was checked"   ניברק

Instructor: The doctor examined us.
Student: We were examined by the doctor.

harofe badak otánu.   הרופא בדק אותנו.
    nivdáknu al yedey harofe.   נברקנו על ידי הרופא.
harofe badak et baalex.   הרופא בדק את בעלך.
    baalex nivdak al yedey harofe.   בעלך נבדק על ידי הרופא.
harofe badak otxem.   הרופא בדק אתכם.
    nivdáktem al yedey harofe.   נברקתם על ידי הרופא.
harofe badak oti.   הרופא בדק אותי.
    nivdákti al yedey harofe.   נברקתי על ידי הרופא.
harofe badak otax.   הרופא בדק אותך.
    nivdakt al yedey harofe.   נבדקת על ידי הרופא.
harofe badak otxa.   הרופא בדק אותך.
    nivdákta al yedey harofe.   נברקת על ידי הרופא.
harofe badak et kulam.   הרופא בדק את כולם.
    kulam nivdeku al yedey harofe. כולם נבדקו על ידי הרופא.
harofe badak et išto.   הרופא בדק את אשתו.
    išto nivdeka al yedey harofe.   אשתו נבדקה על ידי הרופא.
harofe badak otxen.   הרופא בדק אתכן.
    nivdákten al yedey harofe.   נברקתן על ידי הרופא.
harofe badak otan.   הרופא בדק אותן.
    hen nivdeku al yedey harofe.   הן נבדקו על ידי הרופא.

I. Transformation Drill   /nisgar/   "was closed"   נסגר

Instructor: They locked me in the office.
Student: I was locked in the office.

sagru oti bamisrad.   סגרו אותי במשרד.
   nisgárti bamisrad.   נסגרתי במשרד.
sagru otxa veet dov bamisrad.   סגרו אותך ואת דוב במשרד.
   dov veata nisgártem bamisrad.   דוב ואתה נסגרתם במשרד.
sagru et baala šel xána bamisrad.   סגרו את בעלה של חנה במשרד.
   baala šel xána nisgar bamisrad.   בעלה של חנה נסגר במשרד.
sagru otánu bamisrad.   סגרו אותנו במשרד.
   nisgárnu bamisrad.   נסגרנו במשרד.
sagru otax bamisrad.   סגרו אותך במשרד.
   nisgart bamisrad.   נסגרת במשרד.
sagru otxen bamisrad.   סגרו אתכן במשרד.
   nisgárten bamisrad.   נסגרתן במשרד.
sagru et mošе veet david bamisrad.   סגרו את משה ואת דוד במשרד.
   moše vedavid nisgeru bamisrad.   משה ודוד נסגרו במשרד.
sagru ota bamisrad.   סגרו אותה במשרד.
   hi nisgera bamisrad.   היא נסגרה במשרד.
sagru oto bamisrad.   סגרו אותו במשרד.
   hu nisgar bamisrad.   הוא נסגר במשרד.

J. Transformation Drill   /nexšav/   "was considered"   נחשב

Instructor: They considered you a good teacher.
Student: You were considered a good teacher.

xašvu otxa lemore tov.   חשבו אותך למורה טוב.
   nexšávta lemore tov.   נחשבת למורה טוב.
xašvu otax lemora tova.   חשבו אותך למורה טובה.
   nexšavt lemora tova.   נחשבת למורה טובה.
xašvu otam lemorim tovim.   חשבו אותם למורים טובים.
   hem nexševu lemorim tovim.   הם נחשבו למורים טובים.
xašvu otxen lemorot tovot.   חשבו אתכן למורות טובות.
   nexšávten lemorot tovot.   נחשבתן למורות טובות.
xašvu otxem lemorim tovim.   חשבו אתכם למורים טובים.
   nexšávtem lemorim tovim.   נחשבתם למורים טובים.
xašvu otánu lemorim tovim.   חשבו אותנו למורים טובים.
   nexšávnu lemorim tovim.   נחשבנו למורים טובים.
xašvu oto lemore tov.   חשבו אותו למורה טוב.
   hu nexšav lemore tov.   הוא נחשב למורה טוב.
xašvu et išti lemora tova.   חשבו את אשתי למורה טובה.
   išti nexševa lemora tova.   אשתי נחשבה למורה טובה.
xašvu et sára veet raxel lemorot tovot.   חשבו את שרה ואת רחל למורות טובות.
   sára veraxel nexševu lemorot tovot.   שרה ורחל נחשבו למורות טובות.
xašvu oti lemore tov.   חשבו אותי למורה טוב.
   nexšávti lemore tov.   נחשבתי למורה טוב.

REVIEW CONVERSATIONS

A: at yodáat et mispar hatélefon šel david?   א: את יודעת את מספר הטלפון של דוד?

B: lo. kax asimon vehitkašer im modiin.   ב: לא. קח אסימון והתקשר עם מודיעין.

A: eyn kan séfer telefónim?   א: אין כאן ספר טלפונים?

B: ani lo roa séfer telefónim.   ב: אני לא רואה ספר טלפונים.

C: ma hašaa.   ג: מה השעה?

D: ani xošévet šešeš.   ד: אני חושבת ששש.

C: xayegi xaméš'esre vebidki.   ג: חייגי חמש-עשרה ובדקי.

D: amárti lax šehašaa šeš.   ד: אמרתי לך שהשעה שש.

E: hatélefon mekulkal.   ה: הטלפון מקולקל.

F: hitkašri im šeš'esre.   ו: התקשרי עם שש-עשרה.

E: hitkašárti aval hakav tafus.   ה: התקשרתי אבל הקו תפוס.

F: xaygi od hapáam.   ו: חייגי עוד הפעם.

G: hizmánti sixa lexéyfa.   ז: הזמנתי שיחה לחיפה.

H: láma lo hitkašárta yeširot?   ח: למה לא הזקשרת ישירות?

G: efšar lehitkašer yeširot lexéyfa?   ז: אפשר להתקשר ישירות לחיפה?

H: ken, behexlet.   ח: כן. בהחלט.

I: lean ata holex?   ס: לאן אתה הולך?

J: nišláxti lexanut hamakólet.   י: נשלחתי לחנות המכולת.

I: mi šalax otxa?   ט: מי שלח אותך?

J: nišláxti al yedey mošе liknot xalav.   י: נשלחתי על ידי משה לקנות חלב.

K: ma asíta habóker?   כ: מה עשית הבוקר?

L: nifgášti im david.   ל: נפגשתי עם דוד.

K: eyfo nifgášta ito?   כ: איפה נפגשת אתו?

L: nifgášti ito bekafe atára.   ל: נפגשתי אתו בקפה עטרה.

M: hitkašárnu etmol im xáyfa.   מ: התקשרנו אתמול עם חיפה.

N: eyx hem nišmeu?   נ: איך הם נשמעו?

M: šamánu otam heytev.   מ: שמענו אותם היטב.

N: im mi dibártem?   נ: עם מי דברתם?

M: dibárnu im kol hamišpaxa.   מ: דברנו עם כל המשפחה.

O: noda lánu šeat nimcet betel aviv.   ס: נודע לנו שאת נמצאת בתל אביב.

P: meáin noda laxem?   ע: מאין נודע לכם?

O: nir'et bemalon dan.   ס: נראית כמלון דן.

P: ken. ani gára šam.   ע: כן. אני גרה שם.

Q: éyfo háita etmol baláyla.   פ: איפה היית אתמול בלילה?

R: nisgárti bamisrad.   צ: נסגרתי במשרד.

Q: eyx ze kara?   פ: איך זה קרה?

R: hadélet nisgera velo yaxólti liftóax ota.   צ: הדלת נסגרה ולא יכולתי לפתוח אותה.

S: nexšávti lemore tov.   ק: נחשבתי למורה טוב. י

T: éyfo? betel aviv?   ר: איפה? בתל אביב?

S: ken. gam betel aviv xašvu oti.   ק: כן. גם בתל אביב חשבו אותי.

T: vekan?   ר: וכאן?

S: gam kan ani nexšav lemore tov.   ק: גם כאן אני נחשב למורה טוב.

Made in the USA
Monee, IL
10 December 2024

72748599R00131